CHRISTIAN
PREACHING

CHRISTIAN PREACHING

A Trinitarian Theology of Proclamation

Michael Pasquarello III

Baker Academic
Grand Rapids, Michigan

© 2006 by Michael Pasquarello III

Published by Baker Academic
a division of Baker Publishing Group
P.O. Box 6287, Grand Rapids, MI 49516-6287
www.bakeracademic.com

Printed in the United States of America

Library of Congress Cataloging-in-Publication Data
Pasquarello, Michael
    Christian preaching : a Trinitarian theology of proclamation / Michael Pasquarello III.
        p.   cm.
    Includes bibliographical references and index.
    ISBN 10: 0-8010-2760-8 (pbk.)
    ISBN 978-0-8010-2760-4 (pbk.)
    1. Preaching. I. Title.
BV4211.3.P365 2006
251—dc22   2006026221

Contents

Preface

On Changing the Subject

It is good for you to renounce yourself in the praise of God, better than to advance in self-praise.

—Augustine of Hippo, Sermon 145

I suspect that for each of us there is a story behind our questions about, commitments to, and convictions concerning the practice of preaching. So far as I can remember, mine were clarified in earnest about halfway into almost twenty years of pastoral ministry. I was sent to serve a downtown congregation, a proud old church that had suffered through thirty consecutive years of membership decline. It was the most demanding and difficult challenge I have ever faced, a time that was characterized by continual discouragement and more than occasional despair. That pastoral assignment, however, was a true turning point since I was confronted daily by the stark reality that the Triune God, before and above all else, must matter in everything we say and do as his people.

At the same time, I quickly began to realize that perhaps the greatest temptation we face is to avoid paying serious attention to God by focusing on the business of religion. By the business of religion I mean looking for short-term fixes that would deny the church's need for living faith, to know and love God, focusing instead on new programs, activities, and other cosmetic changes to compete in the religious marketplace, thus reducing the church's ministry of evangelization and catechesis to "religious customer service." This relentless pressure to focus on the business of religion is driven by a number of perceived needs: to be more "effective" in attracting visitors, generating enthusiasm (or at least decreasing unhappiness) among members, and most important, increasing financial giving, which might temporarily alleviate the crisis even if it failed to acknowledge our deepest desire, destiny, and delight as creatures—praising and knowing the Triune God, who is the source and end of all things.

Confronted by what clearly seemed to be a desperate situation, I did something I am sure many pastors might find rather strange and perhaps even a waste of time, given the large amount of work that needed to be done. I began to reread the books I used during my seminary days, not as resources for papers or exams, but rather to acquire the kind of Christian wisdom, conviction, and hope to go on in the daily struggle and to think, speak, and act truthfully in service of the gospel. To my great surprise, I discovered that the writers who spoke powerfully to me were those who were dead, and those who had been dead longest spoke most powerfully. And I remembered that one of the virtues I had come to appreciate about John Wesley, the spiritual founder of my own tradition, was his long view of things. By "long view" I mean that while Wesley confessed his desire to be a man of just "one book"—Holy Scripture—he immersed himself in the Christian tradition to discern faithful patterns of Christian faith, identity, and practice congruent with the wisdom revealed and enacted in the servant ministry of a crucified Lord.

Although Wesley is considered by many to be one of the most effective preachers in Christian history, he did not view preaching or its effects as ends in themselves. Rather, he saw himself and the people called Methodists as part of a larger providential story: the creating and redeeming work of God proclaimed and enacted by the church across time. He therefore viewed the Methodist movement as both evangelical and catholic, members of the Holy Catholic Church and participants in the communion of saints; a people graciously called to a common life of praise and adoration defined by the church's confession of the Triune God; a distinctive form of Christian existence or way of life aimed toward the fullness of loving communion between God and humanity. Nor did Wesley see his preaching as standing on its own or revolving around himself since his preaching was grounded in the gospel, which for Wesley was the prophetic and apostolic witness of Scripture interpreted within a pattern of holiness that refers all things to the end of loving God and loving neighbors as oneself.[1]

In a 1789 sermon, "On the Unity of Divine Being," Wesley expressed grave concern over the displacement of the communion of love shared by the persons of the "three one God" by functional forms of religion that manifest themselves as morality derived from human reason and experience but are detached from the church's scriptural and doctrinal wisdom. Wesley's warning anticipates many of the challenges of our time. Today, much popular, pragmatic preaching reduces the church's affirmation of the creating and redeeming activity of the Trinity to manageable size by focusing on and offering principles to apply, rules to follow, and things to do. By promoting their personal and social utility as their primary market value and appeal, these presumably "evangelistic" strategies offer a technological approach to faith. This approach is essentially a form of "moralistic therapeutic deism" that places the sovereign self at the center of salvation, church, and world rather than the Triune God.[2] As Wesley writes,

> Thus almost all men of letters, both in England, France and Germany, yea, and all the civilized countries of Europe, extol "humanity" to the skies, as the very essence of religion. That this great triumvirate, Rousseau, Voltaire, and David Hume, have contributed all their labours, sparing no pains to establish a religion which should stand on its own foundation, independent of any revelation whatever, yea, not supposing even the being of a God. So leaving him, if he has any being, to himself, they have found out both a religion and a happiness which have no relation at all to God, nor any dependence upon him. It is no wonder that this religion should grow fashionable, and spread far and wide in the world. But call it "humanity," "virtue," "morality," or what you please, it is neither better nor worse than atheism. Men hereby willfully and design-edly put asunder what God has joined, the duties of the first and second table. It is separating the love of our neighbor from the love of God. It is a plausible way of thrusting God out of the world he has made.[3]

1. See the excellent collection of essays on Methodism set within a larger ecumenical context in Geoffrey Wainwright, *Methodists in Dialogue* (Nashville: Abingdon, 1995).

2. I have borrowed the term "moralistic therapeutic deism" from Christian Smith and Melinda Lundquist Denton, *Soul Searching: The Religious and Spiritual Lives of American Teenagers* (Oxford: Oxford University Press, 2005); see the excellent discussion of this "technological" approach in D. Stephen Long, *John Wesley's Moral Theology: The Quest for God and Goodness* (Nashville: Abingdon, 2005).

3. *The Works of John Wesley*, Bicentennial Edition, ed. Albert C. Outler (Nashville: Abingdon, 1984–), 4:69.

Christian Preaching has been written with hope toward "changing the subject" of Christian preaching from ourselves to the Triune God. This book is an essay in practical theology, an extended theological reflection on the practice of preaching within the church's trinitarian wisdom or "grammar" of faith. Unlike many books that discuss preaching in terms of homiletic method and technique, I have not written about sermon design, style, delivery, illustrations, PowerPoint, video clips, technology, popular culture, and sociological trends, or any other number of secondary matters that have recently captured our attention.

My aim is much larger and long term. I want to provide theological rather than pragmatic justification for speaking of God, justification that is a trinitarian vision of practice by which our thoughts, words, and lives may be more carefully weighed and made true to the One of whom we speak and more fitting for the people God calls to reflect his glory in the form of Christ crucified and risen—"the Word made flesh." Daniel Hardy summarizes the end or "purpose" to which I have aimed: "to honor God in all knowledge and practice . . . is the best kind of theology. It is God-focused wisdom." I do not presume to have fully accomplished this task, but the joy of attending to the subject matter has certainly been worth the effort, and I will be thankful if my work makes some contribution to this end.

I will use the phrase "speaking of God" as a shorthand definition of Christian preaching, since the source, means, and goal of all we are and all we do is the Word spoken by the Father in the power of the Holy Spirit. Christian preaching, in contrast to "effective communication," is a personally involved, participatory, and embodied form of graced activity that is the Triune God's gift to the church. This is not subject to human mastery and control, but as an expression of doxological speech is gratefully received and offered back to God through the praise and thanksgiving of the Christian community at worship.

In a culture in which there is no shortage of technique or infatuation with our own ingenuity, mastery, and control, God-given wisdom does indeed seem to be in short supply. Contrary to the "conventional wisdom" of our time, I do not believe that preachers need new ideas, techniques, or methods that "work" to make Christianity more intelligible to the world on the world's terms. What we preachers need is for our lives and the lives of those to whom we preach to be more truthfully located within the gospel—the life, work, and speech of the Triune God, who is the source and goal of our very being. Bruce Marshall notes:

> The church is in the gospel; it is part of the gospel, without the inclusion of which the gospel is neither proclaimed nor believed. The claim that the church belongs to the gospel can be the "catholic" counterpart to the "evangelical" claim that salvation is only by faith in this same gospel of God's free mercy in Christ. . . . The gospel is a narrative, specifically the narrative which identifies the particular human being Jesus of Nazareth . . . and extends naturally to include the narratives about Israel, which identify the Father, and the narrative of Pentecost, which identifies the Spirit . . . [and] the mission of the Spirit is to create the church. Therefore the church belongs to the Gospel.[4]

Christian Preaching argues that our greatest homiletic need is for theological wisdom cultivated by inhabiting the narrative world of the gospel. Richard Lischer observes:

> Without the proper grounding in *theologia*, homiletics will continue as a fragmented discipline. Its exegesis will be preliminary technology rather than an exercise in prayerful dialogue with the text. Sermon-design will be reduced to endless rules and formulas for high-impact communication. The sermon will be conceived as a projection of the speaker's personality or as the fabricator of religious consciousness. Preaching is thereby alienated from its home in worship, doctrine, pastoral care, and the sacramental life. It is on its own.[5]

I wish to thank Asbury Theological Seminary for the generous sabbatical support that helped to make this work possible. I also am indebted to colleagues, especially Dr. Lester Ruth, for stimulating conversations. I am grateful to my provost, Dr. Joel B. Green, Bishop William H. Willimon, and Professors Stanley Hauerwas and Richard Lischer for their example and continuing encouragement. Professor Thomas Long willingly served as an external reader; I am grateful for his timely and helpful suggestions, although I bear responsibility for my own shortcomings. I am deeply grateful to Jim Kinney and Baker Academic for their enthusiastic support of this project. In addition, special thanks

---

4. Bruce D. Marshall, "The Church in the Gospel," *Pro Ecclesia* 1, no. 1 (Fall 1992): 27–41.

5. Richard Lischer, *A Theology of Preaching: The Dynamics of the Gospel*, rev. ed. (Eugene, OR: Wipf & Stock, 2001), x.

to Jeff Wittung at Baker for his able assistance throughout the editing process. Finally, I wish to express my deep gratitude for the students with whom I have been privileged to work, first at Duke Divinity School and most recently at Asbury Theological Seminary. Their desire to know and speak of the Triune God is contagious. *Christian Preaching* is dedicated to them with gratitude.

Introduction

Speaking of God:
Preaching at the "End of Religion"

You are great, Lord, and highly to be praised. . . . You stir man to take pleasure in praising you, because you have made us for yourself, and our heart is restless until it rests in you.

—Augustine of Hippo, *Confessions*

Christian Preaching is written within a theological tradition that acknowledges that throughout most of Christian history the practice of preaching was believed to take place in, with, and through the initiative and activity of the Triune God.[1] Human speakers and listeners understood themselves to be responding to and participating in the prior gift of God's speech, the Word spoken by the Father in the power of the Spirit through the witness of the prophets and apostles to build up the church as a doxological community: "But you are a chosen race, a royal priesthood, a holy nation, God's own people, in order that you may proclaim the mighty acts of him who called you out of darkness into his marvelous light" (1 Pet. 2:9 NRSV).

1. Here I have learned much from William M. Thompson, *The Struggle for Theology's Soul: Contesting Scripture in Theology* (New York: Crossroad, 1996); Oliver Davies, *A Theology of Compassion: Metaphysics of Difference and the Renewal of Tradition* (Grand Rapids: Eerdmans, 2001); Robert W. Jenson, *Systematic Theology*, vol. 1, *The Triune God* (New York: Oxford University Press, 1997); Geoffrey Wainwright, *Doxology: The Praise of God in Worship, Doctrine and Life* (New York: Oxford University Press, 1980).

Yet, for many contemporary preachers, the forms of preaching that are most familiar—the inheritance of late modernity—have been separated from a divine-human conversation that is mediated through the light of scriptural witness, theological memory, moral wisdom, and eschatological hope. This conversation is the confession of the God of Israel—the Father, Son, and Holy Spirit—whose self-communication summons the church into a vocation of praise, adoration, and loving obedience that bears witness to the hope of the redemption and final glorification of the world.[2]

A particularly corrosive effect of this separation has been an increasingly anthropocentric emphasis in preaching that is reflected in excessive self-consciousness and dependence on the communication skills, style, techniques, innovative methods, and personality of the preacher, and a correlative preoccupation with the likes, preferences, opinions, and "deeply felt needs" of listeners. During modernity, this human-centered approach to both preaching and listening has proven to be widely effective in creating culturally accommodated forms of religion—forms often maximally cultural yet minimally Christian in both their liberal and conservative manifestations. More recently this approach has shown to be quite successful in developing models for the creation and growth of large or "mega" churches.[3] Stanley Hauerwas comments:

> Christians in modernity thought their task was to make the Gospel intelligible to the world rather than to help the world understand why it could not be intelligible without the Gospel. Desiring to become part of the modernist project, preachers and theologians accepted the presumption that Christianity is a set of beliefs, a worldview, designed to give meaning to our lives. As a result, the politics of Christian discourse was relegated to the private in the name of being politically responsible in, to, and for liberal social orders. We accepted the politics of translation believing that neither we, nor our Christian or half-Christian neighbors could be expected to submit to the discipline of Christian speech.[4]

2. For contributions to the recovery of trinitarian faith and practice, see Basil Studer, *Trinity and Incarnation: The Faith of the Early Church*, ed. Andrew Louth (Collegeville, MN: Liturgical Press, 1993); Luke Timothy Johnson, *The Creed: What Christians Believe and Why It Matters* (New York: Doubleday, 2003), chap. 9; Christopher R. Seitz, ed., *Nicene Christianity: The Future for a New Ecumenism* (Grand Rapids: Brazos, 2001); Roger E. Van Harn, ed., *Exploring and Proclaiming the Apostles' Creed* (Grand Rapids: Eerdmans, 2004).

3. See Ralph C. Wood, *Contending for the Faith: The Church's Engagement with Culture* (Waco: Baylor University Press, 2003).

4. Stanley Hauerwas, *Sanctify Them in the Truth: Holiness Exemplified* (Nashville: Abingdon, 1998), 193.

The discourse of modernity, however, has failed to demonstrate a capacity for speaking of God in a manner necessary for building up the church in conformity to the gospel it presumes to believe and live, a gospel that is the proclamation of a Lord whose self-giving love displays God's power and wisdom through obedience, suffering, and death on a cross, and who in his exaltation at the Father's right hand is the object of the church's worship, which creates the conditions for truthful witness in the world. Nicholas Lash observes,

> All human beings have their hearts set somewhere; hold something sacred, worship at some shrine. We are spontaneously idolatrous—where, by "idolatry," I mean the worship of some creature, the setting of the heart on some particular thing (usually oneself). For most of us there is no single creature that is the object of our faith. . . . Idolatry is the divinizing, the taking of absolute and over-riding of any value, fact, nation, dream, project, person, possession or idea. It matters not what being I take as god and set my heart upon, whether it be freedom or efficiency, yesterday or tomorrow, America or me; to make of some being, of any being, an "absolute," an object of worship, is idolatry.[5]

There is an urgent need in our time for a theological vision of preaching that calls the church to its primary vocation: to turn from idolatry (perhaps no more subtly and therefore dangerously present than in the zealous pursuit of cultural relevance—across the theological spectrum) to the worship of the Triune God, which is the necessary condition for hearing and responding to God's self-communication in Christ. As Brent Laytham observes:

> For us, idolatry is less about visible images of Yahweh. . . . Our idolatry is more about verbal imaginations of Yahweh. . . . The critical danger is not an image of a false god, but a false image of the true God. . . . Christians are more likely to bring the God that they do worship into the orbit of something else. . . . Yet the idolatry hides itself under pious rhetoric that refuses to acknowledge the de-centering of God.[6]

---

5. Nicholas Lash, *The Beginning and the End of "Religion"* (Cambridge: Cambridge University Press, 1996), 21, 134, 245; I have been assisted by the interpretation of Christendom and modernity in Douglas Harink, *Paul among the Postliberals: Pauline Theology beyond Christendom and Morality* (Grand Rapids: Brazos, 2003). See especially the conclusion: "Preaching Paul beyond Christendom and Modernity."

6. D. Brent Laytham, "God Is One, Holy, Catholic and Apostolic," in *God Is Not—: Religious, Nice, "One of Us," an American, a Capitalist*, ed. D. Brent Laytham (Grand Rapids: Brazos, 2004), 124–25.

Located within the conditions created by Christian worship, learning to speak of God within the logic of the gospel, Scripture, and Christian life is intrinsic to the gift of participating in the vocation of praising and knowing God that is a self-forgetful yet fully engaged activity. Preaching is both doxological and doctrinal; liturgical speech uttered in truthful confession, thankful praise, and loving adoration to the Triune God, who in giving and receiving the church's praise communicates himself in the form of Christ through the energy of the Spirit.[7] Eugene Peterson observes:

> We live in an age obsessed with communication. Communication is good but a minor good. Knowing about things never has seemed to improve our lives a great deal. The pastoral task with words is not communication but communion—the healing and restoration and creation of love relationships between God and his fighting children and our fought-over creation. . . . This is hard work and requires alertness. The language of our time is in terrible condition. It is used carelessly and cynically. Mostly it is a tool for propaganda, whether secular or religious. Every time badly used and abused language is carried by pastors into prayers and preaching and direction, the Word of God is cheapened.[8]

Peterson's comments point to the need for a trinitarian vision of Christian speech that will contribute to the recovery of robust and unapologetic preaching in service of the church's worship, faith, and missionary activity within a post-Christendom world.[9] This vision will provide an alternative to one shaped by the Enlightenment and modernity, which in both seminary curricula and the ministry of the church continues to perpetuate itself through a variety of divisions: sacred/secular, theological/pastoral, art/craft, academic/popular, doctrine/exegesis, intellect/will, past/present, text/sermon, content/form, and faithfulness/effectiveness.[10]

7. See the discussion of the liturgical and doxological nature of language in Catherine Pickstock, *After Writing: On the Liturgical Consummation of Philosophy* (Malden, MA: Blackwell, 1998), 47–100.

8. Eugene H. Peterson, *The Contemplative Pastor: Returning to the Art of Spiritual Direction* (Grand Rapids: Eerdmans, 1989), 46.

9. See the collection of essays in *The Strange New World of the Gospel: Re-Evangelizing in the Postmodern World,* ed. Carl E. Braaten and Robert W. Jenson (Grand Rapids: Eerdmans, 2002). "Those who turn to religion are not necessarily finding their way back to church. Most unbelievers in America and other western countries are post-Christians. They have been baptized and brought up in a church, but no longer practice the faith. Hence, the need for re-evangelization" (viii).

10. Here I am following Charles L. Campbell, *Preaching Jesus: New Directions for Homiletics in Hans Frei's Postliberal Theology* (Grand Rapids: Eerdmans, 1997); James Kay, "Reorienta-

Because this inherited vision continues to reinforce compartmentalized ways in which we think and speak of God, ourselves, and the world—often in the name of being "relevant" or "practical"—it should not be surprising that much contemporary preaching embodies these divisions in reduced, manipulative, and even idolatrous forms of discourse that in practice diminish the vision of divine-human communion affirmed in the church's confession of the Triune God. This is not an insignificant matter, as Lash comments:

> If human beings are . . . "hearers of the word" it is by utterance, and hence by sound, that we are constituted—and constituted to be, in every fiber of our being, turned towards, attentive to, the voice that makes us and calls us home. The self-utterance that God is spills over, we might say, into the making of the world. Sound is outgoing: speech and song are for communication, for relationship, for building up communion in the Spirit.[11]

Our contemporary homiletic landscape is characterized by what Lash refers to as "noise" and "idle chatter," careless and even irreverent discourse that is incoherent as Christian speech. Having forgotten the practice of silence or attentiveness appropriate for "hearers of the word," preachers spend much of their time designing sermons as "talks" that communicate forms of abstract, privatized, and individualistic faith fused with moralistic and/or therapeutic "styles" of life. Such strategies, however, betray an assumption that the mystery of salvation by divine grace and the sanctification of humanity in the divine image can be spoken of like any other commodity or activity. Addressing this loss of Christian speech, Stanley Hauerwas has emphasized the need to

> reclaim a voice that speaks with authority, a voice whose power compels without coercion and persuades without denigration. Accomplishing such a feat requires, at the very least, a competence in writing and speaking in such a manner that our language as Christians actually does some work. By "doing work" I mean that our language is not simply a means of "saying what everybody already knows," but is deploying and

tion: Homiletics as Authorized Rhetoric," *The Princeton Seminary Bulletin* 24, no. 1 (2003): 16–35; David J. Lose, *Confessing Jesus Christ: Preaching in a Postmodern World* (Grand Rapids: Eerdmans, 2003), 7–30; Hans W. Frei, *Types of Christian Theology*, ed. George Hunsinger and William C. Placher (New Haven: Yale University Press, 1992), 28–146.

11. Nicholas Lash, *Holiness, Speech and Silence: Reflections on the Question of God* (Aldershot: Ashgate, 2004), 92.

engendering linguistic practices that enable Christians to discuss and simultaneously to bear witness to a reality that we (and all that is) are God's good creation. In short, theological language that "does work" consists of those discourse practices that truly make a difference. (Language that "makes" a difference, of course, does so precisely because it also "reveals" important differences.)[12]

Forms of popular preaching that are presumably designed to communicate to "secular" or "unchurched" people continue to draw from a disparate collection of fragments, discrete bits and pieces scavenged from the remains of a divided, declining Christendom. Spoken from "nowhere" in particular, and with little sense of theological or ecclesial identity, such strategies participate in an "un-churching" of the church in the name of promoting its growth. Despite the popularity of such preaching methods, or at the least their comfortable, convenient familiarity, these contemporary strategies fail to do the kind of work described by Hauerwas. Instead, they contribute to the displacement of God and deformation of the church that characterizes large segments of Western Christianity at the "end of religion."[13] Lash comments on this state of affairs:

> Not the beginning or the end of faith, hope, or charity. Not the beginning or end of prayer or proclamation, of the duty laid upon all humankind to work for peace and justice, and the integrity of God's creation. But the view that "religion" is the name of one particular district which we may inhabit if we feel so inclined, a region of diminishing plausibility and significance, a territory quite distinct from those we know as "politics" and "art," as "science" and "law" and "economics"; this view of things, peculiar to modern Western culture, had a beginning in the

12. Stanley M. Hauerwas, *Wilderness Wanderings: Probing Twentieth-Century Theology and Philosophy* (Boulder, CO: Westview, 1997), 3.

13. Lash, *Holiness, Speech and Silence*, 56–71; see also the excellent discussion of "religion" in William T. Cavanaugh, *Theopolitical Imagination: Discovering the Liturgy as a Political Act in an Age of Global Consumerism* (New York: T&T Clark, 2002); for a good discussion of preaching, see Richard Lischer, "Resurrection and Rhetoric," in *Marks of the Body of Christ*, ed. Carl E. Braaten and Robert W. Jenson (Grand Rapids: Eerdmans, 1999), 13–24; *What's the Matter with Preaching Today?* ed. Mike Graves (Louisville: Westminster John Knox, 2004); Rodney Clapp, *A Peculiar People: The Church as Culture in a Post-Christian Society* (Downers Grove, IL: InterVarsity, 1996), 16–57; an insightful critique of contemporary "religion" is provided in David E. Fitch, *The Great Giveaway: Reclaiming the Mission of the Church from Big Business, Parachurch Organizations, Psychotherapy, Consumer Capitalism, and Other Modern Maladies* (Grand Rapids: Baker, 2005).

seventeenth century, and (if postmodern means anything at all) is now coming to an end.[14]

If the "transition" to a post-Christendom culture is showing us anything, it is that in God's providential activity we may find ourselves at a time and place to begin the humble work of changing the subject, gathering up the fragments of a dying Christendom into a more coherent theological and ecclesial vision engendered by praising and knowing the Triune God. Lash observes:

> We are not incapable, as human beings, of making sense of things, of speaking truth and acting with integrity. But all these things we do from somewhere, shaped by some set of memories and expectations, bearing some sense of duty borne and gifts that have been given. All sense, and truth, and goodness, are carried and constituted by some story, some pattern of experience, some tradition.[15]

Why Have Preachers Stopped Speaking of God?

Our attempts to think about the practice of preaching and the task of speaking of God do not take place "up in the air" but rather situate us in the middle of a longer story of a people called by God. David Yeago's insightful theological analysis serves to illumine the contemporary conditions in which we attempt to speak of God at the "end of religion."[16] Tracing briefly the story of Christianity in the West, Yeago shows that the ongoing effects of Christian schisms, conflicts, and disunity stemming from the Reformation and wars of religion led churches to bind themselves to powers that pervade nation-states, such as culture, ethnicity, and class, in order to seek cohesion. This has created a widespread view that religious convictions and identity only lie on the surface of what is, in reality, a secular world, which is its natural state and description. The result is that in modern societies public reality—presumably the "real world"—has been equated with

14. Lash, *Beginning and the End of "Religion,"* ix.
15. Ibid., 19.
16. David S. Yeago, "Messiah's People: The Culture of the Church in the Midst of the Nations," *Pro Ecclesia* 6, no. 2 (Spring 1997): 146–71; hereafter cited as MP. See the similar argument in Walter Brueggemann, *Cadences of Home: Preaching among Exiles* (Louisville: Westminster John Knox, 1992); Ephraim Radner, *Hope among the Fragments: The Broken Church and Its Engagement with Scripture* (Grand Rapids: Brazos, 2004), 23–54.

the secular, while the church has been relegated to the private realm, where voluntary associations of like-minded individuals practice something "spiritual" called "religion" (MP, 146–48).

Yeago's argument does much to clarify the definition we have inherited and the conditions it has produced—a sacred/secular split—which is the source of the church's "ceaseless crisis of legitimization." He writes, "That is to say, having defined itself as part of the larger public order, the order of modern secular society, the church must then find a reason for being, a justification for its existence in terms of the projects and aspirations of that larger order" (MP, 149).

This assessment of the church in modernity is pertinent to the practice of preaching, since acceptance of this culturally determined function continues to be powerfully influential in shaping Christian speech. For many, the church/culture, message/method, content/form separation and compartmentalization have become the primary if not exclusive context for thinking about the particular kind of discourse called "sermon." Thus the church as a religious institution and the preacher as its designated communicator have become vehicles for delivering discrete fragments of beliefs, values, self-help, and morality that presumably promise meaning and purpose, "messages" packaged and presented in practically applicable, user-friendly forms to facilitate the increase of individual religious understanding and/or spiritual experience (MP, 149–50). Yeago comments on the public status of the church when it allows itself to be defined in this manner.

> Notice that this paradigm effectively gives the nations dominion over the church and its faith. The nations play the role of judges before which the church must plead its case: thus cultures are the authoritative context within which it will be decided whether the faith and life of the church are meaningful and worthy. (MP, 150)

Perhaps no phenomenon in American culture has done more to respond to the "crisis of legitimization" on terms dictated by late modernity than the church marketing movement. As Yeago points out, this diverse, burgeoning movement, despite its "rather stunning intellectual and theological vacuity," exercises a powerful fascination for many in both mainline and evangelical churches. Thus the powerful appeal of church marketing is not only the promise of numbers and money that declining congregations and denominations desperately desire, but it may also be the case that, for many, church marketing "has simply become our destiny" (MP, 164–65). In the name of mission and evangelism, congregations have become vendors of goods and services to aggregates of individuals for whom the market has become the primary means of measuring the relevance of religious products and experiences.[17]

This should not be surprising, however, since both the religious right and religious left have long accommodated themselves to an ecclesial grammar in which the church has sought to justify its existence, a logic that has been grasped and exploited by church managers and marketers with great effectiveness. According to this script, the church, on the one hand, has sought to prove its political relevance for this or that struggle to control and use the coercive power of the state; and on the other hand, the church has sought legitimacy by turning its attention to the private realm of religion, competing as a vendor of religious goods and services according to the criteria of popular demand, namely, the concerns and needs of self-defined, individual religious consumers (MP, 166–67).

Historian Mark Noll has shown that the frontier revivals of the 1770s and 1780s marked the emergence of a voluntarist, individual-ist, and sectarian kind of Protestantism now associated by many with evangelicalism.[18] Newly established American Christians identified themselves with essential qualities of America's founding, which were, as Noll observes, "the democratic, republican, commonsensical, liberal, and providential conceptions by which the founders had identified America." Thus for most of the nineteenth century, American Prot-estantism continued to be aligned with the American political project and its new market economy that provided a welcoming environment for the moralistic zeal of revivalism, which served to legitimate the individuated market and the myth of rational individualism and in-dividual choice.[19]

17. Yeago, MP, 149–50, 165–66; see the excellent collection of essays in Laytham, ed., *God Is Not*; I recommend Darrell L. Guder, ed., *Missional Church: A Vision for the Sending of the Church in North America* (Grand Rapids: Eerdmans, 1998); I am indebted to the discussion in Philip D. Kenneson and James L. Street, *Selling (Out) the Church: The Dangers of Church Marketing* (Nashville: Abingdon, 1992); see also the interesting perspective provided in James B. Twitchell, *Branded Nation: The Marketing of Megachurch, College, Inc., and Museumworld* (New York: Simon & Schuster, 2004), 47–108.

18. See the argument and discussion of relevant literature in D. G. Hart, *Deconstructing Evangelicalism: Conservative Protestantism in the Age of Billy Graham* (Grand Rapids: Baker, 2004).

19. Mark A. Noll, *America's God: From Jonathan Edwards to Abraham Lincoln* (Oxford: Oxford University Press, 2002), 188–95. In this section I am also following Noll, *The Rise of Evangelicalism: The Age of Edwards, Whitefield, and the Wesleys* (Downers Grove, IL: Inter-

This "democratization" of Christianity imbibed deeply of the revolutionary spirit, with the ministry of Charles Finney in the 1830s being the climax of a process that had begun a half century earlier. Finney inspired a "Copernican revolution" that made religion exciting and "audience centered," scorning traditional religion for producing dull and ineffective communication and borrowing instead from the rhetorical techniques of populist politicians. Significantly, he shifted the emphasis from the truth to be communicated to the communication of that truth, thus changing the subject of preaching from message to method.[20] Finney's popular methods, however, were influenced not by the trinitarian, christocentric doctrine and ecclesial way of life adhered to by a Jonathan Edwards or a John Wesley. Rather, Finney was influenced by "commonsense theism," whose vigorous empiricism privileged the facts of the Bible and the facts of individual consciousness and thus presumed to judge Christian tradition and history by their contemporary usefulness.[21]

This commonsense rationality, which was moving toward scientific predictability, is reflected in Finney's *Lectures on Revivals of Religion* (1835), which set forth reliable laws that could be activated within a cause-and-effect religious world, analogous to but abstracted from the natural, sensuous world. "The connection between the right use of means for a revival and a revival is as philosophically [i.e., scientifically] sure as between right use of means to raise grain and a crop of wheat. I believe in fact it is more certain, and there are few instances of failure."[22]

The distinctively American character of Finney's popular, pragmatic program can be seen in his insistence that preaching must always be practical: whatever cannot be made immediately useful is not preaching the gospel. Yet in his zeal for reaching lost souls, Finney's definition of

---

Varsity, 2003); Nathan O. Hatch, *The Democratization of American Christianity* (New Haven: Yale University Press, 1989); Mark A. Noll and Nathan O. Hatch, eds., *The Bible in America: Essays in Cultural History* (Oxford: Oxford University Press, 1982); Jon Butler, *Awash in a Sea of Faith: Christianizing the American People* (Cambridge, MA: Harvard University Press, 1990); William G. McLoughlin, *Modern Revivalism: Charles Grandison Finney to Billy Graham* (New York: Ronald, 1959); George M. Marsden, *Reforming Fundamentalism: Fuller Seminary and the New Evangelicalism* (Grand Rapids: Eerdmans, 1987); E. Brooks Holifield, *Theology in America: Christian Thought from the Age of the Puritans to the Civil War* (New Haven: Yale University Press, 2003).

20. Noll, *America's God*, 190; Hatch, *Democratization of American Christianity*, 197–200.

21. Noll, *Rise of Evangelicalism*, 270–78, 290; Holifield, *Theology in America*, 361–68.

22. Cited in Noll, *America's God*, 236.

"useful" and "practical" was increasingly shaped by a form of biblicism grounded in private judgment and personal experience, a Christian antitraditionalism that represented liberation from the wisdom of the Christian past.[23] This project both exemplified and encouraged a habit of mind that assumed simple solutions could be found for complex problems through a fusion of freedom of conscience and the simple truths of the Bible, but now a Bible read in light of one's own common sense and enlightened reason.[24]

Finney's pragmatism shifted the center of Christian virtue as understood by a Wesley or an Edwards from love for God enabled by the gift of divine grace, to human obedience to God's law, moral self-governance, the freedom of the will, and a natural ability to exercise moral choice to obey God. According to Timothy Weber, Finney's idiosyncratic "arminianized Calvinism" taught that anyone who wanted to could be saved. Salvation, therefore, became an individual decision that could be "worked up as well as prayed down" by use of empirically derived methods and measures: aggressive advertising, gospel music that heightened emotions, and sophisticated organization and planning.[25]

By placing primary emphasis on human agency, voluntarism, and making a decision for Christ, revivalists such as Finney propagated the "sanctification" of choice that prepared the way for the pleasures of modern consumer hedonism and redefined Christianity in terms of the marketplace of felt needs and desire. This contributed to a theology and ethic of consumption, production, and economic efficiency that replaced the providential activity of God and the character or ethos cultivated by a Christian tradition of doctrine, devotion, and disciplined life.[26]

William Willimon has argued persuasively that the kind of pragmatic, utilitarian deployment of preaching that was largely made popular by Finney is manifested in many of the latest communication strategies

23. I am following the definition of "popular religion" provided in Edward Farley, *Practicing Gospel: Unconventional Thoughts on the Church's Ministry* (Louisville: Westminster John Knox, 2003): "An unavoidable idolatry of finitizing the sacred characterizes popular religion and piety" (49). According to Farley this is not limited to a particular social class. However, in describing the particular trajectory characterized by Finney's method, what interests me is, "in its most banal sense . . . religion, lured by success, embracing popular culture, thus becoming slick, market-wise, manipulative, avaricious, and sometimes just plain silly" (50).

24. Noll, *America's God*, 380–83; Hatch, *Democratization of American Christianity*, 182–83.

25. Timothy P. Weber, "Revivals," in *Concise Encyclopedia of Preaching*, ed. William H. Willimon and Richard Lischer (Louisville: Westminster John Knox, 1995), 407.

26. Rodney Clapp, *Border Crossings: Christian Trespasses on Popular Culture and Public Affairs* (Grand Rapids: Brazos, 2000), 136–45.

and homiletic techniques that dominate preaching in our time. He concludes that much contemporary homiletic practice continues, albeit unknowingly, to be situated within a theology/practice split that is embodied in forms of "practical atheism." Following in the trajectory that began with Finney, and driven by method separated from message, form from content, and style from substance, a disguised form of "practical atheism" betrays the "lure of technique" that works through neither the presence nor the power of God.[27]

Practical atheism, then, is the pragmatic use of words that is based on the assumption that in the end ministry is a matter of finding the right presentational technology, the proper approach or method, or the appropriate attitude or personal image, but without having to surrender ourselves and our words to the presence or work of the Word and Spirit.[28] For example, although Finney strongly advocated a split between content and form, message and method, his communication strategy took on the form prescribed by his own pragmatic revivalism: human activity that "works" rather than the persons of the Triune God who act with, in, and through human activity by the divine power and wisdom mediated and defined in baptism, which is *the form of Christ crucified*. This is reflected in Finney's statement regarding the Great Commission, which, significantly, does not mention baptism, resurrection, or the Triune Name:

> When Jesus Christ was on earth, laboring among his disciples, *he had nothing to do with forms or measures*. And when the apostles preached afterwards . . . their commission was, "Go and preach the gospel and disciple all nations." *It did not prescribe any forms*. It did not admit any. No persons can pretend to get any set of forms or particular directions as to measures, out of this commission. Do it—the best way you can—ask wisdom from God—use the faculties he has given you—seek the distinction of the Holy Ghost—go forward and do it. This was their commission. And their object was to make known the gospel in the *most effectual way*, to make the truth stand out strikingly, so as to obtain attention and secure obedience of the *greatest number possible*. No person can find any *form* of doing this laid down in the Bible.[29]

27. Here I have learned much from Joseph Dunne, *Back to the Rough Ground: Practical Judgment and the Lure of Technique* (Notre Dame, IN: University of Notre Dame Press, 1997).
28. Ibid., 15–25.
29. Cited in Gordon W. Lathrop and Timothy J. Wengert, *Christian Assembly: Marks of the Church in a Pluralistic Age* (Minneapolis: Augsburg Fortress, 2004), 124; italics mine.

Rick Warren's *Purpose-Driven Church* and *Purpose-Driven Life* are examples of a popular evangelistic strategy that provide a window for better understanding how contemporary homiletic discourse continues to participate in a trajectory originating with Finney.[30] Arguably the most influential disciple of Finney in our time, Warren's program demonstrates that when separated from the church's theological wisdom, Christian speech is easily reduced to a rhetorical technique for the purpose of effecting predetermined results by means of explanation, prediction, and control.[31]

In a manner similar to Finney's pragmatic revivalism, Warren's method privileges human agency (learning and using purpose-driven principles: information + motivation + application = results) in constructing a practical vision that in both its conception and implementation locates its users outside the narrative of Scripture and the trinitarian economy of grace. This individualistic and sectarian strategy reduces the role of God to an unmediated, disembodied force that acts externally and causally in reaction to the prior activity of human choosers. Warren acknowledges that a tension exists in ministry between two distinct realms: the divine and human, the theological and practical. However, his program fails to show that this split is reconciled and overcome within the trinitarian wisdom of Scripture embodied in Christ and the traditioned practices of the church. Instead, Warren writes:

> I know hundreds of dedicated pastors whose churches are not growing. They are faithful to God's Word, they pray earnestly and consistently, they preach solid messages, and their dedication is unquestioned—but still their churches refuse to grow; it takes skill. . . . The Bible teaches that God has given us a critical role to play in accomplishing his will on earth. Church growth is a partnership between God and man. Churches grow by the power of God through the skilled effort of people. God's power and man's skilled effort must be present. We cannot do it without God but he has decided not to do it without us. God uses people to accomplish his purposes. (*PDC*, 56–57)

30. Rick Warren, *The Purpose-Driven Church: Growth without Compromising Your Message and Mission* (Grand Rapids: Zondervan, 1995). Hereafter references will be included in the text as *PDC*.

31. See the excellent discussion of late modernity's technological environment in D. Stephen Long, *John Wesley's Moral Theology: The Quest for God and Goodness* (Nashville: Abingdon, 2005), 1–36.

The consequence of the grammar that informs Warren's purpose-driven way of configuring the divine/human relationship separates ends and means for the sake of its "effectiveness." This method, in turn, creates an evangelistic strategy underwritten by pragmatic forms of ministry that are ordered to the goal or end of growth of the individual and/or the church. Two additionally important consequences of this strategy are that God is designated as a means in service of the method, while pastoral ministry is redefined as a set of skills guided by instrumental reason and personal choice rather than a practice informed by the theological wisdom of Scripture and the tradition of the church.[32]

Thus driven by a purpose to know "how to" exercise the right means for doing things to and for others—"people don't need Truth, they are looking for relief"—preachers are instructed to seek success in the "job" (the Great Commission), which an arguably depersonalized, "de-trinitized" god, now receded into the background, has presumably handed over to human management and promotion for its success (*PDC*, 64–66).[33]

Joseph Dunne offers a number of helpful insights from the practice of teaching, which in certain forms of educational theory has similarly been subordinated to instrumental reason.

> It is as if the action can be resolved into analysis—that the problems of the first-person agent can be solved from the perspective of the third-person analyst. As a form of action, then, teaching is no longer seen as embedded in particular contexts or within cultural, linguistic, religious or political traditions which may be at work in all kinds of tacit and nuanced ways in teachers and pupils as persons. Or, rather, it is suggested that everything essential in teaching can be dis-embedded from such contexts and traditions, as well as from the urgencies and contingencies of the classroom, and made transparent in a neutral model which, by isolating in precise terms the goals of the activity, provides the teachers with guidelines for controlling efficiency and straightforward criteria for evaluating success. . . . One might teach by this model on the ice but hardly in the rough ground of the classroom.[34]

32. This is the whole point of Kenneson and Street, *Selling (Out) the Church*.

33. For my understanding of the integral relationship between doctrine and life, the pastoral function of Christian doctrine, I have benefited from the argument in Ellen Charry, *By the Renewing of Your Minds: The Pastoral Function of Christian Doctrine* (New York: Oxford University Press, 1997).

34. Dunne, *Back to the Rough Ground*, 5.

The introduction to *The Purpose-Driven Life*, entitled "Journey with Purpose," offers an illustrative example of a theologically unmediated, ecclesially decontextualized form of life abstracted from "the rough ground" of the church's history, tradition, and concrete existence in the world.

> This is more than a book; it is a guide to a *40-day spiritual journey* that will enable you to discover the answer to life's most important question: What on earth am I here for? By the end of this journey you will know God's purpose for your life and will understand the big picture—how all the pieces of your life fit together. Having this perspective will reduce your stress, simplify your decisions, increase your satisfaction, and, most important, prepare you for eternity.[35]

Here it is helpful to focus not only on *what* Warren says but also on *how* he presents this program, since *The Purpose-Driven Life* is seen widely as a model of effective communication that is highly valued for its relevance, practical applicability, and easy access to a user-friendly version of Christianity.[36] However, when viewed in light of Finney's pragmatic revivalism, Warren's purpose-driven method also provides a way of seeing how popular forms of religion work to initiate their users into individualistically and idiosyncratically defined ways of thinking and speaking of God, the church, the self, and the world.[37]

For example, *The Purpose-Driven Life* communicates a way of thinking and speaking of God and God's activity that explains the "purpose-driven" gospel as a way of "salvation" that shapes one's vision and whole way of life that presumably is about glorifying God rather than "you" (the reader).[38] However, the particular form of wisdom in which this claim is explicated fails to show that Warren's description of the "purpose-driven" god and its principles—derived from the "Owner's Manual" (Scripture)—is the Triune God whose identity and activity—which is God's glory—are disclosed in the particular narratives

35. Rick Warren, *The Purpose-Driven Life: What On Earth Am I Here For?* (Grand Rapids: Zondervan, 2002); hereafter references will be given in the text as *PDL*.

36. On Warren's popularity and influence, see Sonja Steptoe, "The Man with Purpose," *Time* 163, no. 13 (March 29, 2004): 54–57.

37. For a good discussion of theology as grammar, see Paul L. Holmer, *The Grammar of Faith* (San Francisco: Harper and Row, 1978).

38. Warren states, "God has not left us in the dark to wonder and guess. He has clearly revealed his five purposes for our lives through the Bible. It is our Owner's Manual, explaining why we are alive, how life works, what to avoid, and what to expect in the future" (*PDL*, 20).

of Israel and Christ, confessed in the church's doctrine, celebrated in its liturgical practice, and embodied in the lives of its saints. Indeed, evidence of such trinitarian teaching and practice is conspicuously absent throughout Warren's work.[39]

Rowan Williams comments on the danger to ourselves of pragmatic reductions of God that prevent God from being himself—from being God, being other, being the life he wants to be for us.

> If we need God simply in order to understand and accept our very reality, then our relation to God in particular circumstances will not be one of need in the ordinary sense, a desperate effort to make God supply this or that desired gratification, physical, intellectual or spiritual. We should instead be capable of receiving God as pure gift, unexpected good news—as the absolutely uncontainable, the irreducibly different: as God.[40]

In addition, Warren's purpose-driven method is supported by approximately one thousand discrete, abstracted Bible verses—used with a minimal amount of interpretation—which for some readers might appear to represent a program that is "biblical." Here it is important, however, to note *how* the Bible is used rather than *how much*. Sermons or other forms of Christian discourse may speak *about* the Bible, perhaps may even use a large quantity of verses *from* the Bible, but this does not necessarily guarantee "biblical" speech in its content, purpose, and scope—that the language of the Bible is being used in the same manner or for the same ends as it has been used by Christians in the past.[41] Like Finney, Warren has been unburdened by the past to create his own tradition, "the purpose-driven life and church," that has its own "canon within the canon"—a highly individualistic, pragmatic way of reading Scripture that is separated from the history of Christian interpretation and its

---

39. Warren's hermeneutical method is fragmentary at best and presents virtually no canonical or theological interpretation of the pieces of Scripture he cites. On using Scripture, he states: "Since the verse divisions and numbers were not included in the Bible until 1560 A.D., I haven't always quoted the *entire* verse, but rather focused on the phrase that was appropriate. My model for this is Jesus and how he and the apostles quoted the Old Testament. They often just quoted a phrase to make a point" (*PDL*, 325). For a study that clearly refutes the method advocated by Warren on theological grounds, see Richard B. Hayes, *Echoes of Scripture in the Letters of Paul* (New Haven: Yale University Press, 1989).

40. Rowan Williams, *On Christian Theology* (Malden, MA: Blackwell, 2000), 75.

41. See the extended discussion of "biblical preaching" in Thomas Long, *The Witness of Preaching* (Louisville: Westminster John Knox, 1989).

enactment by the church.[42] Freed from the Christian convictions and practices it creates and that guide its use, the Bible has been subordinated to individual judgment and experience for the construction of a universal, "one size fits all" program that has been derived from the "Owner's Manual."[43]

The challenge of popular methods such as Warren's lies not in their passion for reaching people but rather in their failure to be sufficiently theological in speaking of God, God's people, and the world according to Scripture and the Christian tradition in light of a trinitarian grammar or wisdom of faith. *It is not sufficient simply to "use" the language of the Bible so long as it works simply to meet deeply felt needs, to offer help, to attract visitors, and to increase church membership. Pastors have a theological responsibility to discern how the use of Christian speech works. It is, after all, a speech that discloses our true status as redeemed but sinful creatures who have been called to praise and delight in God as our highest good and that reeducates our desires toward knowing and participating in the Triune Life revealed in the mystery of Christ, who with the Spirit indwells Scripture and the church for the sanctification of the world.*[44] The church receives this identity and mission as a gift in the liturgical activity of affirming and confessing its belief in the Triune God:

> I believe in God the Father Almighty,
> creator of heaven and earth.
> I believe in Jesus Christ his only Son our Lord,
> who was conceived by the Holy Spirit,
> born of the Virgin Mary,
> suffered under Pontius Pilate,
> was crucified, dead, and buried;

42. In light of the Christian tradition, Warren fails to demonstrate why his purpose-driven account should be considered truthful. From Warren's writings, I assume his ecclesial "tradition" is constituted by Saddleback Church. See chapter 1 of *PDC*. On matters related to reading Scripture in light of tradition, see the good discussion in Stephen E. Fowl and L. Gregory Jones, *Reading in Communion: Scripture and Ethics in Christian Life* (Grand Rapids: Eerdmans, 1991).

43. See the excellent discussion of theological judgment in Craig Dykstra, "Reconceiving Practice in Theological Inquiry and Education," in *Virtues and Practices in the Christian Tradition*, ed. Nancey Murphy, Brad J. Kallenberg, and Mark Thiessen Nation (Harrisburg, PA: Trinity Press International, 1996), 161–84.

44. In *A Better Hope: Resources for a Church Confronting Capitalism, Democracy, and Postmodernity* ([Grand Rapids: Brazos, 2000], 155–63), Stanley Hauerwas discusses the grammar of worship, the significance of not only what we speak but how we speak. See the argument in Kenneson and Street, *Selling (Out) the Church*.

he descended to the dead.
On the third day he rose again;
he ascended into heaven,
is seated at the right hand of God the Father,
and will come again to judge the living and the dead.
I believe in the Holy Spirit,
the holy catholic church,
the communion of saints,
the forgiveness of sins,
the resurrection of the body,
and the life everlasting. Amen. (Apostle's Creed)

In light of the church's trinitarian confession, methods such as Warren's can be seen as having important affinities not only with Finney's pragmatic revivalism but also with the larger liberal Protestant tradition of apologetic theology. Having turned its back on the wisdom of the Christian past, this particular type of apologetic theology separated content and form, thus making the individual the end or goal of the church in its desire to meet the demands of an enlightened "unchurched" world. The tradition of Protestant liberalism (in both its evangelical and mainline expressions) has been characterized by a focus on the autonomous individual separated from the particularity of historical ties and communal traditions that view the church as both divine creation and human witness called to embody God's saving and sanctifying activity with and for creation.[45]

Separated from the narrative of Scripture, the example of the saints, and the wisdom of the Christian tradition, which continue to teach, challenge, and inspire, contemporary biblical interpretation and preaching are subject to any number of powerful but false ideologies, structures, and authorities, most notably, a will to power and status, individual and collective narcissism, and consumerism and the nation-state.[46] Unmeasured by theological wisdom, popular forms of religion

45. See Wood, *Contending for the Faith*, 29–58; see also the excellent argument in Garrett Green, "Kant as Christian Apologist: The Failure of Accommodationist Theology," *Pro Ecclesia* 4, no. 3 (Summer 1995): 301–17.

46. See Stanley M. Hauerwas, *Unleashing the Scripture: Freeing the Bible from Captivity to America* (Nashville: Abingdon, 1993), 35–36; Clapp, *A Peculiar People*, 16–57; referring to fourth-century Arianism, William Thompson refers to this as "pseudo-scripturalism," the use of biblical language as "verbal shells" into which external meaning is poured. William M. Thompson, *The Struggle for Theology's Soul: Contesting Scripture in Christology* (New York: Crossroad, 1996), 250–53; on the reality of the "powers," see the argument in Charles L. Campbell, *The Word before the Powers: An Ethic of Preaching* (Louisville: Westminster John Knox, 2002).

that aim for "relevance" by providing useful methods of obtaining meaning, purpose, and personal affirmation can easily be co-opted into the displacement of the Triune God's providential activity in the world and the disappearance of the church as a sign of the cosmic reconciliation accomplished through the work of Christ and the Spirit: the *missio Dei*.[47]

Speaking of God as Orthodoxy: "Right Praise or Glory"

The Christian practice of preaching is not a homiletic theory, practical technique, or form of religious communication; rather, it is the gift of the Spirit to a reconciled and redeemed humanity, a conversation initiated by God in which the church is addressed by the Father through the Son. This Word is the risen Christ, who summons the church to follow him in bearing witness to creation's true end of praising and knowing the Triune God.[48]

As doxological or praise-centered speech, preaching is a form of discourse that characterizes the identity, vocation, and destiny of a people that is realized in worship, the liturgical gesture of prayer or human dispossession and vulnerability before God. This practice of liturgical formation is best understood as a journey of transformation in which the destination and means of arrival are one and the same: the praise and adoration of God.[49] Inagrace Dietterich comments, "Worship designates the style and purpose, the nature and mission of the church, as the calling and journey of a people who offer praise to the glory of God, which is not a retreat from the world, but . . . which enables Christians to see the world as it really is—the creation of a loving and forgiving God."[50]

47. See the excellent discussion of abstract forms of Christianity in Robert W. Jenson, "What Is Post-Christian?" in *The Strange New World of the Gospel*, ed. Carl E. Braaten and Robert W. Jenson (Grand Rapids: Eerdmans, 2002), 21–31.

48. In my understanding of doxological speech, I am indebted to Daniel W. Hardy and David F. Ford, *Praising and Knowing God* (Philadelphia: Westminster, 1985); Don E. Saliers, *Worship as Theology: Foretaste of Glory Divine* (Nashville: Abingdon, 1994); Aidan Kavanagh, *On Liturgical Theology* (New York: Pueblo, 1984); Wainwright, *Doxology*; Lesslie Newbigin, *Proper Confidence: Faith, Doubt, and Certainty in Christian Discipleship* (Grand Rapids: Eerdmans, 1995), 1–15.

49. Debra Dean Murphy, *Teaching That Transforms: Worship as the Heart of Christian Education* (Grand Rapids: Brazos, 2004), 12–13.

50. Inagrace T. Dietterich, "A Particular People: Toward a Faithful and Effective Ecclesiology," in *The Church between Gospel and Culture: The Emerging Mission in North America*, ed. George R. Hunsberger and Craig Van Gelder (Grand Rapids: Eerdmans, 1996), 364.

Daniel Hardy and David Ford have written extensively of God's glory, the goal of the universe into which humanity is taken up as it turns to the praise, acknowledgment, and affirmation of the Triune God. As they observe, "What is God's glory? Its logic is that of overflowing, creative love, which freely perfects its own perfection and invites others to join this life through praise."[51] Moreover, God's glory disclosed throughout creation and the narrative of Scripture has been revealed definitively in Jesus Christ, for "the Word became flesh and dwelt among us, . . . we have beheld his glory, glory as of the only Son from the Father" (John 1:14). The revelation of God's self-affirmation radically transforms Christian understanding through the scandalous notion of God's glory appearing in a crucified man, thus making the cross central to the practice of orthodoxy ("right praise or glory"). So Hardy and Ford assert, "All the lines of Christianity converge on the Christ-centered worship of God. Renewal has always come through people whose first interest in life has been adoration and realistic attention to God. Any experience of Christianity that does not participate in this has missed the point."[52]

From this perspective, forms of Christianity that attempt to assimilate the concept of divine purpose and glory into human activity and accomplishments must be seen as theologically insufficient expressions of faith. As Leander Keck comments, "The opening line of the Westminster Confession [which declares that the chief end of humankind is "to glorify God and enjoy him forever"] is now reversed, for now the chief end of God is to glorify us and to be useful to us indefinitely."[53] God's purpose and glory, however, cannot be abstracted from the trinitarian economy of salvation—the purpose of the Father enacted through the mission of the Son and the Spirit and exclaimed in the apostolic memory and hope of a people whose very life is doxological.

The divine purpose celebrated in Scripture is the movement of self-giving love in which the Triune God communicates the fullness of his life and glory within the economy of creation and redemption. The foolishness and weakness of the cross provide new criteria for who God is and how God acts in the world through the proclamation of the gospel in the demonstration of divine power, thus revolutionizing our understanding of the glory revealed in Christ and realized through

51. Hardy and Ford, *Praising and Knowing God*, 8.
52. Ibid., 8.
53. Leander Keck, *The Church Confident* (Nashville: Abingdon, 1993), 34.

the Spirit who indwells the church for the salvation and sanctification of the world.

> Blessed be the God and Father of our Lord Jesus Christ, who has blessed us in Christ with every spiritual blessing in the heavenly places, even as he chose us in him before the foundation of the world, that we should be holy and blameless before him. He destined us in love to be his sons through Jesus Christ, according to the purpose of his will, to the praise of his glorious grace which he freely bestowed upon us in the Beloved. In him we have redemption through his blood, the forgiveness of our trespasses, according to the riches of his grace which he lavished upon us. For he has made known to us . . . his purpose which he set forth in Christ as a plan for the fullness of time; to unite all things in him, things in heaven and on earth. (Eph. 1:3–11)

Father Jean Daniélou comments on Ephesians 1,

> The mystery of redemption is the center of the trinitarian plan. Its source is the Father's love for us, it is accomplished through the mission of the Son, and it is fulfilled in us through the gift of the Spirit. Redemption is the work of the Trinity coming to gather up the whole of creation. . . . Here we see God's plan as it unfolds in three moments: first, the preparation for Christ's work in the eternal plan of the Father; next, its realization in the person and mission of Christ; and finally, its fulfillment by the Spirit working in the Church, and guiding God's plan to its completion.[54]

The glory of the Triune God cannot be contained within a program of regulative principles, rules, or motivational talks about what we need to do either for ourselves or for God. God's glory is disclosed through his self-gift in Christ—the divine generosity or "giving away" that we receive and return in being drawn out of ourselves to know the One whose vulnerable self-communication stirs us to amazement, desire, and delight.

God's glory or purpose shines nowhere more resplendently than in the worship of the church, in which our lives are reconstituted as grateful recipients through the gracious activity of Christ and the Spirit present in word and sacrament. In such doxological activity, the Spirit joins us to the Son, who in assuming our human flesh, communicates

---

54. Jean Daniélou, *Prayer: The Mission of the Church*, trans. David Louis Schindler Jr. (Grand Rapids: Eerdmans, 1996), 85.

the radiance of the Father's life and holiness within a contingent, sinful, dying world. Moreover, this is a particular form of glory, *doxa*, which is the blessing and self-giving of the Triune God who draws and transforms us into grateful recipients and passionate speakers of a splendor revealed in the "utterly unglorious" cross of Jesus Christ, to whom our lives and speech are being conformed.[55] Rodney Clapp comments, "Worship is a waste of time. That is the first thing that must be asserted in any careful discussion of the Christian custom of gathering regularly to praise the God of heaven and earth. . . . Worship is distorted and even perverted if it is made instrumental, the means to some other end than glorifying and honoring God. . . . True and right worship (literally orthodoxy) is first and foremost the service of God and needs no further justification."[56]

The doxological speech of the church springs from the worship of the Triune God to constitute the life of the church as a people of praise. Orthodoxy—right praise or glory—generates knowing and doing that is lively and fresh, a joy-filled, ecstatic way of thinking, feeling, and speaking that is freely given by the God of joy and that evokes the fruit of confession. This is not only a confession of human sinfulness and need, but even more important it is a confession of God's praise and glory. It is in being drawn by the Spirit to participate in the knowledge and love of God that we are enabled to transcend the many popular, human-centered forms of ministry that predominate in our time, forms of ministry that reduce preaching to mastery and control by means of skill and technique, reduce the church's mission to a job description, and inhabit the pastoral office with culturally defined "spiritual" executives and entrepreneurs. As Hardy and Ford observe, "Such stoicized forms of Christianity have many allies, especially the nation-state, which is delighted to welcome a religion that is so timid and orderly, leaving the passions free for economics, war, and collective sport."[57]

Perhaps the most offensive and scandalous aspect of speaking the Word of God in our time may be the notion of grace, which announces that from beginning to end our human lives are not of our own making, management, or control. In learning to confess that we are sinful creatures of a gracious God, we discover that our lives are constituted

55. Saliers, *Worship as Theology*, 40–41.
56. Rodney Clapp, "On the Making of Kings and Christians," in *The Conviction of Things Not Seen: Worship and Ministry in the 21st Century*, ed. Todd E. Johnson (Grand Rapids: Brazos, 2002), 109.
57. Hardy and Ford, *Praising and Knowing God*, 144; Fitch, *Great Giveaway*, 27–46.

as gifts rather than possessions, whose purpose is to know and love our Creator. In Christian worship, then, we acknowledge our grateful dependence according to the particular wisdom displayed in the self-giving of Christ, through which the Spirit evokes responsiveness and receptivity to the God who speaks both creation and salvation.[58] Thus, in a time that calls for a strong, robust message of faith, hope, and love, there is no "deeply felt need" more urgent than proclaiming the "foolishness" of the cross—the power and wisdom of the gospel that creates a people of loving praise and glad obedience in whom the Spirit bears witness to the flourishing of humanity before God.

In a recent study of Augustine's theology, Michael Hanby has shown that modernity's "dis-graced" forms of "Pelagian" or "stoicized" religion, predicated on human mastery, explanation, and control, served a "de-trinitized" god without participation in doxological delight, which is the filial union shared by the Son and the Father that is rooted in the body of Christ. This has resulted in the loss of a sense of divine beauty and love that draws us toward the life of God, the longing for divine truth and goodness that makes us happy, and the knowledge and wisdom of Christ, whose adoration and imitation constitute redemption. The theological loss of salvation as the restoration of communion between divine and human being, as union of creature with creator, turned the individual will into "a will to power . . . set over against God's body [Christ and the church] which must be placed under house arrest." A trinitarian vision of divine and human reality is thus reduced to external, self-contained, and functional arrangements in which god "uses" humanity just as humanity "uses" god to achieve predetermined goals. God then becomes an immanent, causal force that in the end leaves everything "up to us" and the graceless autonomy of the human will, which is "the man-god" of religion and a form of "nihilism."[59]

Hanby argues persuasively that for Augustine it is only because of divine grace that the self is doxological, the gift by which we become truly ourselves in God's love of, delight in, and giving of himself. Moreover, it is only through delight in Christ, the gift of mutual delight between the Father and the Son, that "I" can finally and freely be

58. Stanley Hauerwas, *A Better Hope: Resources for a Church Confronting Capitalism, Democracy, and Postmodernity* (Grand Rapids: Brazos, 2000), 155–62; Murphy, *Teaching That Transforms*, 97–220.

59. Michael Hanby, *Augustine and Modernity* (New York: Routledge, 2003), 1–5, 177–79; see the older, but still excellent discussion of Arius in Arthur C. McGill, *Suffering: A Test of Theological Method* (Philadelphia: Westminster, 1982).

both fully myself and fully God's. Augustine contended that the Pelagians introduced another kind of self that was alien to this trinitarian economy of grace, thus reducing divine assistance to knowledge of the law and equating grace with knowing, but doing so without mediating what is known through Christ, the Wisdom of God. Conspicuously absent are the love, joy, and delight of the Triune God whose gracious presence through the self-giving of Christ in the Spirit binds us to the source and end of human desiring and happiness and transforms our humanity into the form or beauty of Christ.

Pelagian "pietism" thus established itself as its own origin and ground without participation in the delight of Father and Son, the union of lover and beloved, and was reduced to a controlled, rational operation of cause and effect through autonomous human understanding and the exercise of "free" will. In practice, this created a moralistic gospel of human duty to obey the new law given by Jesus, who himself was effectively reduced from the incarnate Son of the Father to a human sage who communicates practical instruction and advice and motivation to apply this new law, but without the self-communication of God that engenders and nourishes life.[60]

Convinced that the grammar of faith is given in the form of Christ and generated within the trinitarian economy of grace, Augustine offered an alternative to the Pelagians' moralistic use of words. Speaking of God is a gift of prior grace: the fullness, abundance, and overflowing goodness of God's being and life revealed in the Word, through whom the wisdom of salvation is communicated in Scripture by the witness of the Spirit, who orders human speech to the praise of God.[61]

Speaking of God: A Trinitarian Theology of Preaching

In an important essay,[62] Richard Lischer has written of the fragmentation of theology and its alienation from the life of the contemporary church. He argues that nowhere does this fragmentation impact with greater force and nowhere is the pain felt more deeply than in the

---

60. Hanby, *Augustine and Modernity*, 72–105; see also James K. A. Smith, *Introducing Radical Orthodoxy: Mapping a Post-Secular Theology* (Grand Rapids: Baker, 2004), 108–22.

61. Hanby, *Augustine and Modernity*, 101–5; Hardy and Ford, *Praising and Knowing God*, 6–23.

62. Richard Lischer, *A Theology of Preaching*, 2nd ed. (Durham, NC: Labyrinth, 1992), 1–15.

practice of preaching: "Only the preacher who is rooted in the church's constitutive principles, its doctrine, will be free to address the concerns of living people."[63] Theology monitors the church's proclamation of the gospel and functions as the mediator between exegesis and preaching. Because of the nature and task of preaching, theology and exegesis serve the important purpose of creating and sustaining the life of a community in which the ministry of the Word is the final expression of its theology.[64] Lischer envisions the rediscovery of a practical vision in which an integration of Scripture and theology in the life of the preacher is publicly mediated to the church through sermons ordered around the community's manifold experience of the gospel.

The following interrelated and overlapping chapters attempt to sketch such a vision by means of an extended conversation regarding matters integral to preaching within the trinitarian "grammar" of faith confessed by the church: preaching as a theological practice; preaching as a traditioned practice; preaching as an ecclesial practice; preaching as a pastoral practice; preaching as a scriptural practice; preaching as a beautiful practice; and preaching as a pilgrim practice.[65] An important participant in this conversation will be Augustine, who is joined by Irenaeus, Martin Luther, John Wesley, and numerous contemporary figures. Each chapter ends with a sermon that attempts to reunite the church's trinitarian faith with proclamation; these sermons serve as homiletic expressions of the vision articulated throughout this book. The aim is to exemplify a way of thinking and speaking that will contribute to the renewal of preaching as a gift of thankful praise to the One who alone is worthy of worship. *Christian Preaching* is therefore unapologetically doxological in proclaiming the glory of the Triune God, the divine mystery who is the source, means, and goal of all our feeble attempts to bring Christ to speech.

63. Ibid., 1.
64. Ibid., 14.
65. In thinking through the structure of this book, I have been instructed by Brad J. Kallenberg, *Ethics as Grammar: Changing the Postmodern Subject* (Notre Dame, IN: University of Notre Dame Press, 2001).

1

Speaking of God:
Preaching as a Theological Practice

Grant, Almighty God, that all who confess your Name may be united in your truth, live together in your love, and reveal your glory in the world.

—Book of Common Prayer

For most of Christian history the practice of preaching was believed to have taken place in, with, and through the initiative and presence of the Triune God. Human speakers and listeners understood themselves as standing in the presence of divine mystery in answering God's speech, or Word, moved by the witness of the Spirit, who evokes awe and wonder, confession and lament, joyful thanks and loving adoration.[1] As a trinitarian practice, therefore, preaching begins in prayer and ends in praise, originating in the gift of silence and reverent attention

1. In drafting this chapter, I have benefited from Daniel W. Hardy and David F. Ford, *Praising and Knowing God* (Philadelphia: Westminster, 1985); Geoffrey Wainwright, *Doxology: The Praise of God in Worship, Doctrine and Life* (New York: Oxford University Press, 1980); Aidan Kavanagh, *On Liturgical Theology* (New York: Pueblo, 1984); Peter Brunner, *Worship in the Name of Jesus*, trans. M. H. Bertram (St. Louis: Concordia, 1968); William H. Willimon, *The Service of God: How Worship and Ethics Are Related* (Nashville: Abingdon, 1983).

to God's new language and life incarnate in Christ, which is attested by the whole of Scripture and embodied in the glad obedience of the church.

We therefore listen before we speak, since in the discourse of the Spirit the risen Christ—the Word who dwells among us—speaks, bringing prayerful attentiveness to wonder and amazement in communicating himself in the gifts of faith, hope, and love, and the knowledge of God and humanity.[2] Moreover, because the holy conversation of the Son and Spirit with the Father constitutes our life as church, the language of preaching is not of our own creation. We are summoned and prompted to speak with and after the Word and Spirit so that we are transformed into a word or sermon spoken under the sway of the breath or power of another.[3] Paul Bradshaw comments:

> In the biblical tradition there is little difference between prayer and the proclamation of God's Word. When we pray our prayer of remembrance we are also preaching, and when we read aloud the biblical text or tell of God's work in the world, we are also engaged in the prayer of remembrance. Worship and mission are thus not separate things between which a choice may have to be made. On the contrary, they are the very same activity. To do one is to do the other. To proclaim the gospel is to offer worship to God, and to recount God's mighty deeds in prayer is to preach the good news.[4]

Nicholas Lash has persuasively argued that the primary, although not exclusive, function of Christian doctrine is regulative or grammatical. By this Lash means that Christian doctrine provides identity-sustaining rules of discourse and behavior that govern Christian uses of the word "God" in prayer, praise, and proclamation. The doctrine of the Trinity is the "summary grammar" of the Christian account of creation and redemption, guiding our action and speech so that we may speak and act in relation or truthful reference to the mystery of God in which we live and work, hope and die.

2. See the excellent discussion in David S. Yeago, "The Bible," in *Knowing the Triune God: The Work of the Spirit in the Practices of the Church*, ed. James J. Buckley and David S. Yeago (Grand Rapids: Eerdmans, 2001), 49–94.

3. Here I am indebted to Oliver Davies, *A Theology of Compassion: Metaphysics of Difference and the Renewal of Tradition* (Grand Rapids: Eerdmans, 2001), 189–209; I have discussed the theological wisdom of premodern preaching in Michael Pasquarello III, *Sacred Rhetoric: Preaching as a Theological and Pastoral Practice of the Church* (Grand Rapids: Eerdmans, 2005).

4. Paul F. Bradshaw, *Two Ways of Praying* (Nashville: Abingdon, 1995), 49.

We require some such grammar for our pedagogy, because all the pressures—outside and within—both pressures applied by the structures and mind-sets of individualism and collectivism alike, and pressures derived from fear and egotism, homelessness, ambition, and despair, incline us to opt for "irrelation": to treat persons as things, and to bind the mystery of God into the It-world by mistakenly identifying some feature of the world—some individual, some nation, some possession, some dream, some project, or some ideal—with divinity, with the "nature" of God. We require some "set of protocols against idolatry," against the manifold forms of the illusion that the nature of God lies within our grasp.[5]

From Theological to Technological Preaching

Lash's comments are especially significant for contemporary preaching. One consequence of the modern professionalization of clergy education and formalization of divisions between the theological disciplines was a separation of the study of doctrine and Scripture that reoriented these according to their respective academic guilds and distanced them from ecclesial tradition and practice. Further, these divisions transformed preaching from a form of pastoral discourse in primary theology or godly wisdom—for the praise of God and sanctification of humanity—into a technique shaped more by dependence on rhetorical skills and communication strategies than the trinitarian language and grammar of the church.[6] Paul Holmer writes of the grammar of faith:

Knowing God, then, is a matter of coming to know him in prayer, worship, and praise, and much else that makes up the religious life. Theology, now thinking of it in the grammatical sense, is not a substitute for worship; and it certainly is not a lofty and sophisticated way to acknowledge God in contrast to the vulgar modes of belief and submissive respect. It

5. Nicholas Lash, *Easter in Ordinary: Reflections on Human Experience and the Knowledge of God* (Notre Dame, IN: University of Notre Dame Press, 1988), 260–61; on trinitarian grammar, see the excellent introduction by Philip Turner in *Nicene Christianity: The Future for a New Ecumenism*, ed. Christopher Seitz (Grand Rapids: Brazos, 2001); on the Trinity and preaching, see the essays in *Exploring and Proclaiming the Apostles' Creed*, ed. Roger E. Van Harn (Grand Rapids: Eerdmans, 2004); for a detailed discussion of grammar, see Brad J. Kallenberg, *Ethics as Grammar: Changing the Postmodern Subject* (Notre Dame, IN: University of Notre Dame Press, 2001), 113–214.

6. See James Kay, "Reorientation: Homiletics as Theologically Authorized Rhetoric," *The Princeton Seminary Bulletin* 24, no. 1 (2003): 16–35; Charles L. Campbell, *Preaching Jesus: New Directions in Hans Frei's Postliberal Theology* (Grand Rapids: Eerdmans, 1997).

does not substitute new concepts for those in the story, for that again is no improvement but is invariably a radically different replacement. One might say a new concept changes the entire grammar. . . . Like grammar in more mundane instances of everyday speech, theology is both all that we have—namely, knowing what is right to say—and also the way one secures the identity of God. . . . The true God is known only when his identity is established in a tradition and by a ruled practice of language and worship.[7]

Because words draw their meaning from the company they keep, it is necessary that we recover the primacy of preaching as a theological practice that participates in the scripturally and ecclesially mediated character of truth communicated in Christ, the One of whom we speak.[8] The nature and purpose of preaching is theological and doxological, which requires that we be schooled in the habits necessary for listening to and answering God in the Christian practices of prayer and praise. Our primary need, then, is to be formed in the theological grammar of Christian speech for the ministry of proclamation: speaking with and after God's self-knowledge revealed in the gospel through the wisdom of Holy Scripture. Lash comments:

It is, after all, Jesus who is confessed to be God's Word made flesh; it is his life, and history, and destiny that speak to us, inviting our response. There is no other word in God but this one Word, which finds fully focused form and expression, in the created order, in the history of the Crucified. Nothing is to be gained by attempting, as it were, to listen "beyond" Jesus, for some other word than that which he is said to be. What, might we say, would God utter, but his Word?[9]

One of the most difficult challenges we face is a widespread presumption that the ecclesial activity we call preaching and the listening it engenders requires little training or cultivation of the theological virtues of faith, hope, and love—virtues that allow us to hear the one Word God speaks. There is a widespread view that preaching is no longer intrinsic to the worship of God since, for many, worship has been reduced to a matter of individual "religious" preference or taste—a marketed "style" that functions instrumentally to promote the growth of the

7. Paul Holmer, *The Grammar of Faith* (New York: Harper & Row, 1978), 203–4.
8. Lash, *Beginning and the End of "Religion,"* 23–24.
9. Nicholas Lash, *Holiness, Speech and Silence: Reflections on the Question of God* (Aldershot: Ashgate, 2004), 76.

church or individuals rather than to create and transform a people for the praise and glory of God.

An increasing number of those who occupy both pulpit and pew see themselves no longer standing under the authority of the Word of God as it is found in the story of Israel and the life, death, and resurrection of Jesus Christ. However, if "the end of words" is to become congruent with the Word spoken by the Triune God of whom Christians speak, it must be recovered as a theological practice that attempts "to involve the whole church in eager, grateful listening, as well-schooled and well-crafted hearers of the Word, just as accomplished and prepared as the preacher."[10] This is the "work of the people," the liturgical activity that conforms the church to the Word made flesh.

It is only because of the gracious activity of God and not ourselves that we are able to speak with confidence; thus the Christian faith is shaped by a life of repentance and hope. Moreover, the whole creation continues to long with hope for the revelation of such reconciliation and friendship, to participate in the communion of the Son with the Father through the gift of the Spirit—the extravagance of divine forgiveness and reconciliation poured out in baptismal and eucharistic practice upon a redeemed, sinful people in whom the Triune God is pleased to dwell.[11] Debra Dean Murphy comments:

> Christians are those who worship the Triune God, what we know and how we know are bound together in doxology. The longing to know the truth of God and of ourselves is not merely intellectual but is the deepest desire of our souls, a desire fulfilled only in community, in communion—in the fellowship of Christian sisters and brothers and in the eternal mystery of the God who is our life. . . . Catechesis, in its various forms, helps us to fulfill our mission in the world, for the work of the people—*leitourgia*—is never done.[12]

Such truthfulness in speech and life, the witness of a church "evangelized" over time into the "faith which comes by hearing," is dem-

---

10. See the essays in Stanley Hauerwas, *Sanctify Them in the Truth: Holiness Exemplified* (Nashville: Abingdon, 1998), 19–36, 191–200, 235–40; see also Richard Lischer, *The End of Words: The Language of Reconciliation in a Culture of Violence* (Grand Rapids: Eerdmans, 2005).

11. Aidan Kavanagh, *On Liturgical Theology* (New York: Pueblo, 1984), 73–176; Barry A. Harvey, *Another City: An Eccesiological Primer for a Post-Christian World* (Harrisburg, PA: Trinity Press International, 1999), 135–66.

12. Debra Dean Murphy, *Teaching That Transforms: Worship as the Heart of Christian Education* (Grand Rapids: Brazos, 2004), 219.

onstrated in the gift of repentance, the purification and redirection of all human desire toward God's self-gift in Christ. Such transformation occurs in hearing the one Word God is and speaks, in a living "away" from ourselves to that which is beyond our control or possession, in loving attention to the truth that is mediated through a divine and human conversation initiated by the Spirit.[13] Such listening is a gift bestowed and received within a particular way of life formed by the gospel, which according to the wisdom of the world may sound so strange that many will claim it could hardly be "good news": the announcement that "God has made both Lord and Christ this Jesus who was crucified."[14]

Severed from the mystery of God whose self-communication is mediated through Scripture and doctrine, or the liturgy and life of the church, the practice of preaching has been increasingly held captive by individualistic, abstract, and instrumental aims. This loss has led to a surrender of the distinctive theological wisdom necessary for Christian people to distinguish themselves from false expressions of speech and life. Thus, when situated within the theory/practice split embraced by modernity, preaching is easily reduced to a task of formulaic design, valued primarily for its utility in effecting desired outcomes and goals external to the astonishing scriptural narrative of creation and redemption, a narrative whose author is the Triune God revealed in the mystery of the Word spoken and the Spirit outpoured.[15] Eugene Peterson comments:

> The secularized mind is terrorized by mysteries. Thus it makes lists, labels people, assigns roles, and solves problems. But a solved life is a reduced life. These tightly buttoned up people never take great faith risks or make convincing love talk. They deny or ignore the mysteries and diminish human existence to what can be managed, controlled, and fixed. We live in a cult of experts who explain and solve. The vast technological apparatus around us gives the impression that there is a

13. Rowan Williams, *On Christian Theology* (Malden, MA: Blackwell, 2000), 83–84.

14. Lash, *Beginning and the End of "Religion,"* 164–82, 219–36, cf. Acts 2:36; Stanley M. Hauerwas, *Wilderness Wanderings: Probing Twentieth-Century Theology and Philosophy* (Boulder, CO: Westview Press, 1997), 164–67.

15. Edward Farley, *Theologia: Fragmentation and Unity of Theological Education* (Philadelphia: Fortress, 1983), 72–139; see the discussion of modern biblical scholarship in Stanley M. Hauerwas, *Unleashing the Scripture: Freeing the Bible from Captivity to America* (Nashville: Abingdon, 1993); Robert Louis Wilken, "In Defense of Allegory," in *Theology and Scriptural Imagination*, ed. L. Gregory Jones and James J. Buckley (Malden, MA: Blackwell, 1998), 35–49.

tool for everything if we can only afford it. Pastors cast in the role of spiritual technologists are hard put to keep that role from absorbing everything else, since there are so many that need to be and can, in fact, be fixed.[16]

Removed from the ecology of divine truth and love embodied in scriptural memory, liturgical practice, and doctrinal confession through which the Triune God speaks and acts to form and re-form the church, these "innovative" forms of preaching tend inevitably toward trivialized and even idolatrous forms of speech and life. Richard Lischer comments on this "Gospel of Technology":

> The retreat from the word was fueled by the ideology of a newly professionalized culture and the personal insecurities of the minister. A second retreat from the word is underway, this one in large, successful churches whose members would never dream that the light shows, videos and PowerPoint presentations that accompany the Sunday sermon represent a fundamental lack of confidence in the spoken word of God. The new retreat is guided by a new professional class, the media and communications technicians whose expertise makes the sermon possible every Sunday. . . . The techies have become the most valuable members of the "sermon team" which includes a planning process in which the priestly encounter with the word of God has been displaced by something nearer to a group engineering project.[17]

While such technological methods may indeed appear to produce messages that provide "meaning" and "purpose" to anxious "seekers," in practice they reduce Christianity to a gnostic message that separates the form of the gospel from its content—the biblical narrative of the Triune God disclosed in creation, Israel, Jesus, and his community of disciples. The Word is thus abstracted from human flesh, and Christ is abstracted from his church, resulting in a sacred/secular, spiritual/material split that renders God without a people and the Creator separated from creation.[18] Ironically, this discarnate gospel and domesticated God have contributed to a relentless quest for "relevance" that involves

---

16. Eugene Peterson, *The Contemplative Pastor: Returning to the Art of Spiritual Direction* (Grand Rapids: Eerdmans, 1989), 64.

17. Lischer, *End of Words*, 24–25.

18. See the thorough discussion of Gnosticism in Philip J. Lee, *Against the Protestant Gnostics* (Oxford: Oxford University Press, 1987); see also Rodney Clapp, *A Peculiar People: The Church as Culture in a Post-Christian Society* (Downers Grove, IL: InterVarsity, 1996), 34–36.

discovering new methods of preaching that will meet listeners' needs and close the perceived gap between such compartmentalized forms of Christianity and the presumed "real world." Debra Murphy describes the symptoms of this crisis:

> The market driven character of much of our worship; the dumbing down of the church's historic liturgy; the thoughtless capitulation by Christians to consumer capitalism; the extolling of managerial models of ecclesial leadership; the view of the church as a promoter of "family values" and defender of (abstract) principles of love, justice, and freedom; the facile identification of Christianity and nationalism; the failure to train the imaginations of the young; the devolving of rigorous Christian discourse into pious sentimentality; and the growing trend across Christian traditions toward a vacuous, generic, benign pop spirituality.[19]

Uninformed by the grammar or rule of Christian doctrine, such evangelistic and apologetic strategies, no matter how well intended, fail to discern a problem that is fundamentally theological, since Christian preaching *is* a theological practice. At its heart, preaching is the human articulation of the speech of God, the gospel, through which the Spirit is actively gathering up all things in heaven and on earth under the lordship of Christ for the praise and glory of the Father.

At stake in this "turn to the self" is the vocation of the church to worship the Triune God. This is primarily a theological rather than a stylistic matter, since it is within the economy of salvation that the church has been created as a witness to God's loving purpose of raising a fallen creation to share in his glory. Reinhard Hütter writes:

> The goal . . . is to retrieve an understanding common to almost all Christians until roughly two hundred years ago: that the church is the location where we come to know God, surely not in every possible way, but in the one decisive way; namely, as the One who saves us and draws us into the fullness of the divine life—all of this through faith in the crucified and risen Jesus Christ. The church is nothing other than the thankful creature of God's saving work, not a proud executor but a glad recipient. Yet this receiving embodied in practices is precisely the way in and through which the Holy Spirit works the saving knowledge of God. For this very reason not only the Catholics but also the Reformers could call the church the "mother of faith."[20]

19. Murphy, *Teaching That Transforms*, 23.
20. Reinhard Hütter, *Bound to Be Free: Evangelical Catholic Engagements in Ecclesiology, Ethics, and Ecumenism* (Grand Rapids: Eerdmans, 2004), 44.

When preaching is expressed in forms of teaching that offer explanations of Christian life abstracted from the mystery of Christ narrated by Scripture, the church loses its story—the surprising, astonishing power and wisdom of God whose Word speaks to, with, and in the world to create and sustain a holy people whose presence demonstrates and extends the God-given life of salvation. Abstraction, moreover, separates salvation from the life of God and its historical embodiment in the life of the church, the great communion of praise and adoration raised up to bear truthful, radiant witness to the glory of the Trinity, whose kingdom of peace and righteousness has arrived in the life, death, and resurrection of Christ and outpouring of the Holy Spirit. As Hauerwas states:

> The alternative to explanation and understanding is descriptions made possible by truthful stories. The Christian narrative stands in contrast to explanation and understanding just to the extent that Christians offer descriptions that are unintelligible if our very existence does not come as a gift. . . . That the church is able to offer such a peace has been made possible by the life of the one we call Jesus. For it is in his life we believe we rightly see the end that was "in the beginning." That story, the story of Jesus, we also believe is the story of the church. . . . We were not created for no purpose, but rather for the glory of God. That alone is the story of stories.[21]

Perhaps nothing is more urgent in our time than the recovery of truthful speech in our Christian gatherings. Rowan Williams observes that truthful discourse that speaks of God and our life before God as inhabitants of a moral universe is an inherently political and liturgical matter. Such language, however, is often spoken in the "about" mode, which characterizes the discourse of those driven by a desire for the retention of power, as well as those whose discourse is driven by desire to negotiate a way into the power relations that prevail.[22]

Christian speech is incapable of doing its appointed work in the mode of explanation and understanding because it is language that is received as a gift, and because it stands under God's judgment. Therefore Christian speech must resist the urge to close and finish what is said. Thus if our homiletic discourse is to approach honesty,

21. Stanley Hauerwas, *Performing the Faith: Bonhoeffer and the Practice of Nonviolence* (Grand Rapids: Brazos, 2004), 145–46.
22. Williams, *On Christian Theology*, 5–6.

it must remain close to the particular, taking "as normative a story of response to God in the world and the world in God, the record of Israel and Jesus."[23] The biblical narrative, which tells a story of the re-formation of human responses to God, weaves together history and liturgy; the God perceived in the story of Israel is addressed as well as talked about in a common life of prayer and praise. "The integrity of a community's language about God, the degree to which it escapes its own pressures to power and closure, is tied to the integrity of the language it directs to God."[24]

Truthful vision cannot be divorced from truthful worship, which means that truthful speech emerges from the life of a people who seek God simply for God's sake, to know and love God. This is a desire that needs no other "purpose" for its justification. William Willimon comments:

> To use the church's worship for any purpose other than the glorification of God is to abuse worship. Worship loses its integrity when it is regarded instrumentally as a means to something else, even as a means of achieving the most noble human purposes, even the noble purpose of moral edification. *Leitourgia* must be celebrated for its own sake, not simply as a means of rallying the faithful for *diakonia*. Worship must not be one more "resource" in our pastoral bag of tricks for getting people to be more just or more loving or anything else. Utilitarianism . . . remains the greatest temptation in American Christian worship. . . . Such worship is a human-centered, human orchestrated perversion of what is meant to be a divine-human centered activity.[25]

Without a truthful narrative that exposes our illusions and offers a compelling vision of the Triune God, who is the beginning and end of all that is, and without a truthful story of a crucified and risen Savior and his people that captivates our imaginations and empowers us to stand against the powers of this world, consumer culture offers profound problems for the contemporary church. Belief is systematically misdirected from traditional religious practices into consumption, while believers and seekers alike have been trained to abstract doctrines and practices from the traditions and communal frameworks that connect them to a particular God and a particular form of life.

23. Ibid., 7.
24. Ibid.
25. William H. Willimon, *The Service of God: How Worship and Ethics Are Related* (Nashville: Abingdon, 1983), 42.

Countering this pragmatic, utilitarian deployment of Christian doctrines and practices requires their rightful relocation in the larger narrative of God's providential activity and provision of exemplars whose witness displays the wisdom of truthful practice.[26] The church names such characters "saints" rather than "experts," remembering them not for their effectiveness but for lives marked by holiness, the fruit of charity, and the sacrifice of thanksgiving to the One who alone is worthy to receive such praise.[27]

Re-Theologizing the Word: A More Excellent Way

One such salutary exemplar and saint is Augustine, bishop of Hippo in North Africa (d. 430), whose *De doctrina christiana* (*Teaching Christianity*) was the first substantive theology of preaching. This pastoral treatise has played an enduring role in the formation of Christian leaders to speak of Christ, the Word of God, in the Spirit's power.[28] Augustine's purpose was primarily to teach Christian pastors to praise, know, and love the Triune God by participating in a conversation created by the eloquence of the Spirit and the wisdom of Christ, and thereby to learn the grammar of faith, which is both theological and doxological. As Augustine affirms, "It is not easy, after all, to find any name that will really fit such transcendent majesty. In fact it is better just to say that this Trinity is the one God, from whom are all things, through whom are all things, in whom are all things" (*DDC* 1.5). Moreover, Augustine acknowledges that while nothing really worthy of God can be said, he still accepts and desires for human voices to rejoice in praising him, which is the same as calling him God (*DDC* 1.6).

26. See the insightful argument in Vincent J. Miller, *Consuming Religion: Christian Faith and Practice in a Cultural Practice* (New York: Continuum, 2004).

27. See the excellent discussion in D. Stephen Long, "God Is Not Nice," in *God Is Not—: Religious, Nice, "One of Us," an American, a Capitalist*, ed. D. Brent Laytham (Grand Rapids: Brazos, 2004), 39–54.

28. I am using the edition of *De doctrina christiana* published by the Augustinian Heritage Institute, *The Works of Saint Augustine: A Translation for the 21st Century, Teaching Christianity*, 1/11, ed. John E. Rotelle, OSA, trans. Edmund Hill, OP (Hyde Park, NY: New City, 1996). Hereafter references will be included in the text as *DDC*. I have followed the discussion of *De doctrina christiana* in Telford Work, *Living and Active: Scripture in the Economy of Salvation* (Grand Rapids: Eerdmans, 2002); Frances M. Young, *Biblical Exegesis and the Formation of Christian Culture* (Peabody, MA: Hendrickson, 2002); Luke Timothy Johnson and William S. Kurz, *The Future of Catholic Biblical Scholarship* (Grand Rapids: Eerdmans, 2002); Carol Harrison, *Augustine: Christian Truth and Fractured Humanity* (Oxford: Oxford University Press, 2000), 46–78.

For Augustine, the task of learning to speak of God was a matter of learning to articulate appropriate rules for human discourse, cultivated through attention to Scripture and by perceiving how the practices of Christianity shape our language according to God's activity in creation and redemption.[29] In writing, then, Augustine was about the business of conversion, which involves the formation of Christian understanding and the character of love. This concern with conversion reveals Augustine's commitment to the life-shaping role of Scripture in relation to divine truth and goodness. He believed that Scripture possessed the capacity to transform the speech and life of preachers through an increase of cognitive and affective love for the Triune God, who fully knows and loves his creation. This is the gift of passionate intellect, personal knowledge, and wisdom that so habituates one's thinking and speaking as to become the praise-shout of God's people. As Paul Griffiths notes, for Augustine, "True speech is disowned, relinquished, returned as gift to its giver, definitively and universally not yours. . . . To speak truly is to accept the gift of speech by adoration."[30]

Significantly, Augustine begins by calling attention to the essential subject matter of Scripture, which is articulated in the church's Rule of Faith and embodied in its liturgical life. The Rule of Faith, or Truth, points to the true objects of human praise, love, and enjoyment: the Father, Son, and Holy Spirit, the Holy Trinity—the one Being who is the living God. Thus the Christian God cannot be utilized or treated instrumentally like other objects, idols, or commodities, but is known only through faith in the form of delight and dispossession, desire and self-surrender. The practices of prayer and praise transform Christian people for the grateful reception and "use" of all things as gifts in light of and for that love, thus reordering desires and drawing lives more deeply into the communion of charity that is the source and end of all creation. Here Augustine differs significantly from modern, pragmatic, utilitarian views of God, humanity, and the world.

> Some things are to be enjoyed, others to be used, and there are others, which are to be enjoyed and used. Those things, which are to be enjoyed, make us blessed. Those things, which are to be used, help and, as it were, sustain us as we move toward blessedness in order that we may

29. Lewis Ayres, "The Fundamental Grammar of Augustine's Trinitarian Theology," in *Augustine and His Critics*, ed. Robert Dodaro and George Lawless (London: Routledge, 2000), 53.

30. Paul J. Griffiths, *Lying: An Augustinian Theology of Duplicity* (Grand Rapids: Brazos, 2004), 85.

gain and cling to those things, which make us blessed. If we who enjoy and use things, being placed in the midst of things of both kinds, wish to enjoy those things which should be used, our course will be impeded and sometimes deflected, so we are retarded in obtaining those things which are to be enjoyed, or even prevented altogether, shackled by an inferior love. (*DDC* 1.3.3)

Augustine therefore begins his handbook for preachers with an exposition of Christian orthodoxy, right praise or worship, and the wisdom of salvation. The combination of these three produces a knowledge and love of truth that reorders one's desire from self to God and to the neighbor in God, which is citizenship in the kingdom of charity. Accordingly, Augustine articulates the grand story of God narrated in the incarnation, the "Word made flesh," rehearsing the life, death, resurrection, and ascension of Christ, and the anticipation of his return in glory. Concluding the narrative of salvation, he discusses the gift of the Spirit, the church, forgiveness of sin, and resurrection of spirit and body to eternal life (*DDC* 1.14.13–1.20.21).

Book 1 of *De doctrina christiana* displays Augustine's fundamental commitment to the primary doxological ethos of the church. This ethos is, for Augustine, the praise and adoration of God the Triune Creator, who in Christ and the Spirit overcomes the power and effects of false securities and defenses that are manifested in human pride and sin. These include the aspiration to self-creation and self-love, the temptation to idolatry, the reduction of ourselves to need, and the reduction of others, including God, to our usefulness. Augustine, in contrast, confesses the church's faith by pointing to the truths of revelation that lead to the gift of divine wisdom for the restoration of humanity into God's image and likeness. These revelatory truths include the transcendent end of human existence (life with God), the way to this end (conformity to Christ), life constituted by faith and love (holiness), the affirmation of the Word embodied in a form of life (the church), and participation in the gifts and life of divine grace (the glory of God) (*DDC* 1).

Augustine therefore unites the narrative of the incarnation with an exposition of the law of love, the telos of Christian worship that transforms humanity for intimate friendship with God, the self, and neighbor. This is the sum of truth, the "thing" to which all Scripture points, the law of love for God and neighbor, who are united within Christ's divinity and humanity, the head and his body the church (*DDC*

3.25). Thus no matter how popular or convincing an interpretation, sermon, or way of life, it is mistaken if it does not build up the twofold law of love incarnate in Christ and Scripture. Faith is not simply a matter of believing certain things about God, but is "a matter of setting as our heart's desire the holy mystery disclosed in Christ towards whose blinding presence we walk in company on pilgrimage."[31] The healing of humanity for communion, for love and enjoyment of God and for love of neighbor and creation in and for God, is given through Scripture in the form of Christ, who by the Spirit's love transforms false attachments and redirects inordinate desires that dishonor God, harm the self, and do violence to others.

> Scripture, though, commands nothing but charity and love, and censures nothing but cupidity, or greed, and that is why it gives shape to human morals. Again, if people's minds are already in thrall to some erroneous opinion, whatever scripture asserts that differs from it will be reckoned by them to be said in a figurative way. The only thing, though, it ever asserts is Catholic faith, with reference to things in the past and in the future and in the present. It tells the story of things past, foretells things future, points out things present; but all these things are of value for nourishing and fortifying charity or love, and overcoming and extinguishing cupidity or greed. (*DDC* 3.10.15)

Augustine was convinced that the practice of theology, the knowledge of God signified by Scripture and confessed in the church, must have at its center the inexorable love of God, who desires the return of such love by humble, teachable minds (*DDC* 2.7.9–2.9.14). One learns and grows into Christ, the subject matter of Scripture, by participating in the faith and disciplined way of the church, both of which are gifts of the Spirit: fear or reverence for a holy God, knowledge and love of God, piety or devotion, strength and courage, and purity of vision and wisdom. Most important, preachers must continually seek the Lord's face out of love for the Word, who gives understanding for truthful speech.

> They should familiarize themselves with the kinds of expression employed in the Holy Scriptures and be alert to observe how things are commonly said in them and to commit it to memory. But much more important than that, and supremely necessary is that they should pray

---

31. Lash, *Beginning and the End of "Religion,"* 169.

for understanding. After all, in this very literature, which they are eager to study, they read that the Lord gives wisdom, and from his face come knowledge and understanding. From him indeed it is that they have received their interest and eagerness to study, if it is qualified by loving piety. (*DDC* 3.37.56)

Through the practice of preaching, the Word continues to call, guide, and accompany a pilgrim people, thus illumining a journey whose end is the transformation of all things into the fullness of joy given in the vision of God.

That is why, since we are meant to enjoy the truth, which is unchangeably alive, and since it is in its light that God the Trinity, author and maker of the universe, provides for all the things he has made, our minds have to be purified to enable them to perceive that light, and to cling to it once perceived. We should think of this purification process as being a kind of walk, a kind of voyage to our home country. We do not draw near after all, by movement in place to the One who is present everywhere, but by honest commitment and good behavior. (*DDC* 1.10.10)

According to Augustine we would be incapable of such pilgrimage unless Wisdom herself had seen fit to adapt herself even to such infirmity as ours, providing an example of how to live in the form of our human flesh. And being counted foolish so that we might become wise, she stooped to share our weakness so we might be made strong (*DDC* 1.11.11). This same Wisdom is both our way home and our home country, with great compassion becoming the pavement beneath our feet along which we might travel on this arduous journey (*DDC* 1.17.16). In Christ—the Way, Truth, and Life—we reach the Father, bound by the Spirit to abide in that supreme and unchangeable good (*DDC* 1.38).

Truth appears in the incarnation of the Word, whose being is the sign of God's interior essence and whose being in the world, as Word made flesh, is as speaker of words and as creator of new words and speakers. Moreover, the creating and incarnate Word establishes the realm in which the Spirit, through the gift of love, creates the church and Scripture as his body, as the "grammar" or wisdom of humanity and creation.[32]

32. Ephraim Radner, *Hope among the Fragments: The Broken Church and Its Engagement of Scripture* (Grand Rapids: Brazos, 2004), 14.

Thus, in proposing rules or directions for biblical interpretation, Augustine viewed Scripture as speaking of both Christ and the church, the whole Christ, "the community of God's people from Abraham through the last Christian saint, as this community is one with the crucified and risen One."[33] As Frances Young comments, "Christ and his Body are incorporated in one another, so that the Head saves and the Body is saved. The sufferings of Christ are our sufferings. The Son of God died the real death, which is the lot of mortal flesh, and he was cast forth and forsaken. So God becomes the Lord of salvation."[34] Augustine writes:

> The first one is "about the Lord and his body." We know that we are sometimes being given hints that head and body, that is Christ and Church, constitute one person—after all, it was not without reason that the faithful were told then you are the seed of Abraham, although there is only one seed of Abraham, which is Christ. So according to this first rule we should not let it baffle us when a text passes from head to body and from body to head, and yet still refers to one and the same person. It is one person speaking, you see, where it says, "He placed a turban on my head as on a bridegroom, and adorned me with the ornaments as a bride" (Isa. 61:10) and yet of course we have to understand which of these two fits the head, which the body; which fits Christ, that is, and which the Church. (*DDC* 3.31.44)

According to Augustine, the Scriptures are both magnificent and salutary, so adjusted by the Holy Spirit that they ward off starvation with the clearer passages while driving away boredom with the ones that are more obscure. He thus demonstrates what the Scriptures are and the way in which they are written, which prepares readers for instruction in Christian wisdom, the enjoyment and praise of God in all things (*DDC* 2.7, 2.9–10, 2.14).

Augustine did not presume that the teaching of Scripture is self-evident, but freely acknowledged that our complicity in sin—loving the self by enjoying others and the things of creation rather than enjoying

33. Robert W. Jenson, "Hermeneutics and the Life of the Church," in *Reclaiming the Bible for the Church*, ed. Carl E. Braaten and Robert W. Jenson (Grand Rapids: Eerdmans, 1995), 103.

34. Frances M. Young, *Biblical Exegesis and the Formation of Christian Culture* (Peabody, MA: Hendrickson, 2002), 284; see the discussion by Richard A. Norris Jr., "Augustine and the Close of the Ancient Period of Interpretation," in *A History of Biblical Interpretation*, vol. 1, *The Ancient Period*, ed. Alan J. Hauser and Duane F. Watson (Grand Rapids: Eerdmans, 2003), 380–408.

them for the love of God—leaves us captive to idolatrous, destructive patterns of speech and life. This bondage is overcome only by the spiritual practice of listening to Scripture in a manner congruent with the character of God, a habit that situates the reader within a theological and moral context and thereby under the sovereignty and sway of the law of love rather than one's own authority or self-love.[35]

> But living a just and holy life requires one to be capable of an objective and impartial evaluation of things; to love things, that is to say, in the right order, so that you do not love what is not to be loved, or fail to love what is to be loved, or have a greater love for what should be loved less, or an equal love for things that should be loved less or more, or a lesser or greater love for things that should be loved equally. (*DDC* 1.27.28)

If knowing God is its true end, the study of Scripture must be directed by prayer and adoration. Scripture sanctifies the imagination and speech through constant immersion in its wisdom and attention to its eloquence. Knowing what to speak and how to speak is discerned within the story of God's providential activity, which takes the form of Christ and the church—love of God and neighbor—God's peace manifested in the world.[36] For Augustine, then, the story of Scripture is a sacrament of the mystery of Christ, through which the Divine Speaker breathes forth the Word in love to instruct, delight, and transform, thereby making all things new. Confidence in the efficacy of the Word who speaks through human words made Augustine suspicious of communication strategies that imitated popular arts, fads, and entertainment to accommodate listeners' tastes. Such tactics denied the humility of Christ, the Word who accommodates his voice to the plain language of Scripture, to the church's confession of sin and God's praise, and to the humble sermons of its preachers (*DDC* 4.6.9–4.7.14, 4.20.39–4.21.50).

During a career as a master rhetorician, Augustine learned that technologies of the word are capable of achieving relative and limited goods. After his conversion, he came to see that a relentless temptation to self-love renders such skills capable of doing great harm under the influence of illusion and self-deceit. Shorn of the habits and desires cultivated in attentive listening to the Word of God within the church's

---

35. Alan Jacobs, *A Theology of Reading: The Hermeneutics of Love* (Boulder, CO: Westview, 2001), 16–17.

36. Radner, *Hope among the Fragments*, 15–17.

worship of God, Christian pastors are easily tempted to become "word-smiths" or peddlers of religious goods and wares.[37]

Augustine therefore offered an alternative way by encouraging pastors to take up a life of prayerful attention to the Word with the love bestowed by the Spirit. Prayer, or openness before God who speaks in his Word, cleanses one's vision for acknowledging God's gifts; attunes oneself to the Spirit who anoints human speech; and entrusts one's listeners to the grace of hearing, which grants loving assent to God. In the movement of the heart and mind toward the truth revealed in Christ, preachers are instructed in divine wisdom, becoming themselves echoes of the Word, eloquent sermons that bespeak the gift of charity that is the sum of Christian faith and life (*DDC* 4.3.4–4.5.8, 4.27.59).

Christian preaching, then, is theological rhetoric, a gift of the Spirit in which Christ, the incarnate Word spoken by the Father, condescends to indwell Scripture and the church, himself speaking the restoration and fulfillment of creation by confessing the praise of the Creator. "For Augustine the performance of Scripture in Church is intended by God and empowered by the Holy Spirit to build communal and personal virtue, and to accomplish personal salvation. . . . It moves the reader and hearer from idolatrous alienation into direct presence of the Triune God."[38]

Augustine's theological wisdom points to a robust, unreservedly trinitarian way of thinking and speaking—sacred rhetoric—that is necessary for resisting the false gods that threaten to silence the proclamation of the gospel in speaking of God, the church, and the world. This trinitarian "grammar of faith" constitutes the joyful celebration of a community of wonder and overflows in the presence of the superabundant richness of the being of the Holy Trinity, in whom love is forever given and forever enjoyed in ever new exchanges of God's donation. Such praise is an overflow of that love, a participation in the reality of the Holy Spirit within the life of the community that lives as one in Christ, thus letting God be God. If the church's mission to the nations is at heart to be a witness to the Truth in whom all things have been created and redeemed, it must recover its fluency

37. Harrison, *Augustine*, 68–78.

38. Telford Work, *Living and Active: Scripture in the Economy of Salvation* (Grand Rapids: Eerdmans, 2002), 307; see the excellent discussion of Augustine's view of Scripture in John Norris, "Augustine and Sign in *Tractatus in Johannis Euangelium*," in *Augustine: Biblical Exegete*, ed. Frederick Van Fleteren and Joseph C. Schnaubelt (New York: Peter Lang, 2001), 215–32.

in the wisdom and eloquence of Scripture, the story of stories, for the glory of God.[39]

Nehemiah 8; John 5:19–27, 36–44

Our Lord offered a shorthand way of understanding the story of Israel that we have just heard in Nehemiah 8 when he said: "You search the Scriptures, because you think that in them you have eternal life; and it is they that bear witness to me." In order to communicate the truth of this claim I have moved my preaching classes from our normally assigned seminar room to one of our seminary chapels. I have been pleasantly surprised to see how this change of environment or ethos, which locates our work in a different kind of home, has contributed to a change in students' outlooks, attitudes, and actual performance of the practice of preaching. They are coming to realize that we are not simply looking at something called a text to find an idea or two that might be relevant, or to dig out some principles for application that will work. Rather, our hope is that we are listening to and speaking of God, the Word, as an act of praise—doxological speech from the canon of Holy Scripture that creates the faith, life, and witness of the church, which is the work of Christ and the Spirit.

The chapel where we meet has a large, prominent baptismal font; a communion table; a pulpit flanked by a tall wooden cross; icons of Christ and the apostles Peter and Paul; and a large, stained-glass window with the symbol of a dove. Perhaps I can summarize in a few simple words what I am trying to communicate in response to my students' questions and struggles to make sense of Scripture and preaching: "It's about God!" And I am continually amazed at how these few words are often the most important I may speak during the course of an entire semester: "It's about God!" I have begun to surmise that, for some, my words may authorize a break with the conventional wisdom of our time, that I might offer encouragement to dare to speak of God and the things of God rather than talking about whatever happens to be on our minds or the minds of our listeners. My hope is that in our work together God will raise up men and women to be ministers of the Word in the manner of Ezra, of whom Scripture says: "For Ezra

---

39. Lesslie Newbigin, *Foolishness to the Greeks: The Gospel and Western Culture* (Grand Rapids: Eerdmans, 1986), 143–45.

had prepared his heart to see the Torah of the LORD and to do it" (cf. Ezra 7:10).

The story of God rebuilding Jerusalem from ruin, of God restoring Israel after years in exile, is a major expression of the gospel, of evangelical faith in the scriptural tradition of Israel's witness to the God of Jesus Christ. The story begins with Nehemiah, the cupbearer to the king, a devout man who grieved, wept, and prayed over Israel's condition, calling upon God to remember his promises, to be faithful in his covenant love, to be gracious and merciful toward his sinful people. With confidence, not in himself but in God's character as revealed in God's past actions, Nehemiah reverently addressed the One whom he calls the great and awesome God, boldly approaching the throne of grace to plead:

> Remember the instruction you gave your servant Moses, saying: "If you are unfaithful, I will scatter you among the nations, but if you return to me and obey my commands, then even if your exiled people are at the farthest horizon, I will gather them from there and bring them to the place I have chosen as a dwelling for my Name." (Neh. 1:8–9 NIV)

The first seven chapters of Nehemiah tell this story of rebuilding and regathering in just a period of fifty-two days, a time during which Nehemiah brought organization, political status, and security to the community of returning exiles. At the same time, the story makes it clear that Nehemiah is neither the source nor the center of the action but only its servant and instrument. God is the One whose mercy and power bring an end to exile, just as it is God who welcomes home a displaced and disobedient people, a journey marked by hardship, poverty, suffering, and disappointment.

Many Christians and congregations are in exile today. They have not been physically displaced to another country nor have they been dislocated from their church buildings; for that matter, they may even be numerically and financially successful. But in spite of such culturally approved outward signs, many still feel lost and abandoned in a North American church that continues to forget the Triune God, whom we have been called to worship and serve; a church, in both liberal and conservative expressions, that continues to distance itself from a Christian identity given in Jesus Christ through the work of the Holy Spirit in baptism; a church, in both mainline and evangelical traditions, where many feel like strangers rather than friends who have been graciously invited to gather at the table of the Prince of Peace; a church where many feel more at home in the world that has set itself at odds with God's will revealed in the kingdom proclaimed and established by the Lord, who rules through the power and wisdom of the cross.

It saddens me to see pastors and people just hanging on by a thread, overwhelmed by the chaos of our culture, discouraged to the point of despair by the decline of the church. Many folks seem to be just grasping at thin air for anything or anyone who seems to have an answer, a solution, a new idea, the latest program or method that works; and so we have ten steps, three points, six proofs, and ten principles of purpose. And then there's, Bishop, send us a young minister with children. Deacons, call us a pastor who will visit. Pulpit committee, find us a preacher with charisma, personality, and pizzazz! Do you know what I mean?

But perhaps the greatest need this crisis of homelessness has created is an urgent need to remember the scriptural witness to the story of the Triune God, who creates and saves—the need to return home. And the story of Nehemiah and Ezra brings to memory news that is good, news of what God is doing among us this morning and what God is doing in the world. This gathering is a homecoming. It is the primary means by which God is faithful to his promises, by which God's power of forgiveness restores us, overcomes exile, renews our life for the covenant that God has made through Israel—the life, death, and resurrection of his Son, Jesus Christ, the outpouring of the Spirit to raise up the church as a living temple in whom he dwells, and the kingdom coming on earth as it is in heaven.

And because Christ has died, Christ is risen, and Christ will come again, this gathering is as sacred as all the sacred assemblies in which the Word is read and proclaimed and a holy meal is shared in the presence of our risen Lord, who speaks with such authority that even the dead are raised. Our gatherings are invitations to come home, to remember who we are and whose we are, assemblies in which we are blessed to witness God's power and glory among us in the person and work of Jesus Christ, who continues to draw and gather the nations into his rule of peace and righteousness.

Did you notice that the rebuilding of the wall was only a prelude to the restoration and reconstruction of a people, which is the work of the Word and Spirit? Ezra opened the book in the sight of the people, and when he did so the people stood. Perhaps this means the Torah was held up at this point, just as it is in the synagogue today, just as

Holy Scripture is held up in many congregations when it is read today, "The Word of God for the people of God" . . . "Thanks be to God." A dead ritual, you say. Well, I don't think so. This is a liturgical act; not as in high church or as in low church, but as in for God, for the praise of God: "And Ezra blessed the LORD, the great God; and all the people answered, 'Amen, Amen' [Yes! Yes!]; lifting up their hands; and they bowed their heads and worshiped the Lord with their faces to the ground" (Neh. 8:6). This is not a matter of style or technique. Rather, it has everything to do with the character of God and our identity as God's people, chosen and beloved in Jesus Christ, the living Word who dwells among and within us, the Son of the Father who speaks creation and salvation into being through the Spirit's power.

And Ezra, that faithful scribe, did not simply talk about the Bible; what he did was not simply transmit information, topics, themes, principles, or a list of things to do for practical application—things that still leave us in control. His reading and speaking were acts of worship, speaking of God for both preacher and people to remember, love, and adore God together as one person in holy communion. Holy people were standing in the presence of a holy God lovingly receiving the Word with gratitude and reverence. They were "all ears" as they heard God's voice calling them anew, with fresh power and renewed purpose, out of the past into a future unfolding in their hearing. As Jesus said in his first sermon at a synagogue in his hometown of Nazareth after reading from the prophet Isaiah, "Today this is fulfilled in your hearing." The power of this story is the power of God's Word, who creates and redeems, a story that must be read, proclaimed, and heard as a primary means of grace by which God speaks to seek, find, and restore a homeless people.

What a great story, but what an even greater God. In a situation that outwardly gave every indication of God's abandonment, the Word of God was opened and brought to speech, and this was sufficient to satisfy and nourish those who gathered to listen. And this lively, life-giving Word recalled the story of God and his people, beginning with creation and culminating in Exodus—a story of extravagant love lavished upon a poor, pitiful, rebellious, forgetful community; a story of a love capable of moving even the hardest of hearts and the proudest to tears; a story able to invoke and inspire amazement, and awe in the presence of such goodness and glory. In the face of such goodness, both preacher and people remembered and responded to Torah—the whole story of God—in celebrating a day of Sabbath rest. They remembered

God's graciousness by feasting with holiday food and drink, sharing generously with the needy and poor because God's joy was their strength. And this pattern of assembly has continued to this very day: the presence of God made known through Word and sacrament, the fruit and overflow of which is called mission, our participation in the life of the Triune God for the life of the world.

What a relevant story for us, is it not? In the midst of so much confusion and conflict about the worship of God and the purpose of the church, we have heard a strong, clear Word that works to restore and renew our lives in calling to mind the memory and hope of Scripture, which is the story of God. When we assemble as God's people, he manifests himself with us through the Word spoken and enacted. In hearing the Word, we do as God says, with the effect of the Spirit re-creating us according to Christ, who is God's speech that nourishes and strengthens us to follow him in the days ahead.

And what a strong word of encouragement, is it not? In spite of our loss of memory, identity, vitality, membership, and mission, God continues to be with us through the power of the Word spoken and enacted. God has been faithful in the past, God's steadfast love surrounds us in the present, and God's hope of redemption calls us into a future that only God can give. The Word we have heard is not simply a story from the past; it is the story in which we now live, move, and have our very being—the life-giving power that works among us through Christ and the Spirit today.

This morning Jesus Christ stands among us, speaking and offering himself to us. St. Augustine wrote lovingly of him: "He is our home; and he is our way home, and he is our home away from home; he is the way, the truth, and the life who has come to us in order to lead us to the Father, bound together in love by the Spirit" (*DDC* 1.34.38, my paraphrase). For we are a people called to be holy as God is holy. Through the work of the Spirit we have been drawn into the life of God, whose goodness is revealed in Jesus Christ, the One in whom we have been gathered to be the dwelling place for his name among the nations. It's about God! Amen.

2

Speaking of God:
Preaching as a Traditioned Practice

An appeal to the "past" does not mean that Christians will be faithful today by doing what was done in the past, but by attending to what they did in the past we hope to know better how to live now. Of course, since we believe in the communion of saints it is a comfort to know that our past fore-bearers are present with us.

—Stanley Hauerwas, *Dispatches from the Front*

For over 1,500 years Augustine's *De doctrina christiana* (*Teaching Christianity*) has continued to be a highly valued source of Christian wisdom, providing a theology or grammar of Christian discourse for the witness of preaching enacted in the proclamation of God's Word. Arguably the most widely read handbook of its kind in Christian history, *Teaching Christianity* (*DDC*) invites pastors to join an intellectual and spiritual journey: learning to think and speak of God within a way of life that refers all things to God and the love of God, a theological and ecclesial purpose that embraces doctrine, spirituality, exegesis, and preaching.

For Augustine, learning to think and speak well cannot be separated from learning to pray and worship within a tradition that constitutes a community of confession and praise: the confession of sin and the confession of the praise of God for all things. Thus Christian speakers and speech must be shaped by divine truth and goodness, the gift of wisdom imparted through the Word and Spirit, who indwell Scripture and the church, witnessing to God's love and holiness in the world. Christian preaching, then, is a form of primary theology—knowledge and love of the Triune God—which the church confesses in its faith, enacts in its worship, and embodies in its common life.

God is known truly, moreover, when his identity is given and received in a living tradition of language and worship—an extended conversation that produces faith—which the grammar of theology engenders.[1] Faith thinks with loving assent in personal engagement with the God of Jesus Christ; we cannot love what we do not know, nor do we progress in knowledge if we do not love. For Augustine, a vision of faith that seeks to understand is grounded in the doctrines of Trinity and incarnation, thus uniting theory and practice, wisdom and knowledge, theology and preaching. God's address or Word, in which he conveys his purposes and promises, is not an abstract message, principles, or rules. The Word is the person of Christ, who is heard in history through the gift of faith, and who, as faith's object, re-creates history as its way, truth, and life. Theology, including the practice of preaching, does not aim to be useful but rather seeks to be true to its source, the wisdom of God.[2]

Ephraim Radner argues convincingly that so much of conservative and liberal biblical criticism of the past two centuries has been driven by a lack of memory. This entails a forgetfulness of God's providential activity given in the forms of Scripture, in which the life of the church takes narrative shape within the diversity of its expressions in time, according to God's thinking, seeing, and moving with respect to creation. Within this providential story, the activity of a preacher and listening congregation may be seen as more than an isolated event, but it is woven into the very fabric of the Word enfleshed in history for the renewal and re-creation of the world. Thus Christian preaching speaks out of a past, into a present, and toward a future, lovingly held within the life of the Triune God.[3]

1. Paul Holmer, *The Grammar of Faith* (San Francisco: Harper & Row, 1978), 204.
2. Andrew Louth, *Discerning the Mystery: An Essay on the Nature of Theology* (Oxford: Clarendon, 1983), 2–5.
3. Ephraim Radner, *Hope among the Fragments: The Broken Church and Its Engagement of Scripture* (Grand Rapids: Brazos, 2004), 16–19, 172–75.

Augustine affirmed the significant role of Christian traditioning in the prologue to *Teaching Christianity*. There he states that certain theological rules or wisdom for dealing with Scripture and attaining its end or goal, which is also its means, that is, the knowledge and love of God, must be passed on to those who are willing to learn since reading Scripture or listening to another read and teach is to share within a community of interpreters and speakers. Augustine asserts that even inspired individuals who claim to interpret Scripture by means of a "divine gift" are not autonomous, but make use of familiar conventions of language, letters, and words they have learned from others since birth. Personal inspiration does not rule out the need for preachers to be taught or to receive from others, a point he emphasizes by referring to biblical precedence: Paul was taught by God but was sent to Ananias to receive the sacraments; the centurion was addressed by an angel but was later turned over to Peter; Moses learned from his father-in-law how to govern; Philip explained Isaiah's mysteries to an Ethiopian eunuch.

The most persuasive example, however, is charity, which would not bind together hearts and minds to unite the church were it not for what one person speaks to another; God is pleased for his Word to be spoken through human voices in his temple, through the preaching of the church. According to Augustine, nothing that we have is our own except our falsehood. What we have that is true comes from the One who said, "I am the truth." Augustine asks, "What do we have, after all, that we have not received? But if we have received it, why should we boast as though we had not?" To be made part of the Christian tradition presupposes the gift of faith; it is to belong to a community of truth that is given as grace, a gift that cannot be possessed but requires constant trust, receptivity, and humility (*DDC* Prologue).

Within the Christian tradition, the lively conversation we share with the communion of saints, "the living faith of the dead,"[4] continues to school us in the way of becoming more faithful interpreters of Scripture and speakers of the gospel. The gift of remembering locates us within a conversation integral to the recovering of a robust, unreservedly Christian witness sufficient for the task of evangelization

---

4. Jaroslav Pelikan, *The Vindication of Tradition* (New Haven: Yale University Press, 1984), 65; parts of this chapter are revised material from my *Sacred Rhetoric: Preaching as a Theological and Pastoral Practice* (Grand Rapids: Eerdmans, 2005).

and catechesis in the post-Christian missionary situation in which we find ourselves.[5]

A single picture has increasingly held captive the homiletic imagination of the church in late modernity—technical, scientific reason; managed, useful truth—creating ways of thinking and speaking that tell the story of human freedom from the claims of the past.[6] Ironically, exemplars from this forgotten or rejected past may possess the theological wisdom necessary to break free from the tyranny of the contemporary, and its reductionism, and recover confident speech in service of the gospel: news that is truly good.[7] Nicholas Lash observes:

> Are there not ways of proclaiming our freedom from the past which not only leave untouched the forms of bondage that, in fact, have been inherited from the past but, by asserting such bondage to be illusory, actually contribute to our deeper enslavement? And is there not a lesson here, for those who would proclaim the gospel of humanity's freedom in Christ, concerning the manner of that gospel's effective proclamation?[8]

Rather than continuing in a tradition that continually seeks new methods, techniques, or innovative strategies and styles for "effective" communication, we would do well to expand our conversation to locate ourselves within the story of the larger Christian tradition. There we may encounter Christian speakers whose faithfulness in proclaiming the Word was acquired through prayerful attention to the Triune God revealed in the wisdom of Scripture, the "living and active" instrument of divine self-communication.[9]

5. On the significance of describing the history of Christian practice as a guide for the present, see George A. Lindbeck, "Atonement and the Hermeneutics of Intratextual Social Embodiment," in *The Nature of Confession: Evangelicals and Postliberals in Conversation*, ed. Timothy R. Phillips and Dennis L. Okholm (Downers Grove, IL: InterVarsity, 1996), 221–40; also see the argument for the recovery of tradition in Pelikan, *Vindication of Tradition*; Bruce D. Marshall, "The Church in the Gospel," *Pro Ecclesia* 1, no. 1 (Fall 1992): 27–41; Stephen R. Holmes, *Listening to the Past: The Place of Tradition in Theology* (Grand Rapids: Baker, 2002).

6. See the excellent summary in James Kay, "Reorientation: Homiletics as Theologically Authorized Rhetoric," *The Princeton Seminary Bulletin* 24, no. 1 (2003): 16–35; Charles L. Campbell, *Preaching Jesus: New Directions for Homiletics in Hans Frei's Postliberal Theology* (Grand Rapids: Eerdmans, 1997); Walter Brueggemann, *Finally Comes the Poet: Daring Speech for Proclamation* (Minneapolis: Fortress, 1989), 1–2.

7. See the extended discussion in Brueggemann, *Finally Comes the Poet*.

8. Nicholas Lash, *Theology on the Way to Emmaus* (London: SCM, 1986), 58.

9. See the excellent study by Telford Work, *Living and Active: Scripture in the Economy of Salvation* (Grand Rapids: Eerdmans, 2002).

Indeed, given the widespread "forgetfulness of the Word" that characterizes our time, which results in an all-too-easy, even irreverent, idle chatter that does little serious work in service of the God of the gospel, many pastors are searching for an alternative way of construing the practice of Christian preaching. An increasing number of preachers are expressing a desire to cultivate a homiletic imagination shaped by scriptural memory, colored by moral judgment, and constituted by participation in a living tradition. Moreover, in a time characterized by the extent to which our ingenuity has outstripped our wisdom, Christian people are looking for trustworthy speakers of the Word who will guide them in performing the church's faith in a common life of worship and loving obedience to the Triune God.[10] Robert Webber concludes in his assessment of younger evangelicals: "The road to the future leads through the past."[11]

In a discussion of the church's language of faith, Rowan Williams observes that what is often overlooked in assessments of its contemporary "relevance" is the question of what this language is expected to do. The problem may not be with the language, but with users who have ceased speaking in God's presence, in relationship to truth, and who have instead used Christian language for defending, denigrating, calculating, controlling, and other self-interested ways. Williams cites Dietrich Bonhoeffer's challenge to "religious" language, written in 1944, that holds true in our time:

> Reconciliation and redemption, regeneration and the Holy Spirit, love of our enemies, cross and resurrection, life in Christ and Christian discipleship—all these things are so difficult and remote that we hardly venture any more to speak of them. In the traditional words and acts we suspect that there may be something quite new and revolutionary, though we cannot grasp or express it. That is our own fault. Our church, which has been fighting in these years only for its self-preservation, as though that were an end in itself, is incapable of taking the word of reconciliation and redemption to mankind and the world.[12]

10. I am indebted to the larger discussion of these and related matters in Nicholas Lash, *The Beginning and the End of "Religion"* (Cambridge: Cambridge University Press, 1996); see also the extended discussion in Robert L. Wilken, *Remembering the Christian Past* (Grand Rapids: Eerdmans, 1990); and Holmes, *Listening to the Past.*

11. See the entire discussion in Robert E. Webber, *The Younger Evangelicals: Facing the Challenges of the New World* (Grand Rapids: Baker, 2003).

12. Dietrich Bonhoeffer, *Letters and Papers from Prison*, enlarged ed. (London: SCM, 1971), 399–400, cited in Rowan Williams, *Christ on Trial: How the Gospel Unsettles Our Judgment* (Grand Rapids: Eerdmans, 2003), 37–38.

Williams observes that these words are not mistaken, nor are they "irrelevant," as many are quick to presume. The problem lies with speakers and hearers who themselves have become irrelevant and external to the language, to the story of its life and use, and who do not possess sufficient depth or substance for the words to be voiced or heard as credible and trustworthy. The language of faith, for many, has been reduced to verbal tools, possessions utilized for individually determined aims, but without remembering the great mysteries of the Triune God, the holiness of the church, and the unity of creation, of which they speak.[13] Perhaps the need of our time is not for a new and more relevant language, method, or technique, but is rather a task of situating the language (its speakers and listeners) within the larger Christian story, to rediscover what is truthful and good in relation (relevant) to the Word who is the Truth in person.

The Gift of the Past in the Present

In *An Essay in the Grammar of Assent*, John Henry Newman writes of the importance of trusting the character and wisdom of others who have demonstrated the habits and dispositions that are the fruit of dwelling in the truth of Christian faith.

> Instead of trusting logical science, we must trust persons, namely those who by long acquaintance with their subject have a right to judge. And if we wish ourselves to share in their convictions and the grounds of them, we must follow their history, and learn as they have learned. We must . . . depend on practice and experience more than on reasoning. . . . By following this we may . . . rightly lean upon ourselves, directing ourselves by our own moral and intellectual judgment, not by our skill in argumentation.[14]

As a Christian practice, preaching requires the formation of vision and discernment, a "knowing how" to speak that is shaped by the grammar of faith embodied in a tradition created and sustained by faith in the speech of God, which is the conversation of the Son and Spirit with the Father.[15] As Newman observes,

---

13. Williams, *Christ on Trial*, 37–38.

14. Cited in Joseph Dunne, *Back to the Rough Ground: Practical Judgment and the Lure of Technique* (Notre Dame, IN: University of Notre Dame Press, 1997), 35.

15. D. Brent Laytham, "God Is One, Holy, Catholic and Apostolic," in *God Is Not—: Religious, Nice, "One of Us," an American, a Capitalist*, ed. D. Brent Laytham (Grand Rapids: Brazos, 2004), 118.

> Nothing that is anonymous will preach; nothing that is dead and gone; nothing even which is of yesterday, however religious in itself and useful. Thought and word are one in the Eternal Logos, and must not be separate in those who are His shadows on earth. They must issue fresh and fresh, as from the preacher's mouth so from his breast, if they are to be "spirit and life" to the hearts of the hearers.[16]

Much of the perceived "deadness," "staleness," and "irrelevance" of contemporary Christianity is arguably related to a deep loss of memory and constitutive practices, a lack of freshness, vitality, and personal knowledge that is the fruit of a common life shared in God's presence, shaped by God's Word, sustained by God's Spirit. This loss has resulted in the surrender of Christian faithfulness and a debasement of Christian speech, a loss of reverent attentiveness, wonder, and delight for the Word of God, the most precious resource for creating and sustaining Christian identity in an identity-denying situation. David Steinmetz observes that "a Church that has lost its memory of the past can only wander about aimlessly in the present and despair of the future. The Church needs the past, if only for the sake of the present and the future. . . . Only when we have regained our identity from the past can we undertake our mission in the present."[17]

Moreover, the loss of vital memory has contributed to a pervasive sense of "homelessness" among Christian people, who continue the struggle to maintain an alternative vision, identity, and vocation in an increasingly indifferent and even hostile world.

> In this world each person is obliged only to him or herself. It is a world without plans or purpose, structures without order, information without knowledge, speed without movement and connections without relations. It is a world with a past but no memory of faithfulness; with a future but no patience or hope; and a present but no dispossession or charity. This world will tolerate anything except that which will not tolerate it; that which tells of a world differently founded.[18]

16. John Henry Newman, *The Idea of a University* (London: Longmans, Green, 1925), 426.

17. David C. Steinmetz, *Memory and Mission: Theological Reflections on the Christian Past* (Nashville: Abingdon, 1988), 33–34.

18. Gerard Loughlin, "The Basis and Authority of Doctrine," in *The Cambridge Companion to Christian Doctrine*, ed. Colin C. Gunton (Cambridge: Cambridge University Press, 1997), 51–52.

Such "homeless" behavior among Christians has been described by Charles Pinches as those words or actions of which it is meaningful to ask: "What on earth could that person be saying or doing?" Actions that are intelligible, deliberative, moral activities require a home; they must fit into a whole way of life, or a "narrative," in which they make sense. We are simply at a loss to make any meaningful sense of human activities, including the practices of preaching and worship, when they do not fit into any recognizable human narratives.

Finding a home for such words and behavior by locating them in the characteristics of listeners according to personal preference or opinion has become a common practice in liberal cultures that privilege individual choice and consumption.[19] When the church adopts this strategy, the wisdom of the Christian tradition is easily forgotten in the zeal for producing a faith that is immediately "relevant." This strategy is not theologically neutral, but is embedded in a popular but unacknowledged tradition.

> The anti-tradition stance is often a façade for a "tradition," and quite an anemic one at that. I think here particularly of the degree to which consumerism has become a tradition in the United States: the continual interests in choices, the fetish for the new, the moral justification of questions like, "Well what's wrong with it?" or "Don't I have a right to do it?" None of these raise the question of the nature of the good served by such conduct, although a good is often assumed in the claims. That is, individual choice and the pursuit of privatized interests are the good, and the expectation that they are to be honored as such.[20]

It is not sufficient to limit the scope of either our thinking or our speaking to a conversation with the living, since some of the sharpest challenges to speaking the gospel are themselves challenged by previous experience and struggle within the church's past. For the sake of faithful practice in the present, we must be willing to expose ourselves and our assumptions to the wisdom of the saints. By allowing ourselves to be challenged and taught within this holy conversation in which we remember the past as present, we are better grounded to speak of God within the faith of the whole church catholic and to

19. Charles R. Pinches, *Theology and Action: After Theory in Christian Ethics* (Grand Rapids: Eerdmans, 2002), 158–66.

20. Tex Sample, *The Spectacle of Worship in a Wired World: Electronic Culture and the Gathered People of God* (Nashville: Abingdon, 1998), 90.

help congregations connect with the larger household of faith that is our home.[21]

Back to the Future

In its quest for catholicity, the church describes its speech and actions within a tradition that is constituted by Scripture, the story of its God and a people constituted by a peculiar language, wisdom, and way of life in which certain patterns of activity are meaningfully performed. When words and actions are extracted from their Christian home, they are easily transformed into ideologies or commodities that become odd, homeless behaviors that are distorted beyond recognition and no longer capable of accomplishing their theological and ecclesial purposes.

Christian notions such as worship, biblical interpretation, preaching, and discipleship cannot simply be redefined or reinvented to accommodate contemporary tastes, since these practices call to memory Christian identity and are understood only within the story of doctrine, devotion, and discipleship that they inhabit and by which they are sustained, corrected, and renewed. As Paul Holmer comments, "So the theology of the Christian tradition has as one of its principal tasks to instruct us in that art of living which will free us from slavery to fashion and the danger of restlessly moving with the times."[22] Rowan Williams observes how this approach to the Christian past goes against the grain of current practice for both traditionalists and progressives. Traditionalists do not expect to be surprised by the past, while progressives are not interested. Yet both miss the point that "we are all bound up in the Body of Christ, the community in which each contributes something unique to the life of all. And this means that the Christian will be looking and listening in his or her study of Christian history for what feeds and nourishes belief now."[23]

Thus the shared memory and hope of the church continue to be "traditioned," a living story remembered and handed down as a gift of the Spirit within the communion of saints for faithful reception,

21. See here Wilken, *Remembering the Christian Past*, 1–24, 165–80; Dunne, *Back to the Rough Ground*, 359; Pelikan, *Vindication of Tradition*, 23–43.

22. Holmer, *Grammar of Faith*, 13.

23. Rowan Williams, *Why Study the Past? The Quest for the Historical Church* (Grand Rapids: Eerdmans, 2005), 3.

nurture, and enactment in the future.[24] Moreover, within this living tradition the witness of the saints continues to speak, displaying the dispositions, habits, and commitments necessary for serious participation in the ongoing struggle to hear and proclaim the Word of God in the present.[25] Samuel Wells describes the character of faithful performance, the church's ongoing "improvisation" of the Word that embodies and extends the drama of Scripture through time:

> To be a saint does not require one to have outstanding gifts or talents. All that is required is that one employ all the resources of the church's tradition . . . rather than create them for one's self, and that one long for the glory of the church's destiny . . . rather than assuming one must achieve it oneself. In the present . . . one must seek in all ways to cooperate with the other members of the company, the communion of saints, rather than stand out from them as an isolated hero.[26]

The proclamation or performance of the Word found in Scripture is guided by a key resource, the church's doctrine, which is the grammar, rule, or stage direction for enacting the story that calls it into being: the calling of Israel, and the life, death, and resurrection of Jesus Christ. The enactment of this story is a form of personal knowledge; doctrine is simply the rule and discipline of its communal performance that grew out of trinitarian baptismal creeds and "rules of faith" in the early church.

All later developments, the creeds of the ecumenical councils, the summae of the medieval period, and the sixteenth-century Protestant and Catholic confessions of faith are no different in intent: to rule the proper and faithful telling, following, and participating in Christ's story, which is the life of the church. Doctrine is therefore the grammar of Christian discourse that helps to cultivate the language of faith, the speech through which God the Holy Spirit is pleased to address us, evoking the thanksgiving of right praise (or-

24. See the excellent discussion in Stanley M. Hauerwas, *The Peaceable Kingdom: A Primer in Christian Ethics* (Notre Dame, IN: University of Notre Dame Press, 1983); see also Stephen E. Fowl and L. Gregory Jones, *Reading and Communion: Scripture and Ethics in Christian Life* (Grand Rapids: Eerdmans, 1991), 29–55.

25. On the pastoral office, see William H. Willimon, *Pastor: The Theology and Practice of Ordained Ministry* (Nashville: Abingdon, 2002), 11–53, 331–36; see also the discussion of social characters within a community and tradition in Alasdair MacIntyre, *After Virtue* (Notre Dame, IN: University of Notre Dame Press, 1984), 27–31.

26. Samuel Wells, *The Drama of Christian Ethics: Improvisation* (Grand Rapids: Brazos, 2004), 43–44.

thodoxy) and correcting our propensity to idolatry or false praise (heterodoxy).[27]

For the majority of the church's life, preaching was just such a "storied" practice. It was a homiletic form of pastoral theology enacted within the liturgy of the church, the oral testimony of the Word of God found in Scripture, articulated within the ongoing, lively conversation among worship, doctrine, and Christian life rather than standing alongside them as a separate discipline. Robert Wilken observes,

> For most of the Church's history, theology and Scriptural interpretation were one. Theology was called *sacra pagina* and the task of interpreting the Bible was a theological enterprise. The Church's faith and life were seen as continuous with the Biblical narrative, and the Scriptures were interpreted within the context of a living theological and spiritual tradition. Even the Reformation appeal to "sola scriptura" assumed the Bible was the book of the Church and that its interpretation was to be shaped by the Church's faith.[28]

From the early church through the sixteenth-century Reformers, theology (*theologia*) was a practical habit (*habitus*) or an aptitude of the soul, the human intellect, and heart having the primary characteristic of wisdom. In earlier times some saw this more as a directly infused gift of God, tied directly to faith, prayer, the virtues, and yearning for God. Later, with the advent of formal theological investigation, others saw it as a wisdom that could also be promoted, deepened, and extended by human study and argument. The meaning of theology, however, did not displace the more primary sense of the term—practical *habitus*, or knowledge whose end is salvation, and wisdom that orders our common life toward God and the things of God.[29]

This personal knowledge originates in divine revelation, historically, through the Word—the whole unified narrative of Scripture, the story of the Triune God and his dealings with his people and world—and is received, individually and corporately, through the illumining work of the Spirit in the life of the church. The central activity in which

---

27. Loughlin, "Basis and Authority of Doctrine," 52–57.

28. Robert Louis Wilken, "In Defense of Allegory," in *Theology and Scriptural Imagination*, ed. L. Gregory Jones and James J. Buckley (Malden, MA: Blackwell, 1998), 48.

29. Edward Farley, *Theologia: The Fragmentation and Unity of Theological Education* (Philadelphia: Fortress, 1983), 33–39; see also the survey in Aidan Nichols, *The Shape of Catholic Theology: An Introduction to Its Sources, Principles, and History* (Collegeville, MN: Liturgical Press, 1991).

the knowledge-wisdom is formed is the theological reading and use of Scripture in worship, which serves a community-forming role in constituting the *ecclesia* when read in accordance with its community-constituting grammar.[30] This ongoing tradition of interpretive practice is situated within a larger vocation of bearing faithful witness to God's transformative activity and purpose for humanity.[31]

Within a tradition of prayerful study of Scripture according to the Rule of Faith, theology is exegetical and exegesis is theological, and the end or goal is moral and spiritual—the holiness of the church through participation in the gracious activity of God.[32] When knowledge of God is proclaimed through preaching in the language of faith and interpreted according to its grammar—the praise of God who creates and redeems all things—it too becomes part of the activity of theology in a primary, pastoral sense. As Rowan Williams notes, when we begin with our common life of belonging to the body of Christ, we are better able to direct our attention to the life of the whole church "that points us to that priority of action, to that record of praise and repentance and contemplation that establishes the 'grammar' of the church's language as responsive, as a following and exploring of something once and for all set before us."[33]

Within a common life shaped by liturgy, devotion, and discipleship, people become Christian by hearing and obeying the first-person, participatory language of the Bible, indwelling or making themselves at home in it. When theology is personally appropriated and absorbed through the gift of faith, its hearers are disposed to godliness.[34] Thus the purpose of extending our conversation to include "distant" friends from the Christian past is neither an exercise in nostalgia nor an authoritarian suppression of difference, but rather is a mature, loving conversation capable of cultivating wisdom and engendering hope for faithful speaking in a future that is being shaped by the Word.[35]

30. George A. Lindbeck, "Scripture, Consensus, and Community," in *Biblical Interpretation in Crisis: The Ratzinger Conference on Bible and Church*, ed. Richard J. Neuhaus (Grand Rapids: Eerdmans, 1989), 74–101.

31. Lash, *Way to Emmaus*, 92.

32. See here the excellent discussion in William M. Thompson, *The Struggle for Theology's Soul: Contesting Scripture in Christology* (New York: Crossroad, 1996), 1–32.

33. Williams, *Why Study the Past?* 96.

34. Holmer, *Grammar of Faith*, 203–4.

35. Lash, *Way to Emmaus*, 59–60. Lash argues for neither a childish submission nor an adolescent rejection of the past, but rather a mature but diligent engagement for critical appropriation.

The Loss of the Past

The challenge of the Enlightenment imagined reason's sovereignty to include not only its domain but also everything else, which transformed, respectively, the foundation of Christian teaching and preaching—Scripture and tradition—into history and experience, and left a liberal theology (and its correlative homiletic) that is finally no theology at all. Scripture was no longer understood as mutually constituted by the story it narrates and the community to whom it is narrated—a community already contained within the story, just as the story was within it. Rather, the historical and scientific study of Scripture left it as unreliable and thus looked elsewhere to validate the historical events behind the text, which could be available to anyone with an appropriately informed interest. That Scripture, as the church's canon, should be the subject of theological and pastoral wisdom in its liturgical enactment, and ecclesial embodiment was no longer required since historical criticism, guided by reason, became the new foundation for establishing the basis of Christian teaching.

Tradition was treated in a similar manner. Due to a growing suspicion of the accumulated wisdom of the Christian past, tradition was seen as insufficient for the radically homogeneous world of modernity in which knowledge rests upon the consciousness of the moment. Rather than appealing to Scripture and its interpretation according to the conversations of the past, it was deemed superior to make direct appeal to the experience of fundamentally isolated individuals, since it has the value of being of the moment. As Loughlin comments, "You cannot doubt what you know immediately, and in a world where immediacy matters, who can gainsay your right, nay your duty to believe?"[36] Lost, however, was the most important factor that actually constitutes the religious experience of most people: the communal traditions of story, belief, and practice, of liturgy and ritual, and in the case of the church, the theological witness of Scripture that shapes and molds the character of Christian people within the medium of shared language and life.[37]

Russell Reno has named the story of this loss "Enlightenment Premillennialism."

36. Loughlin, "Basis and Authority of Doctrine," 49.
37. Here I have followed the excellent summary in Loughlin, "The Basis and Authority of Doctrine," 43–52.

Once, a long time ago, a small sect of Jews began teaching strange things about an itinerant sage and miracle worker, Jesus of Nazareth. It would have petered out on its own, but because the mythologies of Roman and Greek culture were at that time losing plausibility in the increasingly complex and cosmopolitan world of late antiquity, the nascent Christian mythic structure filled a need and flourished. The eventual alliance of Christianity and political power, beginning with Constantine, ensured the dominion of the Christian worldview for over a thousand years in the West. However, first in the Renaissance and then with the rise of modern science, this dominance was challenged. Science demanded evidence and reasoned argument, and this soon eclipsed the dogmatic structure of Christianity. The Age of Faith gave way to the Age of Reason. So now one should not expect well-educated modern people to believe the traditional Christian claims about God, creation, salvation, and eternal life.[38]

Hauerwas describes modernity as the story of autonomous, choosing selves. This narrative has only increased the "normal nihilism" that grips our lives, since we lack the Christian practices and imagination to make sense of our lives according to the story of the gospel. We therefore live as people who live as if "they have no story except the story they chose when they had no story. Such a story is called the story of freedom and is assumed to be irreversibly institutionalized economically as market capitalism and politically as democracy." Brueggemann comments:

In our contemporary society we have arrived at a manufactured religion, worshiping a god from whom we dare expect no serious transformation. Indeed we prefer a god who has become a guarantor of the way things are. We absolutize the present and imagine it has always been the way it is. Because we have no memory, we articulate a god who has no history. Because we treasure no past, we cannot recall God's past with us. The erosion of our language about God is rooted in our failure of nerve about our memory, our loss of authority and tradition, our embarrassment about our concrete and therefore scandalous experience.[39]

When as God's people we lose our memory, we also lose congruence of the ends and means of our life; of what we believe, what we do, and

38. R. R. Reno, *In the Ruins of the Church: Sustaining Faith in an Age of Diminished Christianity* (Grand Rapids: Brazos, 2002), 49.
39. Walter Brueggemann, *Israel's Praise: Doxology against Idolatry and Ideology* (Philadelphia: Fortress, 1988), 127.

how we do it; of what we believe, what we speak, and how we speak it. For example, Eugene Peterson has called to memory the enduring significance of contemplation: prayerful, reverent attention to God as revealed in Scripture and the practices of Christian worship that enable us to think, speak, and live well.[40] According to Peterson, this "traditioned" form of Christian spirituality refers to something much more substantive than many contemporary accounts bearing that name.

> If we have a nation of consumers, obviously the quickest and most effective way to get them into our churches is to identify what they want and offer it to them. . . . The cultivation of consumer spirituality is the antithesis of a sacrificial, "denying-yourself" congregation. A consumer church is an anti-Christ church. It's doing the right thing—gathering a congregation—but doing it in the wrong way. (TL, 24–25)

Christian spirituality refers to the way of life embodied in the Christian tradition across time—the practice of faith, hope, and love—Christian living that cannot be reduced to ideas, beliefs, and rules that depend upon our application for their effectiveness. Christianity is a corporate way of life that is made possible through constant engagement with the Triune God, who graciously indwells the life of the church and the lives of Christian people. Our need is not for more talk "about" God that is technically applicable and efficient. Our need is for a recovery of reverence and care in our speaking "of" God—the Father, Son, and Holy Spirit—the source and end of Christian prayer, praise, and proclamation, whom to know is more important than purpose, blessings, peace of mind, satisfaction, self-improvement, or any other material and spiritual benefits we may hope to derive from believing (TL, 25–26).

The majority of the Christian tradition supports this view. Being Christian is not primarily about becoming a better person, citizen, worker, family member; developing a more spiritual life; or finding meaning and purpose for ourselves. Rather, being Christian is about knowing God, the source and goal of Christian living. Through Christ and the Spirit we are joined to God, with, in, and for God. "Only when we do the Jesus truth in the Jesus way do we get the Jesus life" (TL, 21). On this point the gospel challenges many powerful assumptions that drive many churches in North America.

---

40. Eugene H. Peterson, "Transparent Lives: The Contemplative Christian," *Christian Century* 120, no. 24 (November 2003): 20–27; hereafter, references to this article will be cited as TL.

We are called to participate in not only what God is doing (God's purpose), but to do what God is doing, in God's way, by listening to God, responding to God's Word, focusing on God, depending upon God, praising God, giving ourselves over to God, and loving God. God is always the primary actor who cannot be reduced to an expert adviser or instructor. God speaks, summons, invites, addresses, judges, forgives, commands, promises, empowers, and blesses through the ministry of Christ and the Spirit in word and sacrament to build up the church. God's presence is gift, the Spirit who creates in us faithful obedience to follow Jesus in the way of the cross, which is self-giving love (TL, 24–25).

Thus the key to being Christian is not efficiency, shortcuts, convenience, comfort, control, manageability, or quick results in discovering "purpose" or "meaning in life." For Christian people the "how" must be discerned in a manner that is congruent with the character of the One in whom we believe and worship: prayerful attention; personal, communal response; the obedience of faith that requires patience, hope, humility, and silence; a capacity to wait on Christ, who communicates himself through the presence and gift of the Spirit (TL, 25–26). The Triune Creator does not relate to creation in general or humanity in particular through an external manner (purpose) that works through impersonal principles with the force of cause and effect.

Equally good is the news that God is not a pragmatic utilitarian who does things for people so that people will then be obligated to do things for God. Such mistaken views are driven more by our own fear and self-importance than by the gospel; they easily become means by which we seek to explain or establish ourselves at the center of our world (even in the name of reaching or changing the world) without having to yield to God and God's activity.[41] Put simply, the Triune God cannot be reduced to a tool or a number.

The wisdom of the Christian tradition affirms that the Triune God is perfect goodness, wisdom, beauty, abundance, fullness, fruitfulness, happiness, and holiness, whose being in communion is mutually indwelling, self-giving love—generously poured into our lives by the Holy Spirit. Moreover, God desires our love for no other purpose than that we know, enjoy, and delight in God, and that we share God's goodness through participation in God's love and enjoyment (use) of all things for the praise of God's glory. Because the Triune God has come to be

41. Nicholas Lash, *Easter in Ordinary: Reflections on Human Experience and the Knowledge of God* (Notre Dame, IN: University of Notre Dame Press, 1988), 225.

with us in Jesus Christ as the Mediator who is the way, truth, and life, preaching that is reduced to packaging and presenting information in the form of "how to" rules and principles is no preaching at all.

To become a preacher of the Word, then, is to be transformed into a certain kind of person for service within a distinctive community. It is to be made part of the history of a practice and a bearer of its tradition. It is to acquire the intellectual and moral skills necessary for stewardship of the gospel and its gifts, which we have received through the work of the Spirit and the witness of the saints. As Hauerwas comments, "The authority of Scripture is mediated through the lives of the saints identified by our community as most nearly representing what we are about. Put more strongly, to know what Scripture means, finally, we must look to those who have most nearly learned to exemplify its demands through their lives."[42]

Holmes notes that we are not as far removed from the saints as we might think, since we share the same story with them, which enables us to learn through the practice of listening "to hear their voices, as our sisters and brothers, members of the same body, sharers in the one Spirit, seeking and claiming to possess the same mind of Christ." However, this requires the humility to acknowledge that the Spirit has been active in guiding the church in the past. In our zeal for change and our impatience with the past, we would do well to exercise care, to not be so quick to embrace the novel or innovative because of its "contemporary" status.[43]

As preachers, we have been made members of a community created and sustained by the Word within a holy conversation whose end is to worship, love, and serve the Triune God. Our communal memory of preaching is doxological. It is the proclamation and celebration of the gospel, the announcement of news about God and the world that is good, the story of the crucified and risen Christ, in whom we live, move, and bear witness as forgiven, reconciled, and graced participants and speakers.

As a people who follow Christ, the Word made flesh in time, we are dependent upon the hard-won judgments of our ancestors, whose wisdom will often have the beginning word, since all we have is the past.[44] Our commitment to speaking of God, the vocation of speaking

42. Hauerwas, *The Peaceable Kingdom*, 70.
43. Holmes, *Listening to the Past*, 31, 160–61.
44. Ibid., 134.

the truth in love, "obligates us to risk the recovery, in changing circumstances, of the fundamental aims and commitments of past generations
of Christians and, first and last, of Jesus himself."[45] Lash concludes that
"to attribute unique and unsurpassable revelatory authority to God's
action in Jesus, is to attribute authority to an aspect of the past, not
because it is past, but because this past event is perceived, even today,
to embody God's promise for the future."[46] In the proclamation of the
gospel, the voice of the risen Christ continues to speak the story of a
people whose very existence is for the praise and glory of the Father.

Luke 24:13–35

Well, here we are, just a little over halfway into the Great Fifty
Days, the season of Easter, the church's extended celebration of the
resurrection of Jesus Christ from the dead. CHRIST IS RISEN! Do
you remember Easter? It has not been that long. In fact, it was just a
few short weeks ago. But resurrections have never been that easy to
understand or to figure out, nor do they lend themselves easily to our
management and control. Easter is not a product we package and market, but is the mightiest act of God, who has created us and empowers
our lives and mission in union with Jesus Christ.

For example, I wish I could just lower the big screen and provide
you with a nifty PowerPoint outline on how to apply the resurrection
to your everyday lives, or how the resurrection can help you discover
your purpose, or perhaps give you five principles for understanding
how Easter can help you realize your potential. And then, maybe I
could take today's gospel story, the road to Emmaus, and craft a few
practical tips on how the journey with Jesus can lift your spirits and
restore your self-confidence.

Don't you find it amazing how embarrassed we preachers are by the
strangeness of Easter? Perhaps nothing reveals our human vulnerability
more than a God who will not be handled or manipulated; perhaps
there is nothing more terrifying than a God so free and elusive that
not even the power of death working through the powers of this world
could hold him down. Just think of Good Friday, when that all-too-
familiar mix of politics, religion, and popular opinion joined forces

45. Lash, *Way to Emmaus*, 60–61.
46. Ibid., 53.

to nail the Son of God to a cross—the cross that God has made the very sign of his victory, his self-giving love, the power and wisdom by which he now rules all things.

Now, I say these things because I am guilty of them. I remember all too well my early years in pastoral ministry and how hard I worked to make sense of Easter for my people. I finally gave up, in large part because my futile efforts to explain the mystery of grace hidden throughout the ages simply failed to live up to the matter at hand, the mystery of God with us in Jesus Christ, crucified and risen.

But I am happy to tell you that over the years I have received a good bit of help by paying attention to the preaching of the apostles in the book of Acts. Now, that is a novel concept, is it not? Let Scripture interpret Scripture, listening to the witness of the whole canon offering its many voices in concert, welling up into one resounding crescendo, a mighty praise shout, a great alleluia, a sacrifice of love and adoration to the Word, Jesus Christ, crucified and risen, Lord of heaven and earth. For a long time it did not occur to me that giving more attention to Scripture and less to my own ideas, plans, and strategies might actually open the way for discovering the kind of wisdom I longed to communicate through my preaching.

For example, take today's Scripture lesson from the book of Acts. Here, one of our all-time favorite preachers, Peter the apostle, is at it again. Have you ever noticed how much preaching is generated by the resurrection of Jesus? While there is virtually no explanation or application of Easter, the kind of communication that is so popular today, in the book of Acts there is a whole lot of proclamation going on. Proclamation: the announcement of startling, surprising, astonishingly good news; proclamation as call and response; and proclamation as personal address and answer. Christian proclamation is good news, the gospel message and activity of the Word and Spirit by which the world is being saved. And generated by the proclamation of Easter, there is a whole lot of storytelling going on. Perhaps Scripture is trying to tell us something; perhaps the only way we can get at this mysterious happening called Easter, or resurrection, is by means of story, narrative, witness, and testimony.

Perhaps there is something going on here that is so big, so deep, so grand and glorious that our feeble attempts to render it easy and accessible simply cannot do it justice. Did you hear today's preacher, Peter, newly reconciled, restored, and recommissioned by Jesus, the Lord whom he denied, betrayed, and abandoned? Peter is not an innocent bystander in the story he tells. In fact, even his own rather pathetic story of call, response, failure, fall, and forgiveness followed by a miraculous new beginning is part of the much larger and more important story of Jesus Christ, whom Peter proclaims with extraordinary boldness, confidence, clarity, passion, and urgency.

Listen carefully, he says, and get his story straight. There is no longer room for doubt. This Jesus whom you killed on a cross God has raised up and made him Lord and Christ. Now that's not a bad sermon introduction, is it? Nothing boring about this story; it is actually quite interesting. This Jesus whom you killed on a cross has been raised up to rule as God's Christ; there is no mistaking this claim anymore.

And listen to the kind of response this startling, astonishing announcement evokes. No one says, "Well Peter, do you think you might be able to explain that a little bit?" No one says, "Now slow down, Peter; we are still trying to fill in the handouts from our bulletin." No one says, "Peter, which point are you on now?" No, the announcement of such shocking news, the resurrection of Jesus, the One whom we killed on a cross, captivates the attention of hearers and evokes its own fitting response.

Cut to the heart, they ask the preacher: "So what shall we do?" You know, when we are able to acknowledge that we do not know what we need or what we should do, we are finally in a position to do serious business with God. Left to ourselves we simply don't know what we need or what we should do. Better to ask, What does God want us to do? What does God think we need if this story is true? Well, being the good preacher that he is, Peter is ready with an answer.

"It's time to change your lives; it's time to turn to God; it's time to get baptized in the name of Jesus Christ; it's time for your sins to be forgiven; and it's time to receive the gift of the Holy Spirit. It's time because the promise of God, spoken to Abraham and Sarah, to Moses and Israel, is in fact spoken through the crucified, risen Jesus to you and your children. And even more, this promise is extended to all nations and people, near and far, whomever our Lord calls. It's not just for you."

The book of Acts says Peter went on for a good while, telling the story of the God of Israel—who raised condemned, crucified Jesus from the dead—and unfolding the promise and faithfulness of Israel's God from Abraham all the way down to Jesus and up to the present, to even include us, the whole creation, and those both near and far. Something big has happened, something that exceeds all our expectations. Something so large and lasting, so earthshaking and life changing that to hear and believe the story is like entering into a whole new world. In fact, being taken into this story is to be made a new creature within a new creation, a new heaven and a new earth that God is bringing about and will consummate under the gracious rule of Jesus Christ.

So by now it's not all that surprising to hear Peter say, "Get out while you can! Get out of this sick, dying old world. Give up its wisdom and its ways. Be different, for a whole new world has come and is now on the way to glorious fulfillment in the Lord Jesus Christ—for he is God's Lord and he is God's Christ." Well, three thousand people took Peter's story to heart, were baptized, and signed up with the Lord Jesus to be members of his kingdom. And God, in the person of the risen Lord and the power of the Holy Spirit, continued to be with them, still ruling and serving as they practiced being church together, gathering around the apostles' teaching (i.e., the whole story of God that centers on Jesus); forming a life together, patterned on the story of Jesus; sharing a common meal of friendship and fellowship created by the love of Jesus; and gathering for prayer, which is participating with Jesus in the communion of mutual love, joy, and delight that unites the Father and the Son.

Their whole way of life was enlivened by the power and wisdom of Jesus Christ crucified as they gladly placed themselves in the presence of God each day, praising and thanking him, listening and responding to his voice, remaining open to the movement of his Spirit in order to live more deeply into God's story for the life of the world. Friends, we are no longer citizens of a world run by and for people, and by the world's wisdom and ways. We are no longer members of a sick, dying, old world that insists that we are the only authors of the story of our lives. We have been born anew to a living hope; our faith and confidence are in the living God, for in our baptism we have been created afresh by God's living Word, Jesus Christ, who has conquered the powers of sin, evil, and death.

My brothers and sisters, today I want to invite you to hear anew the story of Jesus Christ, the One whom we killed on a cross, the One whom God has raised up and made Lord and Christ, the One in whom the promise of God's kingdom coming on earth as it is in heaven is a great resounding "Yes" and "Amen." And this promise is for us, and those near to us, but it is also for those far off, whomever the Lord may call.

The story of the disciples on the road to Emmaus is the story of Jesus Christ, the story into which we have been enfolded with the whole creation through his life, death, and resurrection from the dead. This is the story in which we now live: the eighth day of creation. And so every Lord's Day, God's people gather, a pilgrim people who, since the first call was spoken to Abraham and Sarah, have journeyed toward our true and lasting home, communion with the Triune God. And every Lord's Day, which is a little Easter, a day of resurrection, we gather to converse with each other about the journey we share. And when we gather, what was true then is still true today; we have all kinds of questions and serious matters on our minds. Questions about our problems, our needs, our longing for meaning, purpose, and community. Questions about how to get along with others in all of our brokenness, of how to make our lives work better, and how to find answers and solutions to the things that frustrate and confuse us. We have long discussions about what we need to do to make our churches more effective, or to make our ministries more productive, or to take our congregations to the next level, and in some cases, what we need to do just to pay the bills and keep the doors open.

In the end this all sounds rather hopeless, does it not? It sounds a lot like, "We had hoped he was the one." Too often we sound as if the Lord has abandoned us and is gone, leaving us to ourselves and our own devices. Our conversation often sounds as if God is absent, filled only by our sincerity, our good intentions, our passion, our plans, our programs, our purposes, our dreams, our disappointments, but still an absence filled only by our pathetic, little stories.

Thank God we are not the whole story, for the risen Lord still continues to make his presence known among us. Thank God that he comes to be with us, not because we deserve it, for we surely do not. Rather, he comes out of the abundance of mercy and goodness he shares with the Father and the Spirit. And he speaks to us through the whole narrative of Scripture and the story of the church, not because we are smart or clever, but because his Spirit opens our minds and hearts to hear and respond to his voice.

He enables us to sense, enjoy, and delight in his loving, intimate presence with us, not because we have chosen to sing the right kind of songs or worship in the right kind of style, or because we have had the right kind of emotions or experience, but because he chooses, freely, out of the fullness of triune love, to show himself and share himself with us when we take, bless and break bread, eating and drinking together, remembering the grand story of God—his great love for the whole world in assuming suffering, crucified flesh.

And because we are graced to hear, touch, taste, sense, and recognize him in our midst, we now live with confidence that on this long pilgrimage we share we do not travel alone. Now every place we go and every conversation we have is an opportunity to hear his voice and speak his word; every path we take can lead to Emmaus; every encounter with a stranger is an opportunity to welcome and be welcomed by God; every meal is an occasion for sharing, enjoying, and being nourished by God's friendship with others. But you still have to admit, Easter is indeed a strange story. Thank God, the stranger whom we welcome this morning is Jesus Christ, the mystery of God with us; for he is the gift of salvation, God, given for the life of the world. *Alleluia! Christ is risen*. Amen.

3

Speaking of God:
Preaching as an Ecclesial Practice

The church has a mission to see to the speaking of the gospel, whether to the world as message of salvation or to God as appeal and praise.

—Robert Jenson, *Systematic Theology, vol. 1: The Triune God*

As doxological speech, preaching is the work of the whole church that, drawn by the Spirit in response to the living Word, the risen Lord, offers itself in prayer and praise and so constitutes and is constituted as the body of Christ. The saving power of God's revealed speech is experienced and rooted in worship. Animated by divine grace, the church attends to the gospel by speech and enactment, its affirmation and adoration evoked by an astonishing glory, goodness, and love.[1] Thus the proclamation of the Word is an ecclesial practice. It is public speech that acclaims the divine glory for the salvation and sanctification of all creation, the wonder and witness of living communion enjoyed by the church within the life of the Holy Trinity.[2]

1. Walter Brueggemann, *Israel's Praise: Doxology against Idolatry and Ideology* (Philadelphia: Fortress, 1988), 26–28.
2. John Behr, "The Trinitarian Being of the Church," *St. Vladimir's Theological Quarterly* 48, no. 1 (Fall 2004): 67–88.

Such dramatic announcement and communal celebration is indeed the work of evangelism, the "publicity" or astounding news that in the call of Israel and the life, death, resurrection, and exaltation of Jesus Christ, God has defeated the false gods and powers of this world and enthroned Christ as Lord of heaven and earth.[3] Joined with Christ by the Spirit, who indwells Scripture and the church, liturgical celebration of the gospel through word and sacrament is both a witness and blessing to the nations, a compelling invitation and urgent summons to join the great vocation of praise as God's good creation.

The Church as Sacrament of Salvation

Martin Luther (d. 1546) is a salutary exemplar of pastoral leadership, whose preaching was conducted as an ecclesial practice for which Scripture, sacraments, church, episcopacy, teachers, and councils constituted the one stream of apostolic tradition, guided by the Holy Spirit, in which Scripture has primacy. Luther's passionate desire for scriptural reform of the church included a high regard for the necessity of remembering the Christian past: "We do not reject everything that is under the dominion of the Pope. For in that event we should also reject the Christian Church. . . . Much Christian good, nay, all Christian good, is to be found in the papacy and from there it descended to us."[4]

Scripture and tradition are thus two sides of the same process of transmitting the Word of God. The tradition of the church is the exegetical, hermeneutical, and ultimately dogmatic practice of interpreting and communicating Scripture, whose authority creates and requires ecclesial virtue. Luther can even assert that the Christian church, a visible assembly, "is the Mother that begets and bears every Christian through the Word of God. . . . Where Christ is not preached, there is no Holy Spirit to create, call, and gather the Christian Church, and outside it no one can come to the Lord Christ."[5]

3. Reinhard Hütter, *Bound to Be Free: Evangelical Catholic Engagements in Ecclesiology, Ethics, and Ecumenism* (Grand Rapids: Eerdmans, 2004), 37–40.

4. Cited in Heiko A. Oberman, *The Dawn of the Reformation: Essays in Late Medieval and Early Reformation Thought* (Grand Rapids: Eerdmans, 1992), 285; see the discussion in Paul Hinlicky, "The Lutheran Dilemma," *Pro Ecclesia* 8, no. 4 (Fall 1999): 394–98; part of this section is revised material from my *Sacred Rhetoric: Preaching as a Theological and Pastoral Practice* (Grand Rapids: Eerdmans, 2005).

5. Cited in Hinlicky, "The Lutheran Dilemma," 400.

For Luther, therefore, proclamation is the center of all the church does and the central point of its theology and mission; it is the oral address of the gospel, the divine and human communication of God's gracious promises in Christ for the salvation of the world. In this particular form of Christian speech, derived from Scripture and enlivened by the Spirit, Christ gives himself and his gifts, the "joyful exchange" of his righteousness for human sinfulness that opens the "gates of heaven" for all the continued gracious workings of the Triune God.[6]

The preaching of the gospel, moreover, is the message of the cross and resurrection, which is received and grasped through the gift of faith. This is the message of Christ and what he has done, which by the work of the Spirit snatches listeners away from themselves to participate in the gracious reign of the One who has acted on their behalf.[7] For Luther, bringing together the cross and life in the presence of God defines the distinctiveness of Christian praise and adoration. This distinctiveness is simply faith being freely itself before God. The Christian fellowship and living that flow from this, then, are described as a matter of gratitude before God.[8]

Faith is a living, daring confidence in God's grace, so sure and certain that a man would stake his life on it a thousand times. This confidence in God's grace and knowledge of it makes men glad and bold and happy in dealing with God and with all his creatures; and this is the work of the Holy Ghost in faith. Hence a man is ready and glad, without compulsion, to do good to everyone, to serve everyone, to suffer everything, in love and praise of God, who has shown him this grace.[9]

6. See the discussion in Fred W. Meuser, "Luther as Preacher of the Word of God," in *The Cambridge Companion to Martin Luther*, ed. Donald K. McKim (Cambridge: Cambridge University Press, 2003), 136–48; Richard Lischer, "Preface," in *Faith and Freedom: An Invitation to the Writings of Martin Luther*, ed. John F. Thornton and Susan B. Varenne (New York: Vintage Books, 2002), xiii–xxvii; Dennis Ngien, "Theology of Preaching in Martin Luther," *Themelios* 28, no. 2 (Spring 2003): 28–48; Brian A. Gerrish, *The Old Protestantism and the New: Essays on the Reformation Heritage* (Chicago: University of Chicago Press, 1982); Jaroslav Pelikan, *Luther the Expositor: Introduction to the Reformer's Exegetical Writings* (St. Louis: Concordia, 1959); American edition of *Luther's Works*, ed. Jaroslav J. Pelikan and Helmut T. Lehmann (Philadelphia: Fortress; St. Louis: Concordia, 1955–86), hereafter LW; *Communio Sanctorum: The Church as the Communion of Saints: Official Catholic-Lutheran Dialogue*, trans. Mark Jeske, Michael Root, and Daniel Smith (Collegeville, MN: Liturgical Press, 2004).

7. Gerhard Sauter, *Gateways to Dogmatics: Reasoning Theologically for the Life of the Church* (Grand Rapids: Eerdmans, 2003), 124.

8. Daniel W. Hardy and David F. Ford, *Praising and Knowing God* (Philadelphia: Westminster, 1985), 64.

9. Cited in Hardy and Ford, *Praising and Knowing God*, 64.

Indeed, Luther's commitment to the oral, sacramental nature of the Word was such that he devoted himself with single-minded purpose to breaking open the words of Scripture so that the gospel, the voice of God speaking in the risen Christ and the Spirit, might become a shout of praise in the church, reaching not only the minds but also the very hearts and souls of its listeners: faith that comes only by hearing the Word.[10]

For example, in a sermon from John 14, Luther articulated this profound theological and pastoral vision of the Word of God, which is Christ himself present in and through ecclesial doctrine and life, and the union of salvation and the church.

> When Christ commands His apostles to proclaim His Word and carry on His work, we hear and see Him Himself, and thus also God the Father; for they publish and proclaim no other Word than that which they heard from His lips, and they point solely to Him. . . . The Word is handed down to us through the agency of true bishops, pastors, and preachers, who received it from the apostles. In this way all sermons delivered in Christendom must proceed from this one Christ. . . . For it is all from God, who condescends to enter the mouth of each Christian or preacher and says: "If you want to see Me or My work, look to Christ; if you want to hear Me, hear this Word." . . . There you may say without hesitation: "Today I beheld God's Word and work. Yes, I saw and heard God Himself preaching and baptizing." To be sure, the tongue, the voice, the hands, etc., are those of a human being; but the Word and the ministry are really the Divine Majesty Himself. (*LW* 22:66–67)

From Prayer to Praise

Luther considered such confidence to speak of God as a gift of the Spirit received in prayerful study of Scripture within and for the life of the church. This is the Word of God spoken in Christ, who in judgment

10. David C. Steinmetz, "Luther and Formation in Faith," in *Educating People of Faith: Exploring the History of Jewish and Christian Communities*, ed. John Van Engen (Grand Rapids: Eerdmans, 2004), 252–62; Heiko A. Oberman, *Luther: Man between God and the Devil*, trans. Eileen Walliser-Schwarzbart (New York: Bantam Doubleday Dell, 1992); William H. Lazareth, *Christians in Society: Luther, the Bible, and Social Ethics* (Minneapolis: Fortress, 2001), 31–57; Oberman, "Preaching and the Word in the Reformation," *Theology Today* 18, no. 1 (April 1961): 16–29; John W. O'Malley, "Luther the Preacher," in *The Martin Luther Quincentennial*, ed. Gerhard Dunnhaupt (Detroit: Wayne State University Press, 1985), 3–16; Stephen H. Webb, *The Divine Voice: Christian Proclamation and the Theology of Sound* (Grand Rapids: Brazos, 2004), 141–46.

and mercy restores us to our primary vocation of ceaseless praise and adoration.[11] Thus the path leading to truthful speech requires submission to the pathos of transformation. One must learn to be attentive to God's Word, standing under Scripture to be interpreted rather than standing over Scripture as judge. Luther's "Preface to the Wittenberg Edition of Luther's German Writings" invites students to learn this particular habit of theological study: "This is the way taught by holy king David (and doubtlessly used by all the patriarchs and prophets) in the one hundred-nineteenth Psalm. They are *Oratio, Meditatio, Tentatio.*"[12]

"My lips will pour forth your praise, because you teach me your statutes. My tongue will sing of your promise, for all your commandments are right" (Ps. 119:171–72 NRSV). Luther insisted that every student in theology should meditate on Psalm 119 once a day, the psalm sung daily in the monastic liturgy of the hours. The prayer of God's people, the communion of saints, is the primary context in which our tongues are healed and we ourselves are changed to speak the truth in love to the praise and glory of God.[13]

Prayer. Students of Scripture must humbly pray for the Holy Spirit to give understanding, turning from the self to wait on God, whose presence is mediated through Christ's promises to the church. This was exemplified by David, who in praying, "Teach me Lord, instruct me, lead me, show me," allowed God, the true teacher of Scripture, to perform the work of the narrative of salvation in his life (Lull, 66).

Meditation. Students of theology must prayerfully meditate on Scripture, indwelling the language of the Word in the practices of the church, making room for God's saving activity. Meditation requires constant repetition, careful attention to Scripture's speech, or discourse, and patient reading and re-reading of its words. Through meditation, the Spirit unites the one who prays with the Word that is prayed (Lull, 66).

Temptation. Temptation is the touchstone that cultivates knowledge and understanding—an external experience—which when suffered demonstrates the credibility and power of God's Word. Although pub-

---

11. Hütter, *Bound to Be Free*, 179–80.

12. Timothy E. Lull, ed., *Martin Luther's Basic Theological Writings* (Minneapolis: Fortress, 1989), 65; hereafter cited in text as Lull. *Oratio, meditatio, tentatio* mean "prayer, meditation, temptation" (cf. *LW* 34:283–88). Here I am indebted to the discussion in Reinhard Hütter, *Suffering Divine Things: Theology as Church Practice* (Grand Rapids: Eerdmans, 2000), 72–75; and David C. Steinmetz, *Memory and Mission: Theological Reflections on the Christian Past* (Nashville: Abingdon, 1988), 164–73.

13. Hütter, *Bound to Be Free*, 180.

lic exposure to the Word is certain to provoke assaults and afflictions from the powers that struggle against the reign of Christ, these are the conditions in which God makes true doctors of Holy Scripture.

True theologians of the church, those who seek and love God's Word, are thus equipped for the task of preaching to young, imperfect Christians on the one hand and to mature and perfect ones on the other. Listening humbly to the Word cultivates wisdom for speaking of God to and within diverse conditions of humanity: the young, old, sick, healthy, strong, energetic, lazy, simple, and wise. Above all else, preachers must guard against the temptation of pride—thinking too highly of one's own wisdom and seeking the praise of others—since in Holy Scripture only God is worthy to be praised: "God opposes the proud, but gives grace to the humble" (Lull, 67–68).

Luther's invitation to the study of Scripture was shaped by years of monastic practice and piety, and informed by a deep knowledge of patristic and medieval theology. This habit fused theological study with prayer for the purpose of transmitting living faith and strengthening Christian existence.[14] Moreover, this was not simply for the individual because it presupposed the church. Ecclesial in scope, its goal is the unity of God and his people, a fellowship or communion identified and constituted by particular practices, or marks, of the church.[15]

On the Councils and the Churches is Luther's mature account of ecclesial existence (prayer, word, and discipleship), a gospel-centered theology embodied in the church, the visible life of God's holy people created and sanctified through Christ in the Spirit.[16] Accordingly, Luther begins by discussing the tablets of the law, which are written on the hearts of believers rather than on stones. The first tablet deals with the proper knowledge of God, while the second tablet deals with the sanctification of the body. Thus the seven marks refer to the first tablet and are to be understood as being constitutive for the church:

> That is called a new, holy life in the soul, in accordance with the first table of Moses. It is also called the three principle virtues of Christians, namely, faith, hope and love: and the Holy Spirit, who imparts, does

14. Oberman, *Martin Luther*, 172; see also Heiko A. Oberman, *The Two Reformations: The Journey from the Last Days to the New World*, ed. Donald Weinstein (New Haven: Yale University Press, 2003), 40–43; Kenneth Hagen, *Luther's Approach to Scripture as Seen in His "Commentaries" on Galatians, 1518–1538* (Tübingen: Mohr, 1993), x–xi.

15. Hütter, *Suffering Divine Things*, 75–76.

16. Hütter, *Bound to Be Free*, 36–37.

and effects this (gained for us by Christ) is therefore called sanctifier or life-giver. For the old Adam is dead, and in addition has to learn from the law he is unable to do it and that he is dead, he would not know this himself. (Lull, 543)[17]

Luther turned to the Apostles' Creed to define the church: "I believe in a holy Christian church, the communion of saints, that is, a multitude or gathering of people who are Christians and holy." The church is a regular assembly whose worship is the essence of its life, a Christian community that believes in Christ and has the Holy Spirit. The Spirit sanctifies the church daily through the forgiveness of sins and through the putting off of, purging of, and putting to death of sins, from which they are called to be a holy people (Lull, 540–41).

Christian people, moreover, have the holy Word of God, the public proclamation of the gospel of Christ: "We are talking about the outward word, orally preached by human beings like you and me. Christ has left this behind as an outward sign by which one is to recognize his church or his Christian holy people in the world." In addition to the external, orally proclaimed Word by which the church is recognized in the activities of preaching, hearing, believing, and confessing, there are corresponding actions—baptism, the Lord's Supper, the power of the keys in community discipline, the church offices and ordination, worship and instruction, and discipleship in suffering and temptation (Lull, 545–63). David Yeago comments:

> For Luther, these practices not only identify the church, they constitute it as church, as the holy Christian people. Luther speaks of these seven practices as *Heilthümer*, perhaps best translated as "holy things." Luther is saying, in effect, that these seven practices are true "miracle-working" holy things through which the Spirit fashions a holy people in the world. The holiness of the church is not merely a note of a purely forensic imputation to Christians of the holiness of Christ. . . . The church is sanctified by holy practices, which make up its common life through which practices the inward gifts of faith and the Holy Spirit are bestowed on the gathered people.[18]

The true character of the church consists in the Word of God and the knowing act of faith, which constitute the *communio sanctorum*. As

---

17. Cf. *LW* 41:143–78.
18. David S. Yeago, "A Christian, Holy People: Martin Luther on Salvation and the Church," *Modern Theology* 13, no. 1 (January 1997): 110.

a creature of the Word, the one catholic and apostolic church is holy, although not because it claims holiness as its own intrinsic attribute. Such holiness is attributed only to the sanctifying work of the Spirit, who authenticates the church's witness to the gospel in its affirmation of the first commandment and rule of Christ. It is the Spirit who enables the church to share in the being of Christ and participate in the life of the Triune God.[19]

As Yeago argues, these holy practices that constitute, sanctify, and therefore identify the church are all related to public worship, the enactment of the liturgy. The proclamation of the Word of God, the celebration of baptism, the Eucharist, and doxology—public praise of God—are liturgical acts. The office of the ministry is essentially an office of liturgical enactment; the public exercise of the keys, church discipline, excludes unrepentant sinners from the Eucharist and re-admits the penitent. The cross, or suffering, is imposed on the church because of exclusive loyalty to Christ confessed, celebrated, and enacted in public prayer and praise.[20]

Ecclesial Catechesis and Preaching

Reinhard Hütter has persuasively argued that Luther's marks of the church, or core practices, and doctrine are interrelated, which, by the Holy Spirit's work, equally instantiate the church as an *ecclesia*, or public, in its own right.[21] Moreover, Luther's catechisms, which were written for a church that was being reformed around the gospel, articulate the basics of his pastoral or ecclesial theology, uniting Christian doctrine to ecclesial practices that mediate the saving knowledge of God communicated in preaching.[22]

19. Christoph Schwobel, "The Creature of the Word: Recovering the Ecclesiology of the Reformers," in *On Being the Church: Essays on the Christian Community*, ed. Colin E. Gunton and Daniel W. Hardy (Edinburgh: T&T Clark, 1989), 118–21; Yeago, "A Christian, Holy People," 118; Yeago, "Ecclesia Sancta, Ecclesia Peccatrix: The Holiness of the Church in Martin Luther's Theology," *Pro Ecclesia* 9, no. 3 (Summer 2000): 352–54.

20. Yeago, "A Christian, Holy People," 110.

21. Hütter, *Bound to Be Free*, 37–42.

22. Timothy J. Wengert, "Introduction," in *Harvesting Martin Luther's Reflections on Theology, Ethics, and the Church*, ed. Timothy J. Wengert (Grand Rapids: Eerdmans, 2004), 3; Steinmetz, "Luther and Formation in Faith," in *Educating People of Faith: Exploring the History of Jewish and Christian Communities*, ed. John Van Engen and Dorothy Bass (Grand Rapids: Eerdmans, 2004), 263–69.

The material in the Large Catechism originated in 1529 as sermons on the basic texts of Christian faith and life: the Ten Commandments, the Apostles' Creed, the Lord's Prayer, and sometimes the Ave Maria. To these Luther added instruction on baptism and the Lord's Supper.[23] The preface to the Large Catechism exhorts pastors to allow its doctrine to inform the task of preaching and teaching since it "provides a brief summary and digest of the entire Holy Scripture." Luther confessed his own continuing need to learn as a child, to repeat daily the Lord's Prayer, the Ten Commandments, the creed, and the psalms, which are the "ABCs" of God and his Word that drive away the devil and evil thoughts. Since God himself commands this practice (Deut. 6:7–8), God himself is its teacher. To learn the Ten Commandments in this manner is to know the scope of the Scriptures, of which the writings of the prophets and apostles are sermons or expositions that yield wisdom, counsel, and judgment (*Concord*, 409–10).

The creed, moreover, is a summary of the gospel, and the gospel, in turn, is a narrative: it proclaims the history of God's gracious dealings with humankind in creation, rendering Christ and the gathering of a people, the church, through the Holy Spirit. Thus the creed is based on the Rule of Faith, and the faith of the creed is based on the Trinity.[24] Because the creed sets forth all that must be expected and received from God, it offers grace or help in doing what the Ten Commandments require. This is summed up in three main articles, which correspond to the three major divisions of the biblical narrative in its Christian trinitarian version: "I believe in God the Father, who created me; I believe in God the Son, who has redeemed me; I believe in the Holy Spirit, who makes me holy."

George Lindbeck notes that by preaching on particular biblical narratives throughout the liturgical year, the details of this grand trinitarian

23. The Large Catechism and Small Catechism (1529) in *The Book of Concord: The Confessions of the Evangelical Lutheran Church*, ed. Robert Kolb and Timothy J. Wengert (Minneapolis: Fortress, 2000); hereafter cited as *Concord*. See the discussion in Martin Brecht, *Martin Luther*, vol. 2, *Shaping and Defining the Reformation, 1521–1532*, trans. James L. Schaaf (Philadelphia: Fortress, 1985–), 259–79; David C. Steinmetz, *Luther in Context* (Bloomington: Indiana University Press, 1986), 85–97; Gottfried Seebass, "The Importance of Luther's Writings in the Formation of Protestant Confessions of Faith in the Sixteenth Century," in *Luther's Ecumenical Significance: An Interconfessional Consultation*, ed. Peter Manns and Harding Meyer (Philadelphia: Fortress, 1984), 71–80.

24. Here I am indebted to the exposition of Luther in George Lindbeck, "Martin Luther and the Rabbinic Mind," in *The Church in a Postliberal Age*, ed. James M. Buckley (Grand Rapids: Eerdmans, 2002), 21–37.

narrative are filled in. Such catechetical preaching identifies God and enables Christian people to refer to him and rightly talk to him in prayer and praise. Moreover, to learn the language of faith requires personal appropriation, *pro me*, in order to become one's own story that elicits fear, love, and trust to the praise and glory of God above all things, which is the sum and substance of the first commandment.[25] The Decalogue, therefore, provides the scaffolding for a form of life with the gospel at its center, "which teaches us to know God perfectly . . . in order to help us do what the Ten Commandments require" (*Concord*, 411).

The Gospel: Preaching for the Praise of God

Luther's preface to *A Brief Instruction on What to Look for and Expect in the Gospels* provides a concise summary of the gospel narrative:

> Gospel is and should be nothing less than a discourse or story about Christ. . . . Thus the gospel is and should be nothing less than a chronicle, a story, a narrative about Christ, telling who he is, what he did and what he suffered. . . . For at its briefest, the Gospel is a discourse about Christ, that he is the Son of God and was made man for us, that he died and was raised, that he has been established as Lord, of all things. (Lull, 105)[26]

The gospel is a book of promises; when opened, read, and proclaimed in the church, Christ himself comes to listeners through the Scripture and sermon, and listeners are brought to him by the Spirit to know and love the Father. Robert Jenson comments on Luther's conviction: "For the preaching of the gospel is nothing less than Christ coming to us, or we being brought to him. . . . Christ speaks in preaching; and it is in rendering the person of Christ, the living Word, that God is his own Word, the 'good things' in God's Word are God himself; moreover, we are the 'good things' we hear in the gospel, by attending to them with faith we are shaped to what we hear."[27] According to Luther, the most fitting response to the gift of Christ, who is both sacrament and example, is to offer one's faith to God and one's love to the neighbor,

25. Ibid., 29–31.
26. Cf. *LW* 35:117–24.
27. Robert W. Jenson, "Luther's Contemporary Theological Significance," in *The Cambridge Companion to Martin Luther*, ed. Donald K. McKim (Cambridge: Cambridge University Press, 2003), 283.

treating him or her in the same manner God in Christ has dealt with all humanity—by raising up a Christian, holy people (Lull, 108).

For Luther, preaching was an ecclesial practice situated within a larger web of Christian believing, willing, and acting. Luther confessed and celebrated the good story or report of the gospel, the Spirit-effected speech of Christ the risen Lord, who rules over and in the midst of the battle between God and the devil for the life of the world. His focus was the decisive action of God in Christ, the Word authorized by apostolic witness and the narrative of salvation interpreted within a tradition of Christian doctrine and practice.[28] Speaking of God with confidence in the power of the gospel to open the eyes of even the most hardened hearts, Luther trusted the Spirit to work the miracle of hearing among a holy people "who sing, thank and praise God, and are glad forever, if only they believe firmly and remain steadfast in faith" (Lull, 27).

Luther's ecclesial vision provides a salutary example of how Christian practices mediate God's Word to form the church, a holy people who embody the confession of faith articulated in prayer, praise, and proclamation. As a "sacrament of salvation," the church is where faith is born, nourished, and lived in communion with the Father through the Son and in the Holy Spirit. Because of the particular God whom it worships, the church is a particular people in which the Spirit makes Christ effectively present through Word and sacrament to glorify the Father in the world, which is the heart of ecclesial practice and evangelical witness.[29]

From Ecclesial Practice to Pragmatic Evangelism

George Lindbeck has written of the urgent need for the church to engage in the practice of evangelization—conversion and Christian catechesis—at a time when Christianity is in an awkwardly intermediate stage in Western culture, where having once been culturally established, it is still not clearly disestablished. In our present time of de-Christianization (but not without increasing enthusiasm for private spirituality and religiosity), the overwhelming temptation of the church is to accommodate the prevailing culture rather than to convert it,

28. Hinlicky, "The Lutheran Dilemma," 383–84.
29. Ola Tjorhom, "The Church as the Place of Salvation: On the Interrelation between Justification and Ecclesiology," Pro Ecclesia 9, no. 3 (Summer 2000): 294–96.

which is directly related to a deep loss of common memory, of shared public language and life.[30]

This loss of "mother speech" and identity has provoked a crisis of relevance that renders the church vulnerable to temptations of despair or accommodation, a vulnerability whose origin is twofold. On the one hand, it arises out of embarrassment in the face of contemporary challenges; on the other, it emerges from anxiety regarding the church's future. Thus alternative forms of speech and life appear to offer more culturally credible and pragmatically effective means of securing ecclesiastical success.[31]

However, renewal programs and evangelistic strategies that substitute forms of speech and life less substantive than the language and claims of the gospel inevitably result in a loss of the church's public voice and visibility. This leaves the church without a distinctive way of speaking since a distinctive people no longer exists to speak, thereby relinquishing the public space of the church to the inner spaces of privatized religion. William Willimon writes of the temptations that accompany the church's desire to evangelize the world:

> The way I read church history, most of our really great theological mistakes were made in the interest of evangelism. In so wanting to lean over and speak to the world, sometimes we fall in facedown. We give away the store. We pare down the gospel to something that can fit on a bumper sticker, letting the consumer be the judge of just what can be demanded, said, and expected in the name of Jesus. We use the world's means of speaking only too late to realize that the medium has changed the message rather than the message transforming the world.[32]

When the end or goal of the church is no longer a shared, public life of doxology—the offering of right praise to God for God's sake and knowing and loving God out of love for God—preaching, as an ecclesial practice, yields to pragmatic strategies deemed useful for addressing needs, crises, limitations, or other problems. This lack of doxology leads to a gospel that fills the gaps in one's life or repairs things that have gone wrong and is practical in a host of ways. Thus a praise-centered gospel easily becomes

30. George A. Lindbeck, *The Nature of Doctrine: Religion and Theology in a Postliberal Age* (Philadelphia: Westminster, 1984), 128–34.

31. Walter Brueggemann, *Cadences of Home: Preaching among Exiles* (Louisville: Westminster John Knox, 1997), 2–14.

32. William H. Willimon, "It's Hard to Be Seeker-Sensitive When You Work for Jesus," *Circuit Rider* 27, no. 5 (Sept.–Oct. 2003): 5.

problem-centered. This approach is highly seductive since there is indeed good news for every problematic situation and person, and members are added and the institution grows.[33] In the end, however, forms of pragmatic evangelism may actually work to choke out true growth if the church does not embody the grace it offers, since a church that makes growth its primary end contradicts the cruciform way of life it presumes to proclaim: For "we preach Christ crucified" (1 Cor. 1:23).

Ironically, by continually reinventing itself to attract self-directed consumers in the name of "relevance," the church risks becoming increasingly irrelevant to God's larger saving purposes revealed through Christ and the Spirit for the life of the world. *Rather than being in but not of the world, the church ends up being of but not in the world.* Pursuing a strategy that only perpetuates this "crisis of relevance," an obsessive concern for self-preservation by doing "whatever works" runs the danger of pushing aside all other values, including the apostolic vocation of being the church together in communion with the churches of all time whose primary purpose is to praise, know, and love the Triune God.[34] *Such strategies do not tell us of the mystery of grace, of God's redemptive purpose enacted through Christ and the Spirit to create, judge, and renew the church as a sacrifice of thanksgiving in voicing creation's praise; nor do they tell of the Spirit's work in building up and indwelling a holy people whose unique presence, worship, and way of being proclaim the gospel of Christ's lordship to the world and its powers.* As Brueggemann comments:

> There is little doubt that religious idolatry is matched by social ideology in which the American dream is the goal of life. . . . This powerful combination of idolatry (of a god who has no history and will not act) and ideology (of a social arrangement that will not change and cannot be criticized) is conveyed well in the doxologies of civil religion in which the living God becomes the patron of the status quo, and the present system feels very much like the kingdom. The religious seduction of civil religion is found not only in the powerful propagandas of consumer advertising but is also present in much of the church, which is simply an echo of and guarantor for the controlling ideology.[35]

33. Hardy and Ford, *Praising and Knowing God*, 150.

34. Gordon W. Lathrop, *Holy People: A Liturgical Ecclesiology* (Philadelphia: Fortress, 1999).

35. Walter Brueggemann, *Israel's Praise: Doxology against Idolatry and Ideology* (Philadelphia: Fortress, 1988), 128.

John Wesley: Ecclesial Evangelist

Interestingly, many church growth advocates will often invoke the name of John Wesley as an exemplar of evangelistic preaching who was effective in attracting seekers into the church. Such enthusiasm for emulating Wesley's presumably pragmatic methods and replicating his obviously impressive results typically fails to pay attention to the theological convictions that informed his judgment and practice. Albert Outler notes:

> Traditionally, Wesley has been viewed (by Methodists and non-Methodists alike), rather more in the light of the consequences of his career (i.e., as founder and patriarch of the Methodists), than in the light of his involvements in the crowded forum of eighteenth century theological debate. What have been missed thereby are his deep roots in the Christian tradition, and his refocusing of this tradition in an age of radical transitions.[36]

Wesley was adamant in his insistence that Methodist preachers adhere to the biblically informed manner of Christian believing and speaking displayed from the movement's very beginning. For example, in December 1751 Wesley responded in writing to an inquirer on the subject of "preaching Christ," offering a description theological in both its substance and scope.[37] He tells the story of the gospel—the love of God for sinners demonstrated in the life, death, resurrection, and intercession of Christ and his blessings—and the law—the command of Christ to follow him in active discipleship, particularly in steadfast communal adherence to the teaching of the Sermon on the Mount.

Wesley goes on to reveal the kind of particular homiletic judgment he exercised in addressing sinners, the justified, the diligent, the careless, and the feebleminded, his knowledge of both the law and gospel and how they work in preaching, as well as his pastoral sensitivity to a wide range of spiritual and moral conditions. Derived from the liturgical tradition of the church, such wisdom set him against those whom he viewed as mere "gospel preachers."[38]

36. *The Works of John Wesley: Bicentennial Edition*, vols. 1–4, *Sermons*, ed. Albert C. Outler (Nashville: Abingdon, 1984–87), 1:xi.

37. *The Works of John Wesley*, ed. Thomas Jackson, 3rd ed. (Grand Rapids: Baker, repr., 1978), 1:486–92; hereafter cited as PC.

38. See the discussion of Wesley's dependence on the Anglican tradition in Robert E. Cushman, *John Wesley's Experimental Divinity: Studies in Methodist Doctrinal Standards* (Nashville: Kingswood, 1989).

John Wheatley was one such popular "gospel preacher," who according to Wesley was neither clear nor sound in Christian faith and whose sermons sounded like "an unconnected rhapsody of unmeaning words" and "verses, smooth and soft as cream, in which there was neither depth or stream." Wesley viewed such preaching as both a debasement of Christian speech and a deformation of Christian life, even though its crowd-pleasing style was increasingly contagious (PC 487–89).

"Gospel preaching" promised much but asked little in return. It "corrupted hearers, vitiated their taste for the gospel, ruined their desire for sound teaching, spoiled their spiritual appetites, feeding them 'sweetmeats' until the genuine wine of the kingdom seemed quite insipid." Although such listener-friendly communicators were adept at drawing large crowds, they offered mere "cordial upon cordial" that destroyed listeners' capacities for retaining and digesting the pure milk of the Word of God in Christ (PC 491).

Wesley's description provided a clear alternative for construing both law and gospel for preaching as an ecclesial practice capable of building up a holy people to praise God in joyful obedience through union with Christ in his death and resurrection. This way of preaching invited listeners to enter by faith into a story of salvation that transforms the whole of life by God's grace and for God's glory. Wesley asserts: "God loves you; therefore love and obey him. Christ died for you; therefore die to sin. Christ is risen; therefore, rise in the image of God. Christ liveth forevermore; therefore live to God, till you live with him in glory" (PC 491–92).

Such ecclesial preaching, moreover, served to evangelize those not yet converted and to exhort unto holiness of life the justified, who were supposed to be "going on to perfection." To advance this purpose, Wesley set out to provide the Methodist people, preachers and laity alike, with everything they needed to continue in a life of holiness. This plan amounted to a great deal; Wesley expected his ministers to invest as many as five hours daily in prayerful study. But the key to this catechetical and pedagogical program was Wesley's own published sermons, which provided practical wisdom for speaking of God, salvation, the life of the church, and its mission to the world.

If, for Wesley, oral sermons were to serve proclamation, invitation, and conversion to Christ, then written sermons were for nurture and education, that is, homiletic training for preaching Christ. The sermons were to be his main medium for communicating what the people called

Methodists were all about, providing wisdom for ordering communal speech and life in grateful, obedient response to the grace of God in Christ through the Spirit's work.[39]

It is impossible, however, to understand Wesley's vision and practice of preaching apart from the ecclesial tradition, the Church of England, that was of primary importance in nourishing his faith and understanding. The standard collection of Anglicanism's theological teachings was the two *Books of Homilies* published under Edward VI and Elizabeth, formularies to which Wesley was ever eager to confess his allegiance. The homilies introduced an evangelical economy of salvation in which sermons, *ex opere operata,* played the central part. This was a practical wisdom for evangelical doctrine and life, ordered according to essential topics derived from Scripture to promote disciplined Christian speech, thus providing regular opportunities for listeners to be incorporated into Scripture's drama of salvation.[40] During the latter years of his ministry, after returning from a tour of Methodist societies throughout England and Ireland, Wesley reported:

> The book, which next to the Holy Scriptures was of greatest use to them in settling their judgment as to the grand point of justification by faith, is the book of Homilies. They were never so clearly convinced that we are justified by faith alone till they carefully consulted these and compared them with the sacred writings [i.e., Holy Scripture].[41]

However, Wesley's indebtedness to the Anglican tradition had already been evinced almost fifty years earlier when the Methodist movement was in its infancy and he was forced to refute antinomianism. Wesley distributed a printed extract that included "Doctrine of Salvation" and "Faith and Good Works" from the *Homilies of the Church of England*. This was something of a theological manifesto, a position from which he never would waver. It was the fusion of salvation and ethics: living faith in Christ that works through joyful obedience to God's commands, a doxological and disciplined way of life embedded in particular communities of Christian practice.

39. Albert C. Outler, "Introduction," in *Works of John Wesley*, ed. Outler, 1:1.

40. John N. Wall, "Godly and Fruitful Lessons: The English Bible, Erasmus' Paraphrases, and the Book of Homilies," in *The Godly Kingdom of Tudor England: Great Books of the English Reformation*, ed. John Booty (Wilton, CT: Morehouse-Barlow, 1981), 47–138.

41. Cited in *Certain Sermons or Homilies (1547)* and, *A Homily against Disobedience and Wilful Rebellion (1570)*, ed. Ronald B. Bond (Toronto, ON: University of Toronto Press, 1987), 121–33.

Wesley thus utilized the wisdom of the homilies to call preachers' attention to the Word of God—the wisdom of the crucified and risen Christ, whose presence is mediated through Scripture—and to cultivate confidence in the witness of the Holy Spirit, who creates a holy people in and for the love of God.[42] The road to the future therefore led through the past. The tradition of the Church of England provided a grammar of Christian speech for evangelization and catechesis; while the Bible was the chief source of the homilies, the worship of God was their home. The rhythms of common prayer, praise, and thanksgiving were joined to confession, repentance, and forgiveness—a robust, liturgical life of singing, praying, preaching, and testifying that created an ethos of living faith. Common worship was a graced response of amazement to the astonishing, abundant overflow of divine love, creating a trinitarian "grammar" that constituted the evangelical and sacramental character of Methodism.[43] As Ralph Wood observes of the Wesleys' learned piety,

The Wesleys like their medieval counterparts understood that preaching helps to guarantee the reciprocal relationship of heart and head. Instead of asking what can God do for us—how we might come to feel more pious or to be more holy or to act more spiritually—doctrinal preaching enables us to ask the far profounder question: What does God want to do through us? The Good News is that God is determined to create a radically redemptive community, a new people whose benefits are not primarily for themselves but for God and the world. This transformed Body is sustained by wisdom the world regards as folly—the preaching of Christ crucified (1 Cor. 1:23). Hence Paul's insistence that the Gospel is not something to be preached as much as it is preaching itself: "Faith comes from what is heard" . . . *fides ex auditu* (Rom. 10:17).[44]

Evangelization for Wesley, then, was the fruit of a larger purpose: the faithful proclamation and enactment of the gospel within a trinitarian

42. Albert C. Outler, ed., *John Wesley* (New York: Oxford University Press, 1964), 121–33.

43. For a discussion of Wesley's leadership in providing doctrinal and liturgical texts, see Richard P. Heitzenrater, *Wesley and the People Called Methodists* (Nashville: Abingdon, 1995); see also the excellent discussion in E. Byron Anderson, *Worship and Christian Identity* (Collegeville, MN: Liturgical Press, 2003), 4–6, 151–56, 180–88; see also the good description of the Wesleyan "medium and message" and the close fit among theology, practice, and style in David Hempton, *Methodism: Empire of the Spirit* (New Haven: Yale University Press, 2005), 86–108.

44. Ralph C. Wood, *Contending for the Faith: The Church's Engagement with Culture* (Waco: Baylor University Press, 2003), 180.

economy of grace. His sermons were therefore homiletic expressions of extended, prayerful attention to the canon of Scripture, the Christian tradition, and lives of the saints, as well as public acclamations of praise for the extravagant love of the Father who sends the Son and Spirit to create, judge, and perfect a holy people to be a living sacrifice of praise and witness to the divine rule and mission for the world.

Such ecclesial and evangelistic preaching of the Word, "plain truth for plain folk," evoked new conversions and fresh re-turnings that in response to the promptings of the Spirit deepened into mature, disciplined love for God, the self, and neighbors. The gift of living faith working through love was evinced within a wide range of conditions, but especially among the poorest where surprising manifestations of moral and social transformation were witnessed. These public expressions of divine grace and human gratitude evoked such "wonder, love and praise" so as to call attention to their source and goal: the glory of the Father, Son, and Holy Spirit indwelling redeemed sinful people.[45]

For Wesley, such startling acts of personal conversion, social change, and numerical growth were not the end or goal, but rather were seen as a concrete, visible witness to gracious beginnings and signs pointing to eternal life, the kingdom coming on earth as it is in heaven: the love, enjoyment, and happiness of communion with the Triune God, creation's true end or goal, whom to know through praise and adoration is "One thing needful." Wesley celebrates this truth in his sermon on the Holy Trinity:

> The one perfect good shall be your ultimate end. One thing shall ye desire for its own sake—the fruition of him who is all in all. One happiness ye shall propose to your souls, even an union with him that made them, the having fellowship with the Father and the Son, the being "joined to the Lord in one Spirit." One design ye are to pursue to the end of time—the enjoyment of God in time and eternity. Desire other things so far as they tend to this. Love the creature—as it leads to the Creator. But in every step you take be this, the glorious point that terminates your view. Let every affection, and desire or fear, whatever ye seek or shun, whatever ye think, speak, or do, be in order to your happiness in God, the

45. Hardy and Ford, *Praising and Knowing God*, 148–52; see the discussion of Wesley, worship, and Methodism in "Worship, Evangelism, Ethics: On Eliminating the 'And,' " chap. 10 in Stanley Hauerwas, *A Better Hope: Resources for a Church Confronting Capitalism, Democracy, and Postmodernity* (Grand Rapids: Brazos, 2000), 155–62; Horton Davies, *Worship and Theology in England*, vol. 2, *From Watts and Wesley to Martineau, 1690–1900* (Grand Rapids: Eerdmans, 1996), 184–209.

sole end as well as the source of your being. Have no end, no ultimate end, but God. Thus our Lord: "One thing needful."[46]

Matthew 14:14–36

Has anyone sitting here today ever had the feeling that church is boring? Now, be honest with me, all you good church members; in your heart of hearts, have you ever grown tired of the routine? Of singing, saying, and doing the same old things, week after week, month after month, year after year? Some of you tell me that the number one problem with churches is that they are boring; they lack excitement, passion, energy, and vitality. What we need to do is to make church entertaining and interesting so that we can keep up with the competition for our time, attention, commitment, and money.

What do you think? Do the church and its faith in Jesus Christ as Lord make a claim on your whole life that is convincing, compelling, challenging, and even life changing? Well, let's be honest with each other, especially we who have been in church for as long as we can remember. We have our dry spells; we have our stretches of boredom and indifference. Why, we even have times of occasional unfaithfulness and disobedience to God's will, have we not? But according to the Gospel, when who we are and what we do as God's people cease to move us and inspire us, when our identity and life as God's people fail to command our attention against the competing claims the world places on us, the solution is not to be found in changing the Christian faith and its way of life to fit our interests. According to Jesus, and so according to the Gospel, we are what needs to be adjusted or changed, so that our lives are more fitting or relevant for the Triune God, whom we worship.

This is what happens in the Gospel lesson for this morning. It is a story about Jesus and his followers, which is also a story about Jesus, you, and me—the church—today. It provides a picture of what our Lord is doing with us as he did with the disciples. Did you notice how the story begins? Matthew writes, "As soon as the meal was finished." After Jesus multiplies loaves and fishes to feed and satisfy a hungry,

46. See the sermons "On the Trinity" and "The New Creation" in *The Works of John Wesley*, 2:373–86, 500–510; on Wesley and Christian conversion, see William H. Willimon, "Suddenly a Light from Heaven," in *Conversion and the Wesleyan Tradition*, ed. Kenneth J. Collins and John H. Tyson (Nashville: Abingdon, 2001).

needy crowd of thousands, he insists that the disciples get into a boat to go over to the other side while he stays behind to dismiss the people and then to pray.

Well, the followers of Jesus—and remember, they are us—do what most of us would do: they obey him and climb into the boat. They respond to the words of Jesus even though they do not know where they are going. But since he has just fed them and strengthened them with a miraculous meal, they trust him enough to get into the boat. At the end of the service of Holy Communion in the Book of Common Prayer, the church prays:

> Gracious Father, we give you thanks for this Holy Communion of the Body and Blood of your Beloved Son Jesus Christ, the pledge of our redemption; and we pray that it may bring forgiveness of our sins, strength in our weakness, and everlasting salvation; through Jesus Christ our Lord.

The eucharistic meal we share together with Christ calls us to remember and be thankful for his mighty acts for our salvation centered in his death and resurrection. But the meal doesn't call us back in time, now does it? Rather, it calls us forward into a future that comes to us from God's sovereign hand through the risen Lord in the power of the Holy Spirit.

To put this in a different way, to say it as Matthew tells the story of Jesus, our being fed at his table is not an end; it is a fresh beginning each time, and it is for a purpose and filled with promises. We are sent out into the world in the name of Christ to go in peace to love and serve the Lord, rejoicing in the Spirit. This is our direction from Jesus, and it is why we must first get into the boat. But this is also when things start to get interesting, because being sent by Christ is like being sent on a journey marked by mystery, uncertainty, risk, not knowing, and surprising newness. Look what happens: they end up far out at sea where it is stormy, dark, and dangerous, and where they are scared to death. Now, I ask you, what kind of peace is this?

And the poor disciples—the poor little church—are huddled together, convinced their end has come. This is what we get for listening to Jesus. This is what we get for taking chances with him. This is what we get for daring to step out with him but without any guarantees. And Jesus is nowhere to be seen, his voice is silent, the feeling of his absence in the midst of their desperate situation is simply overwhelming. What they cannot see is that Jesus had gone off to pray to the Father on their behalf.

Now we need to hear this part of the story, as uncomfortable as it may be. There is a popular view of the Christian life and the church that tells us that we should have no reason to worry, to be anxious, to fear, to doubt, or to feel that living by faith, by trust in God and his Word, is often much like being out of control. No, if we only have faith or faith in our faith, everything will turn out all right; everything will remain within our control; we will have no reason to feel anxious about anything. Have you ever heard such things? I do all the time.

But as Christian people, we receive our life from a crucified and risen Lord. Yes, he feeds us at his table, but he feeds us with his own life, the life we were given in our baptism when we were joined with him and plunged into the deep waters of his death and resurrection. And this is what God is now doing with us. He is remaking us, conforming our lives to the image of Jesus Christ, which will take some doing. It requires our death to the old self and resurrection to a new life in the new world brought by Christ, in the kingdom that he rules from an ugly, wooden cross. And even more, what he is doing with us is just a part, an example and witness to his work, of redeeming the whole creation to praise and adore him as king of the whole universe, both now and forever.

Perhaps we have been fooled. Perhaps we have become bored with church because we are no longer willing to take the risk of faithful obedience to Jesus. Perhaps the renewal of our lives as Christians, as God's people, awaits us if we will only get into the boat, or back into the boat, embarking on the journey and way that has been charted by Jesus, the destination and outcome of which we receive from his gracious hand. As our psalm for this morning led us to pray with God's people throughout the ages: "Above the floodwaters is God's throne, from which his power flows, from which he rules the world. God makes his people strong; God gives his people peace" (Ps. 29:10–11 *Message* 944).

These words do not come easily; they are a gift, words God's Spirit prompts us to pray in our need for deliverance, for rescuing, for salvation. And this is what happened to Peter. While he sees Jesus, he is still not sure, so he decides to test him, to find out for himself: "Master, if it is you, call me to come on the water." And Jesus calls him, "Come on, Peter." Peter jumps out and begins to walk on the water to Jesus, but when he turns to glance at the waves towering over him, he feels the force of the wind on his face, he hears the roaring thunder and chaos all around him, and he begins to sink, "Master, save me!"

I have always been told that this story is about Peter. And like Peter, if we will only keep our eyes on Jesus, we too can do great things for God. We too can build the kingdom; we too can overcome the storms of life; we too can win out over worry. Does this sound familiar? Well, the truth of the matter is that Peter actually belonged in the boat with the others, where Jesus had placed him! His walking on water, at least for a few seconds, was not an act of heroic proportion; it was a display of his refusal to trust Jesus to come to their rescue, to remain faithful to them, not to abandon them in their helplessness.

Friends, we all belong in the boat because that's where Jesus has placed us, in his church, so that he can lead us safely through the waters of baptism, into his death and resurrection, until we all attain to the fullness of God's life in Christ and are made holy as God is holy. But the key is Jesus; because we are his people, we can control neither our life nor our destiny.

St. Augustine, speaking as bishop of Hippo in northern Africa, told his people in a sermon:

> Therefore my brothers and sisters, I would implant this in your hearts: if you wish to live in a devout and Christian way, adhere to Christ according to that which he became for us, so that you may reach him according to that which he is and according to that which he was. He came to us that he might become this for us; for he became for us this upon which the weak may be carried and may cross the sea of the world and reach their homeland where there will be no need of a ship because no sea is crossed.[47]

"For no one can cross the sea of this world unless carried by the cross of Christ."[48]

Friends, it is Jesus our risen Lord who has come to us today saying, "Take heart, it is I, do not be afraid" (Matt. 14:27 NRSV). Just as it was God who spoke to Moses, directing him to tell Israel when they stood on the edge of the Red Sea with Pharaoh's army breathing down their necks, "Take heart; do not be afraid" (cf. Exod. 14:13). Just as

47. *Tractates on the Gospel of John* 2.3, in *St. Augustine, Tractates on the Gospel of John, 1–10*, trans. John W. Rettig, The Fathers of the Church 78 (Washington, DC: Catholic University of America Press, 1988), 62–63.

48. Augustine, *Tractates on the Gospel of John* 2.2.

it was God who said to Moses at the burning bush, "I am who I am" (cf. Exod. 3:14 NRSV). Just as it was God who spoke to the prophet Isaiah, telling him to announce to disobedient, exiled Israel, "Be not afraid; when you pass through the waters, I will be with you" (cf. Isa. 43:1–2). "It is I" echoes time after time in the Gospel of John when Jesus says, "I am . . . I am . . . I am Resurrection and I am Life" (cf. John 11:25). Just as it is Christ, the risen Lord, who announces through the vision of John in the book of Revelation, "Do not be afraid, I am the first and I am the last. I am alive. I died, but now I live, and my life is forever" (cf. Rev. 1:17–18).

The major actor in this story of the wind and the waves is Jesus Christ, the Lord of heaven and earth, the One whom even the dark, deadly powers of this world obey; the One to whose name every knee will bow and tongue confess that he is the strong Son of God, the Lord of life and death, to the glory of the Father. And so when Peter began to sink, when he cried out, "Lord, save me!" without hesitating, Jesus reached down to take firm hold of Peter's grasping hand. And then he asked, "Faint of heart, what has gotten into you?"

Peter and the others remind me of how we often respond to our contemporary challenges. My own denomination has lost a third of its membership in a little more than a generation; we have closed thousands of churches and have been forced to restructure, downsize, and discontinue ministries. But even more than these numerical losses has been a decline in missional commitment and activity that has caused some observers to call us a sideline rather than a mainline church. Many of our clergy and laity act and speak as if our situation is truly desperate, that we are like the disciples, cast out at sea, left alone to fend for ourselves, and certain to perish unless we do something to ensure our survival or success as a religious institution.

In this Gospel, Jesus says to us, "Faint of heart, what has gotten into you?" And this is the word of the Lord to us today. He is the One who has placed us in this boat, called us to this adventure, set us in motion on a peculiar way of life as his people called church, and he has promised to never leave or forsake us. He is the One who knows our destiny because in his life, death, and triumphant resurrection he has gone before us and made a way for us to share in the life of love that is his with the Father and the Spirit. Truly, he is the Son of God. And if we worship him, how can church ever be boring?

4

Speaking of God:
Preaching as a Pastoral Practice

> I, for my part, give thanks to our God that in these four books I have set
> out to the best of my poor ability, not what sort of pastor I am myself,
> lacking many of the necessary qualities as I do, but what sort of pastor
> should be him who is eager to toil away, not only for his own sake but
> for others, in the teaching of sound Christian doctrine.
>
> —Augustine, *De doctrina christiana*

Preaching as a pastoral practice is not simply a call to believe something,
to learn something, or to do something. Rather, it is to be made a truthful witness to Christ, knowing and loving the Word that shapes our
lives and gives shape to all the words we speak. In Augustine's words,
the pastor is to become an "eloquent sermon," a holy performance
that invites the church into truthful, enlivening conversation with God
the Father, Son, and Holy Spirit.[1] Thus the paradox of preaching as a

---

1. *De doctrina christiana* 4.27.59, in *The Works of Saint Augustine: A Translation for the
21st Century,* 1/11, *Teaching Christianity: De doctrina christiana,* ed. John E. Rotelle, OSA
(Hyde Park, NY: New City, 1996); hereafter references will be included within the text as *DDC.*
For a good introduction to Augustine's pastoral theology, see Mark Ellingsen, *The Richness of
Augustine: His Contextual and Pastoral Theology* (Louisville: Westminster John Knox, 2005); for

pastoral practice is that in listening to God more than their people, pastors are better equipped to direct others to hear the voice of the Triune God, whose Word and Spirit lead a pilgrim people through time.

To assist pastors in cultivating the necessary wisdom for speaking the truth in love, Augustine locates pastoral ministry within the activity of prayer and praise—the doxological ethos that constitutes the church's being in relation to God—educating human desire and nurturing a disposition for receiving the Word. Indeed, worship creates the ecology of praise in which the Father speaks the Son through the gift of the Spirit to create the grace-filled conditions for responding to and participating in the mystery of salvation. In the pedagogy of worship shaped by baptism and Eucharist, doctrine and life are made one through doxological participation in the Son's response to the Father, which occurs through receiving the gift of the Spirit shared by the Father and the Son.[2] Not surprisingly, Augustine begins the *Confessions* with prayerful adoration of the Trinity, the foundation and goal that unites thinking, speaking, and doing:

> Give me, O Lord, to know and understand whether first to call upon you or praise you, and whether first to know you or call upon you. For if I do not know you I may call upon some other rather than you. . . . Yet how will they call upon you, in whom they have not believed? Or how are they to believe without someone preaching? And they will praise the Lord who seek him. For the ones seeking find him, and the ones finding praise him. Let me seek you, Lord, calling upon you, and let me call upon you, believing you. For you have been preached to us! My faith calls upon you, O Lord, the faith, which you have given me, which you have breathed into me through the humanity of your Son, through the ministry of your preacher.[3]

Debra Murphy has suggested that the *Confessions* be read as a liturgical book that renders joyful praise for the truth, wisdom, and love revealed in Christ—knowledge of God and knowledge of the self—which is a gift received in turning to behold the glory of the Triune Creator.

---

a good introduction to pastoral theology that unites doctrine and practice, see Andrew Purves, *Reconstructing Pastoral Theology: A Christological Foundation* (Louisville: Westminster John Knox, 2005).

2. Here I am following the interpretation of Augustine in Michael Hanby, *Augustine and Modernity* (New York: Routledge, 2003), 90–106.

3. Saint Augustine, *Confessions*, trans. and intro. Henry Chadwick (New York: Oxford University Press, 1991), 1.1.1. Hereafter references will be included in the text as *Confessions*.

The God who is at the center of our life . . . is a God first prayed to, a God first worshiped, a God revealed to us as a community of persons. . . . Catechesis, then—our coming to know who and whose we are—is inseparable from doxology, the worship of Christ, the praise and adoration of Father, Son, and Holy Spirit. It is in worship, in the eucharistic assembly of Christ's body the church, that we are incorporated into the divine economy and given the gift of our very selves so that we might be the gift of Christ's body to and for the world. We are not and we know not apart from this communion.[4]

The church's doxological activity and theological understanding shape pastoral character as a habit, disposition, and way of life cultivated through living in the truth of God and the things of God. This pastoral vocation has a sense of personal truth and participatory knowledge, the gift of divine wisdom embodied in faith, hope, and love that draws and directs the church toward its destiny, the enjoyment and glory of God.

Bespeaking the Wisdom of God

In the *Confessions*, Augustine wrote of an intensive seeking for wisdom before his conversion to Christianity. This passionate love of philosophy in pursuit of eternal truth was his commitment to a way of life, an intellectual, moral, and emotional awakening and inner healing facilitated by the spoken or written words of ancient sages. Following his baptism and incorporation into the body of Christ, Augustine wrote of the intellectual vanity fostered by his love for philosophy, confessing his prideful illusion that human reason is capable of ascending unaided to divine wisdom and happiness.[5]

In his work as a Christian bishop and preacher, Augustine retained the pedagogical insights he learned as a student and teacher of philosophy. Assimilating these to the doctrine of the incarnation, revealed in the church's "folly of preaching" and cruciform way of life, he proclaimed the true "philosophy" of Christ—God's Wisdom, the principle of creation and means of its redemption.

---

4. Debra Dean Murphy, *Teaching That Transforms: Worship as the Heart of Christian Education* (Grand Rapids: Brazos, 2004), 112.

5. William Mallard, *Language and Love: Introducing Augustine's Religious Thought through the Confessions Story* (University Park: Pennsylvania State University Press, 1994); see also Ellen Charry, *By the Renewing of Your Minds: The Pastoral Function of Christian Doctrine* (New York: Oxford University Press, 1997), 120–52.

And so it was in the Wisdom of God that the world was unable to come to know God through wisdom. So why did she come, when she was already here, if not because it was God's pleasure through the folly of preaching to save those who believe? . . . That is how the Wisdom of God treats the ills of humanity, presenting herself for our healing, herself the physician, herself the psychic. So because man had fallen through pride, she applied humility to his cure. We were deceived by the wisdom of the serpent; we are set free by the folly of God. On the one hand, while her true name was Wisdom, she was folly to those who took no notice of God; on the other hand while this is called folly, it is in fact Wisdom to those who overcome the devil. (*DDC* 1.12–14)

Augustine's affirmation links the person and work of Christ to humanity and is congruent with the Catholic faith confessed by the church. The whole life and ministry of Jesus is the work of God in which the Son of God takes to himself our fallen world, our sinful, human flesh, and lives a life of faithful, loving praise on our behalf, doing the will of his Father, walking according to God's wisdom, and following God's way. In this vocation, Jesus learned for us the wisdom we have lost through sin and foolishness, overcoming our idolatrous and destructive ways, restoring and bringing to completion our life and destiny as creatures made in the image of God. Fully God, he descended into ignorance and humiliation; fully human, he advanced in wisdom and character to demonstrate his full participation in our creaturely life for us and for our salvation, which is communion with God.[6]

Martha Nussbaum has argued that the Hellenistic philosophical schools in Greece and Rome—Epicureans, Skeptics, and Stoics—conceived of philosophy as a way of simplicity and study that addressed the most painful problems of human existence. Teachers of wisdom were viewed as compassionate physicians whose linguistic arts—psychagogy (guiding souls), moral reasoning, practical wisdom, and persuasive speech—were capable of clarifying and healing many pervasive types of human suffering. The ancient practice of philosophy, therefore, was not for the purpose of detailed intellectual debate dedicated to the display of one's brilliance or cleverness, but rather was seen as a practical, pastoral art that grappled seriously with diverse expressions of human misery, and promoted human flourishing.[7]

6. Colin E. Gunton, *Theology through Preaching* (Edinburgh and New York: T&T Clark, 2001), 79–84.

7. Martha Nussbaum, *The Therapy of Desire: Theory and Practice in Hellenistic Ethics* (Princeton: Princeton University Press, 1994), 3–19.

This line of thought has been taken up by Pierre Hadot, who has persuasively argued that early Christianity, in both its Eastern and Western expressions, absorbed the practice of philosophy as a way of life: the love of Christian wisdom (i.e., Christ himself) as an expression of thought, will, and one's whole being that led to radical conversion through participation within a particular community. Christianity therefore presented itself as *philosophia*. In fact, it presented itself as the true *philosophia* (philosophy or love of wisdom), or a pastoral art of training people to see the world in a new way, and which offered a new way of speaking and living in the presence of the Triune God, whose glory fills all things. Hadot's work provides a strong reminder of how ancient Christianity facilitated the acquisition of habits of the mind and heart that focused the attention of readers and speakers on doctrinal wisdom that served to nourish spiritual and moral virtue in communion with God and others. Thus no clear distinction existed between theology and philosophy—the knowledge of God and wisdom (or way of life fitting for such knowledge).[8]

Augustine followed this classic pattern in *De doctrina christiana*, depicting the Christian way of life as conformity to the church's confession of faith in the Father, Son, and Holy Spirit, and loving surrender to Christ, who is the mystery of divine wisdom that indwells the communion of saints (*DDC* 1.12–14). He therefore sought to persuade pastors to yield themselves to a particular manner of believing, desiring, and speaking that constitutes the *habitus*, or habits, of the mind and heart, a type of *habitus* that is a form of theological judgment necessary for serving Christ and his people. This "knowing how" comprised the enactment of truthful practice and guided pastors in the conduct of their ecclesial responsibilities. Both knowledge and love are required to grasp divine wisdom, or the grammar of God revealed in Christ and the Spirit that informs pastoral practice and the healing of humanity in the communion of the church.[9]

Augustine, moreover, was no stranger to the wisdom and healing power of Christ in the ministry and fellowship of the church. Through an extended process of repentance, confession, and forgiveness, Augustine's mind was changed to see that human love and desire, which is a restlessness that seeks certitude and control through attachment

---

8. Pierre Hadot, *Philosophy as a Way of Life: Spiritual Exercises from Socrates to Foucault*, ed. Arnold I. Davidson, trans. Michael Chase (Oxford: Oxford University Press, 1995), 47–144.

9. Charry, *Renewing of Your Minds*, 3–34.

to created things rather than to their Creator, is satisfied only when reoriented and drawn into communion with God in loving friendship with others. Thus only the gift of faith enables acknowledgment of one's sinfulness, limits, and death when seen within the larger story of God's goodness and love. Such understanding increases in direct proportion to the degree one acknowledges dependence upon and belonging to God and God's people.

Human lives therefore become truthful when yielded up as acts of praise and thanksgiving to the Father in union with Christ. As Augustine states in his *Confessions*, "You have made us for yourself, and our heart is restless until it rests in you" (1.1). Christopher Thompson comments,

> The normative guiding principle guiding the *Confessions* is the doctrine of the Church concerning God as the Triune Creator of all that exists and Redeemer of all who seek reconciliation. . . . The overriding motif of any narrative of Christian experience is the claim that "God has made us for himself." . . . This is the drama of the revelatory narratives: that I find in them, not confirmation of myself, but the very constitution of myself. I do not place the actions of God within the horizon of my story; rather, I place my story within the action of God.[10]

Augustine's new identity was constituted by a new narrative in which the separate worlds of God and humanity were at last made indivisibly one in the story of Christ enacted by the common life of the church, which was the context for his vocation as pastor and preacher. This new world, however, was not of Augustine's making but was a fresh gift of divine love, a new language and way of life created by faith in the incarnation, and constituted by a particular way of rendering the world as God's good creation. For Augustine this new language was Holy Scripture.[11]

Augustine remained deeply grateful for having been drawn into relationship with this world by the preaching and example of Ambrose, Bishop of Milan, and by the joyful singing and thunderous praise of the Christians in Milan (*Confessions* 9.6). Within the liturgical life of the church, newly given faith and understanding were influenced by

10. Christopher Thompson, *Christian Doctrine, Christian Identity: Augustine and the Narratives of Character* (Lanham, MD: University Press of America, 1999), 99, cf. 78–91.

11. William H. Willimon, *Pastor: The Theology and Practice of Ordained Ministry* (Nashville: Abingdon, 2002), 199–200.

the laws of prayer and believing (*lex orandi*, *lex credendi*), distinct but correlative expressions of one grace that creates Christian identity and activity, *lex operandi*: "faith originating in God and communicated incarnationally through human means which were themselves suffused with faith."[12] In the eucharistic sacrifice of praise and thanksgiving, Augustine experienced life in Christ's one body as one person, participating with God's people in the intimate union of God's being and activity in the world, *theologia* and *oikonomia*.[13]

> So then, the true sacrifices are acts of compassion, whether towards ourselves or towards our neighbors, when they are directed towards God. . . . This being so, it immediately follows that the whole redeemed community, that is to say, the congregation and fellowship of saints, is offered to God as a universal sacrifice, through the great high priest who offered himself in his suffering for us—so that we might be the body of so great a head—under the form of a servant. For it was this form he offered, and in this form he was offered, because it is under this form that he is Mediator, in this form he is the Priest, in this form he is the Sacrifice. . . . This is the sacrifice of the altar, a sacrament well known to the faithful where it is shown to the Church that she herself is offered in the offering, which she presents to God.[14]

Moreover, the language of Trinity and incarnation, which was derived from the whole economy of salvation culminating in Christ, offered not only a disciplined way but also a compelling nearness in the Word. The vitality of divine revelation—God's truth, beauty, and goodness—drew Augustine beyond himself to delight in Christ's gracious presence manifested in the apparent lowliness of the church—its Scripture, sacraments, sermons, and saints. Such concrete expressions of humble self-giving overcame Augustine's fear of conversion to a holy life, thus melting his pride and self-determination, moving him to delight in divine grace, and reorienting his vision to acknowledge the Triune God as creator and redeemer of all things.[15] He confessed:

> I sought a way to obtain strength enough to enjoy you; but I did not find it until I embraced the "mediator between God and man, the man

12. Aidan Kavanagh, OSB, *On Liturgical Theology* (New York: Pueblo, 1984), 98–99.
13. Hanby, *Augustine and Modernity*, 17–18.
14. Augustine, *City of God*, ed. David Knowles, trans. Henry Bettenson (New York: Penguin, 1972), 10.6.
15. Mallard, *Language and Love*, 135–36.

Christ Jesus" (I Tim. 2:5), "who is above all things, God blessed for ever" (Rom. 9:5). He called and said "I am the way and the truth and the life" (John 14:6). The food, which I was too weak to accept he mingled with flesh, in that "The Word was made flesh" (John 1:14), so that our infant condition might come to suck from your wisdom by which you created all things. (*Confessions* 7.18.24)

It is impossible to understand the theological wisdom embodied in Augustine's pastoral ministry apart from this radical conversion through faith in the incarnation, the humble, self-giving love of Christ: his life, death, resurrection, and ascension, and his bodily presence on earth as head of his body, the church. Augustine believed that within this continuing story the Spirit makes audible unadorned words of and about Christ declared by Christian preachers, just as the Spirit makes Christian speech visible in the hearing and doing of ordinary Christian people to reveal the mystery of grace at the heart of creation.[16]

Peter Brown has written of the manner in which bishops like Augustine presented Christianity to the ancient world. They did so by offering a universal way of salvation that was gathering all nations and classes into its bosom, *populari sinu*. The Bible itself, with its layers of meaning, was a microcosm, a textual world of the social and intellectual diversity to be found in Christian churches. Augustine exclaimed, "Its plain language and simple style make it accessible to all. . . . This book stands out alone on so high a peak of authority and yet can draw the crowds to the embrace of its inspired simplicity."[17] In his pastoral ministry, Augustine attended to the incarnate Christ who indwells Scripture to create a Christian populism, or simple words endowed with divine authority for large, unlearned segments of the empire.[18]

Augustine thus embodied in both language and life a form of pastoral theology or wisdom shaped by the bending, reaching, and embracing Word he proclaimed: the *sermo humilis*, humble speech, which he had come to "see" in the incarnate Christ with the eyes of his heart that were cleansed and illumined by divine love. *Sermo humilis*, then, is a fitting expression for the means and end of this transformation, for both the

16. See the excellent discussion in Karlfried Froehlich, "Take Up and Read: Basics of Augustine's Biblical Interpretation," *Interpretation* 58, no. 1 (January 2004): 5–16; Ellingsen, *Richness of Augustine*, 116–17; A. D. R. Polman, *The Word of God according to Augustine* (Grand Rapids: Eerdmans, 1955).

17. Augustine, *Confessions* 12.31.41.

18. Peter Brown, *Power and Persuasion in Late Antiquity* (Madison: University of Wisconsin Press, 1988), 74–76.

content and form that addressed the social and cultural *humilitas* to which the Christian message was directed, and those who were prepared to respond to it. In Augustine's ministry these included pagans, the penitent, illiterates, the dispossessed, and the ineloquent. Thus the humble, seemingly artless form of pastoral speech and compassionate care that invoked the memory of Christ and his prophets served to bridge the gap between the high and low—the divine and human—and signified the existence of Christ on earth after his resurrection. The hidden things of God are set forth in a "lowly" vein; a humble style is the medium most fitting to bring sublime mysteries within the reach of sinful humanity.[19]

Just as God stooped down to our human level in the incarnation, taking on human flesh, so also has God stooped down to indwell human language. This humility made the person of Christ available to all in the truth and goodness of the church's Scriptures; even the humblest of the earth should be drawn to them, moved by them, at home in them. The diversity of Christian congregations, the simplicity of Christian Scriptures, the lack of culture of many Christian heroes, and the Christian care of the poor lent a sense of concreteness to the grand outlines of the Christian imagination. Thus a church empowered and guided by God's providence was capable of absorbing and reconciling all levels of Roman society as a sign of Christ's cross encompassing the spread of Christian mission.[20]

Christian gestures such as preaching and extending hospitality to the poor and weak communicated a basic level of human solidarity, just as God, in the person of the Son, freely identified with humanity, assuming and elevating human flesh without being consumed by its sinful condition. Christ's descent to suffering and death displays the fittingness of God's justice and the greatness of God's love to restore creation, through the person of the Son and power of the Spirit, to the exchange of love between the Father and the Son, which is now extending into the church's vocation of praise and service.[21]

Pastoral ministry, then, is a human sign of salvation lovingly and justly bestowed, pointing to the humble presence of Christ who indwells the reality and mission of the church, thus communicating the

19. Eric Auerbach, *Literary Language and Its Public in Late Antiquity and in the Middle Ages*, trans. Ralph Manheim (Princeton: Princeton University Press, 1965), 49–50.

20. Brown, *Power and Persuasion*, 76, 153. Peter Brown, *Authority and the Sacred: Aspects of the Christianisation of the Roman World* (Cambridge: Cambridge University Press, 1995), 10–11.

21. Hanby, *Augustine and Modernity*, 49–71.

Father's continuing commitment to the creation. Pastoral ministry, moreover, involves one in becoming a certain kind of person: a person in whom occurs both the cultivation of pastoral wisdom and virtue and the cultivation of the intellectual and moral capacities necessary to unite thinking and speaking of God. On the one hand, this involves unlearning sinful habits and judgments that turn one's vision away from God and a life ordered to goodness; on the other hand, this involves acquiring new habits of thinking, desiring, and speaking that are formed within the narrative of God's providential drama of salvation (*DDC* 1.14.13–21).

The constant immersion of oneself within the church's story of doctrine, discipleship, and devotion nourishes one's proficiency in Scripture, which is a "sense" of speaking simply and wisely with the authority of personal communication that bears witness to the risen Lord among his people. Purity of heart and the gift of understanding sustain constancy and patience, which involve a habitual way of seeing the good as well as a sense of knowing how to speak in a manner that both shows forth and forms Christ in the concrete witness of the church.[22] Rebecca Weaver comments:

> Stated otherwise, if the message of scripture is the double commandment of love as joined in the incarnation, then those who are still running the way of Christ, the pavement of Christ's humanity, toward its union with the deity of Christ, the triune God, must reinterpret and renew in each new circumstance the love for God and neighbor. The way that Christ provides must be looked at anew, for even Christ himself, as human, lived a life in process. As such, he serves as a guide for both interpreting and communicating the message. . . . Scripture must at all times be read anew for the Spirit's guidance on how that dual love is to be enacted today.[23]

Augustine's discussion of learned piety—loving God with both heart and mind—demonstrates the kind of insightfulness necessary for creating congruence between the means by which we speak and live and the ends to which we have been called: charity (the source of life) that

22. Andrew Louth, *Discerning the Mystery: An Essay on the Nature of Theology* (Oxford: Clarendon, 1983), 79–85; see the discussion on the moral wisdom necessary for reading and speaking in Stephen E. Fowl and L. Gregory Jones, *Reading in Communion: Scripture and Ethics in the Christian Life* (Grand Rapids: Eerdmans, 1991).

23. Rebecca Harden Weaver, "Reading the Signs: Guidance for the Pilgrim Community," *Interpretation* 58, no. 1 (January 2004): 40.

points to Christ crucified, the One who came to provide a way to God (the means of life), in whom humanity alone finds completion in happiness and holiness (the ends of life). The humble way of Christ, who himself is both the end of this story and the way to the end of this story, establishes the relation between the Word and human words, the church's message and mission, the interpretation of Scripture and its performance by God's people. As united within the incarnation, Christian identity and discourse must possess a particular character that is faithful to Christ and the church's distinctive way of life in him as its head.[24]

Pastoral Pragmatism and the Loss of Congruence

Eugene Peterson has commented extensively on the contemporary lack of congruence between ends and means in ministry, between who we are and what we do, and between what we do and how we do it. By congruence Peterson means a sense of wholeness, rightness, and fittingness between being Christian, speaking as Christians, and living as Christians. In a manner similar to Augustine, Peterson cites John 14:6, "I am the way, and the truth, and the life," to discuss the incongruence of Christianity in North America, whose expressions of faith have changed the subject from God to the self.[25] In addition, this change has effected a huge paradigm shift in pastoral vocation, a shift from the person of Christ to the person of the pastor, who in much of contemporary practice is increasingly identified as a marketing manager of religion. In other words, the pastor is seen as one who, experienced in the instrumental use of technical reason, facilitates numerical growth of the church in terms of "effectiveness."[26]

It is not surprising, then, given this separation of theological wisdom and pastoral practice, that the tasks or means of ministry are detached from their source and end: increasing the growth of the church is detached from knowing and loving God, evangelism from worship,

24. Carol Harrison, *Augustine: Christian Truth and Fractured Humanity* (Oxford: Oxford University Press, 2000), 37–39; Mallard, *Language and Love*, 219–29.

25. Eugene H. Peterson, *Christ Plays in Ten Thousand Places: A Conversation in Spiritual Theology* (Grand Rapids: Eerdmans, 2005), 334–38; see also Peterson, *Under the Unpredictable Plant: An Exploration in Vocational Holiness* (Grand Rapids: Eerdmans, 1992); and Peterson, *The Contemplative Pastor: Returning to the Art of Spiritual Direction* (Grand Rapids: Eerdmans, 1989).

26. Peterson, *Unpredictable Plant*, 174–76.

human insight from divine wisdom, responsiveness to human needs from receptiveness to God's Word. This dichotomy between divine power and human effort betrays a basic incongruence between faithfulness to God and effectiveness in ministry—a matter left unresolved in favor of doing the merely practical—and an implicit "theological" judgment that reduces ministry to method. *This pragmatic solution, however, does not sufficiently acknowledge the theological and redemptive nature of the church in communion with Christ and the Spirit. Nor does it show how the wisdom of theology, the knowledge and goodness of God incarnate in Christ, personally permeates and transforms the person of the pastor for the purpose of becoming a living sign and witness to the story of his life, passion, death, and resurrection.*

Peterson provides a way of resolving this tension by situating ministry within the larger activity of the Triune God. This divine activity is a world in which we participate through prayer, adoration, receptivity, and responsiveness to the grace of God. Theology, then, becomes knowing, hearing, and doing the Word God speaks in Christ and the Spirit.

> Prayer and spirituality feature participation, the complex participation of God and the human, his will and our wills. We do not abandon ourselves to the stream of grace and drown in an ocean of love, losing identity. We do not pull strings that activate God's operations in our lives, subjecting God to our assertive identity. We neither manipulate God . . . nor are manipulated by God. . . . We are involved in the action and participate in its results but do not control or define it. . . . This is the contextual atmosphere in which we find ourselves loved and loving before God.[27]

Peterson suggests that in the pervasive contemporary split between theology and practice, between who we are and what we do, much how-to expertise deemed necessary for becoming a "successful" pastor has been dominated by the social-economic mind-set of Darwinism: market-orientation, competitiveness, and survival of the fittest. Such methods form their "users" to have a capacity for discerning instrumental relations between means and ends, a pragmatic vision that cultivates a particular kind of person who must acquire particular virtues or strengths, such as personal appeal, promotional savvy, mastery, control, and most important, expertise in exercising cause-and-effect power through the practical application of techniques and skills to achieve results.[28]

27. Peterson, *Contemplative Pastor*, 104–5.
28. Peterson, *Unpredictable Plant*, 174–82.

Although typically defended as "value-free," morally neutral "means" that "work," many technological and managerial strategies are external and even antithetical to the servant ministry of Jesus and the vocation of the church as his body. Such unreflective activity invariably distracts pastors and congregations from their true end—participation in the life and mission of the Triune God—and produces forms of leadership that, when evaluated in light of the wisdom incarnate in Christ, are neither theological nor pastoral.[29]

Just as troubling is the way in which the marketing/managing pastoral paradigm alters Christian proclamation into flattened, trivialized truth, taking categories of biblical faith and representing them in manageable shapes without the material substance of the Word, Christ himself, incarnating preacher or people. Discrete abstract topics packaged and transmitted through presumably "value-free" methods of delivery reduce the mystery of God to problems and solutions, and to spiritual help and techniques that reinforce self-interest and stimulate human restlessness for certitude and control. Moreover, how-to strategies for "effectively communicating" closed, managed, and useful truth easily subject the Word to uncritically examined ideology that legitimizes the cultural status quo, its marketplace of needs and desires, and supports the powers of this world, which include the power of the speaker over the powerlessness of listeners.[30] In the end, marketing privatized religion transforms Christian proclamation into the work of gnostic technicians. Incongruence between theology and pastoral practice depersonalizes God, displaces the work of Christ and the Spirit, and consequently diminishes humanity.[31]

Becoming a Living Sermon

When God's praise is replaced by God's utility—worshiping God as means to rather than end of all things—pastors abandon the church's

29. I am indebted to the insights of Philip D. Kenneson, "Selling (Out) the Church in the Marketplace of Desire," *Modern Theology* 9, no. 4 (October 1993): 319–48.

30. See the extended discussion in Walter Brueggemann, *Finally Comes the Poet: Daring Speech for Proclamation* (Philadelphia: Fortress, 1989); Brueggemann, *Biblical Perspectives on Evangelism: Living in a Three-Storied Universe* (Nashville: Abingdon, 1993); see also the excellent discussion in Rowan Williams, *Christ on Trial: How the Gospel Unsettles Our Judgment* (Grand Rapids: Eerdmans, 2003), 38–47.

31. Rodney Clapp, *A Peculiar People: The Church as Culture in a Post-Christian Society* (Downers Grove, IL: InterVarsity, 1996), 34–36, 205–8.

primary vocation of bearing witness to a world beyond manipulation, control, idolatry, and ideology: "the delightfully purposeless, pointless, nonutilitarian purpose of the glorification and enjoyment of God."[32] The end or purpose of pastoral vocation is defined by the vocation of the church—worship—locating all of life within the narrative of the Triune God, who orders the thoughts, affections, and actions of his people to the wisdom of salvation, Jesus Christ. In worship we meet God, who graciously comes to meet us: the love of the Father creates the possibility of prayer that begins in praise and thanksgiving. To pray with and through Christ is to be given the gift of life by the Spirit within God's own self-gift.

Thus constancy in communion with the Triune God—adoration and praise, pouring out oneself in service to the neighbor—is one, and not two different kinds of love: "You shall love the Lord your God with all your heart, soul, mind, and strength; and your neighbor as yourself" (cf. Luke 10:27). Don Saliers observes, "Entering into one requires entering the other. Compassion for neighbor and adoration of God are not separate intentions of two worlds; they are the modes of intending and receiving the love of God in its double manifestation. . . . In rendering glory to God we learn to glorify him in all the commonplaces of life."[33]

Augustine himself was no stranger to the struggle with the self-love and illusion that create divided loves, disordered desires, and idolatrous expressions of human vanity and glory. As a child he concluded that human beings live in two separate worlds with two separate ways of thinking and speaking, both of which are creations of the imagination. In this arrangement, God is kept in heaven, at a distance, thus removed from ordinary human activity, while human beings take hold of the world of knowledge and power to their advantage. Augustine reasoned that if God is secluded in religious affairs, human beings are then free to compete for control of a world ruled by pride, arrogance, and self-assertion.

Moreover, within this division of worlds, even religion is capable of becoming a system of domination and control. Language separated from its embodiment serves partisan and vested interests, since the

32. William H. Willimon, "Ritual and Pastoral Care," and Rodney Clapp, "On the Making of Kings and Christians," in *The Conviction of Things Not Seen: Worship and Ministry in the 21st Century*, ed. Todd E. Johnson (Grand Rapids: Brazos, 2002), 108 and 109–10, respectively.

33. Don E. Saliers, *The Soul in Paraphrase: Prayer and the Religious Affections* (New York: Seabury, 1980), 70–73.

acknowledged loves, desires, and commitments people have inevitably form the character of their community. In his pastoral ministry, Augustine was aware of the moral incongruence presented by a powerful temptation to use God and others as means of obtaining less important things—even advancing the life of the church—and the persistent challenge to learn the proper ordering of human desires by loving God and others within the love of God, who is the true end of life.[34] He writes in his handbook for pastors:

> Thus all your thoughts and your whole life and all your intelligence should be focused on him from whom you have the very things you devote to him. Now when he said *with your whole heart, your whole soul, your whole mind*, he did not leave out any part of life, which could be left vacant, so to speak, and leave room for wanting to enjoy something else. . . . And if God is to be loved more than any human being, we all ought to love God more than ourselves. . . . Now if all those who are able to enjoy God together with us, some we love as people we can help, some as people we can be helped by, some as ones both whose help we need, and whose needs we help to meet. . . . Still, we ought to want all of them to love God together with us, and all our helping them or being helped by them is to be referred to that one (God) in the end. (*DDC* 1.22.21)

The Great Commandment, the grammar of loving God and neighbor, cultivates moral wisdom for resisting the relentless temptation to manage God and to use others without referring their lives to the love of God. Faithfulness in pastoral ministry requires moral strength even more than technical skill, since it is God's wisdom that orders practice to goodness, or nothing less than full or perfect love of God (*DDC* 1.26–30). Augustine advises, "Temperance is love keeping itself entire and incorrupt for God; fortitude is love bearing everything readily for the sake of God; justice is love serving God only . . . ; prudence is love making a right distinction between what helps it towards God and what hinders it."[35] Through the ministry of the incarnation, God has provided not so much a set of rules to follow but rather wisdom that is a way of life; in other words, love wisely ordered according to the work of Christ and the direction of the Spirit. In his death Christ overcame the devil, not by power, but by justice, to teach humanity the

34. Mallard, *Language and Love*, 2–24, 78–80, 125–32, 161–65.

35. Augustine, *On the Morals of the Catholic Church* 25, cited in Eric O. Springsted, *The Act of Faith: Christian Faith and the Moral Self* (Grand Rapids: Eerdmans, 2002), 121.

proper relation of charity, power, and humility. Thus the Word's incarnate example trains us in virtue. Through his life and death he shows the grace of God toward humanity, and by his humility he overcomes human pride. Faith loves the image of God in the Word made flesh, just as faith contemplates the Son of God, becoming like the One who is adored. Christ is loved as the paradigm for pastoral wisdom; he is the Wisdom of God incarnate, who speaks through human weakness, enabling us to attune ourselves and others to God.[36]

Augustine's wisdom points us toward a recovery of transformed judgment that has been lost through the pervasive influence of technique-driven pastoral practice. Paradoxically, the more the practical tasks themselves are focused upon as the primary goal of the church's ministry, the less pastors will possess the discernment necessary to carry their vocation in ways "relevant" or fitting for their true end: a world in which theology and pastoral practice are united within the life of the Triune God, in love of God and neighbor, and in graced participation through faith in the mystery of Christ and the Spirit indwelling the church.[37]

The theological unity of pastoral wisdom as participatory knowledge has been discussed by Servais Pinckaers, who argues that Augustine's early works link the steps to such transformed judgment, joining prayerful study of Scripture with the Beatitudes of the Sermon on the Mount and with the gifts of the Holy Spirit. Pinckaers views Augustine's teaching on the Beatitudes as mirroring the bishop of Hippo's own journey following his conversion, a long pilgrimage that led him toward Christ, the wisdom of God, for whom he longed with all his heart.[38]

Augustine therefore joined his instruction on the connection of the Beatitudes and the gifts of the Spirit to the petitions of the Lord's Prayer, since without the help of the Spirit, Christian pastors can neither grasp the truth of Scripture nor follow the way of the Beatitudes and Christian

36. Springsted, *Act of Faith*, 139–47.

37. For a good discussion of contemporary issues, see David E. Fitch, *The Great Giveaway: Reclaiming the Mission of the Church from Big Business, Parachurch Organizations, Psychotherapy, Consumer Capitalism, and Other Modern Maladies* (Grand Rapids: Baker, 2005); on the need for "transformed judgment," see the excellent discussion in L. Gregory Jones, *Transformed Judgment: Toward a Trinitarian Account of the Moral Life* (Notre Dame, IN: University of Notre Dame Press, 1990); see also the excellent discussion of practical wisdom in Kevin J. Vanhoozer, *The Drama of Doctrine: A Canonical-Linguistic Approach to Christian Theology* (Louisville: Westminster John Knox, 2005), 324–44.

38. For this section I follow Servais Pinckaers, OP, *The Sources of Christian Ethics*, trans. Sr. Mary Thomas Noble, OP (Washington, DC: Catholic University of America Press, 1995), 141–63.

virtue. Moreover, we cannot obtain this end without continual prayer as modeled in the Our Father taught by Christ, the perfect prayer that bends our lives toward God. And it is God who is the One who shapes us according to our truest needs and desires: becoming children of God, reflecting the holiness and glory of God, gladly obeying the will of God in Jesus, living with gratitude for daily bread and gifts and forgiveness, resisting the powers of this world, overcoming evil with good, praising God as a citizen of the reign of God in this life and the life to come.

Augustine depicted the Beatitudes as a journey leading the reader of Scripture from humility—poverty of spirit—to wisdom, and at last to the vision or knowledge of God that is communion. He attributed charity and the gifts of the Spirit to Christ, the One who grants peace with God and neighbor, and the grace of faith that works through love. Augustine also interpreted each petition of the Our Father, the prayer of the Son inspired by the Spirit, with a Beatitude and gift, moving from the gift to the petition in order to unite speaking the truth with prayerful thinking, holy living, and loving address to God. The gift of the Word, God's self-gift, is for conversation, relatedness, and building up communion in the Spirit. In other words, God's self-communication in Christ constitutes the church's identity within the mission of the Triune God.[39] Pinckaers coordinates Augustine's instruction as follows:

Gifts and Beatitudes	Petitions of the Lord's Prayer
Fear of the Lord gives happiness to the poor through the promise of the kingdom.	Hallowing of the divine name through chaste fear.
Piety gladdens a humble heart of those who will inherit the earth.	That God's kingdom may come. That God's will may be done in our souls and bodies, so that we may be established in our struggles.
Knowledge gives joy to those who mourn through the consolation it brings.	Request for daily bread to sustain us with sufficient nourishment.
Fortitude gives happiness to those who hunger and thirst, and satisfies them.	Forgiveness of others' debts to us and of our own by God.
Counsel gives joy to the merciful.	Avoidance of temptations that create duplicity of heart; the simplicity of a heart fixed on God.
Understanding delights the pure of heart.	
Wisdom brings happiness to the peacemakers, the children of God.	Deliverance from evil frees us to be children, crying out: Abba, Father!

39. Nicholas Lash, *Holiness, Speech and Silence: Reflections on the Question of God* (Aldershot: Ashgate, 2004), 92.

Augustine's teaching points to what is arguably the greatest need for cultivating pastoral wisdom in our time: the recovery of contemplation; the gifts of wonder, love, and praise; prayerful attention and receptivity to the Word, who creates and calls to salvation.[40] Standing in the presence of God's self-disclosure in Christ, the holy mystery that draws us out of ourselves, contemplation unites theology *and* prayer, knowledge *and* love, being *and* doing. "Full knowledge of God, the contemplation of God, comes by shifting the center of moral gravity from oneself to God. One comes to know God by willing to be taught and led by God."[41] Prayer is neither a technique nor a means to an end; prayer is making ourselves available to being taken up into God's own life, energized by the vision and power of God's goodness and glory.

God, moreover, is the truth teller who sheds light on human darkness. To turn one's gaze or vision toward God is to be filled up from outside oneself; it is to become a participant in loving conversation with the Word, the source of truth.[42] As Augustine prayed in the *Confessions*, "I do not believe I could speak truthfully under inspiration from anyone other than you, since you are the Truth, whereas all human beings are liars. Thus anyone who tells lies is speaking from what is his own; and in order to speak the truth, I must speak what is yours" (13.25.38). Pinckaers comments on Augustine's advice that pastors be prayers before speakers: "Unless you pray you will not understand."[43]

Learning to pray with Christ in the eternal conversation between the Father and the Son brings together theology, human speech, and action. Within the Triune life of self-giving love, the Spirit unites the activities of listening to God, knowing the things of God, and speaking of God in the love and delight the Father has for the Son. Knowing God through prayerful thought and loving obedience fosters the gift of humility, a capacity to acknowledge that our truest and best speech lies beyond explanation and control. Thomas Long notes, "To speak truthfully about God is also to enter a world, a world in which God

40. See the excellent discussions by Josef Pieper, *Leisure: The Basis of Culture*, trans. Gerald Malsbary (South Bend, IN: St. Augustine's Press, 1998); Lash, *Holiness, Speech and Silence*; Peterson, *Contemplative Pastor*.

41. Springsted, *Act of Faith*, 124.

42. Paul J. Griffiths, *Lying: An Augustinian Theology of Duplicity* (Grand Rapids: Brazos, 2004), 73–80.

43. Pinckaers, *Sources of Christian Ethics*, 163.

is present and can be trusted. To speak about God is to live in that world and speak out of it. . . . Authentic speech about God, therefore, can be said to be a form of prayer."[44]

Pastoral speech calls a pilgrim people to "walk in love, as Christ loved us and gave himself up for us, a fragrant offering and sacrifice to God" (Eph. 5:2), participating in a world spoken into being and formed into the purposes of salvation by God. Augustine writes:

> That is why we are meant to enjoy that truth which is unchangeably alive, and since it is in that light that God the Trinity, author and maker of the universe, provides for all the things he has made, our minds have to be purified, to enable them to perceive that light, and to cling to it once perceived. We should think of this purification process as being a kind of walk, a kind of voyage toward our home country. We do not draw near, after all, by movement in place to the one who is present everywhere, but by honest commitment and good behavior. (*DDC* 1.10.10)

As Christian speech that is congruent with the One of whom and with whom we speak, preaching is primarily a receptive activity: responsiveness to the Word in the Spirit of the risen Christ, who breathes life into texts and contexts, into speaking and listening, thereby assimilating hearts, minds, and bodies into the truth and goodness of God. Only the Holy Spirit can transform gatherings of listeners into a body of people capable of hearing and being formed by the Word. It is foolish to think that we can make a "preaching event" happen or create "meaningful" experiences for listeners. Preaching is an activity of confession and praise, the surrender of self-possession and control of our words to Christ, the mystery of God's Word revealed in human speech and life. Thus the truest sign of pastoral "effectiveness" is the Word's embodiment in the practice of priestly listening and prophetic speech that does work to create a holy people whose common life praises God and proclaims God's salvation for the world.

Philippians 2:1–13

One of the common complaints we hear from people outside the church is that Christians always seem to be fighting with each other.

---

44. Thomas G. Long, *Testimony: Talking Ourselves into Being Christian* (San Francisco: Jossey-Bass, 2004), 11.

They read the paper, watch the news, and most important, talk with their friends, family members, and coworkers, only to discover that life among God's people is often just as divisive as the rest of the world.

I remember this well from the years I served as a pastor in a small town where everyone knew everyone else. During a typical trip to the grocery store, I would receive an up-to-date report from town members regarding just who, from among our congregation, was not getting along: "Aren't you the Methodist preacher?" I was asked one day in the Piggly Wiggly; "I hear your people are fighting again."

This is not a new thing among Christians. In fact, it is as old as Adam, and it certainly was not a new problem among the churches of the New Testament. The apostle Paul was apparently very aware of this problem among the congregations that were given birth through his preaching of the gospel, and the Scripture we heard this morning from Philippians shows just how much this was on his mind.

Paul's concern was that the life of his Christian friends in Philippi— their whole way of being and living, not just what they did on Sunday—would be consistent with what they believed, that their walk and their talk would be one, as we like to say. He was concerned that their character was being made consistent with the One whom they claimed to worship, the God of Jesus Christ. But, apparently, members of that congregation were at odds with each other and continued to hold grudges as a result of their stubbornness and pride. And so Paul writes from a particular perspective that he calls the mind of Christ, the wisdom of God revealed in the cross, the self-giving love of Jesus, which by God's grace enabled Paul to see that a whole new world had come through Christ's death and resurrection and that this divided, dying, old world is now being reconciled and reunited for the praise and glory of God. And it is for this reason that divisions and quarreling among Christian people present a major scandal to a watching, listening world; it compromises our witness to the saving work of God, the reconciliation of heaven and earth under the lordship of Jesus Christ.

I thought about such things earlier this summer when I saw the most wonderful movie, *The March of the Penguins*. It is a fascinating documentary about the life of penguins at the South Pole. It tells the story of their life together and how, in following the wisdom of God in creation, they are united as one in answering the call of the Creator, giving themselves in the most remarkable expressions of sacrifice, suffering, and even death as the very means of their life as God's creatures. As the narrator states at the beginning of the movie, "This is not simply a story of nature or survival of the species; this is a story of love."

I will not forget the picture of a long line of penguins, strung out in single file, alternatively shuffling along upright, as if all dressed up in their tuxedos and on their way to a grand, formal occasion, and sliding along the ice on their bellies, like children happily riding their sleds after a winter snowfall and the cancellation of school. It's a wonderful picture of unity, not simply being together in the same place, but unity in action, unity as a matter of life or death.

The march of the penguins is like a band of pilgrims on a long, demanding, and dangerous journey. Yet year after year something calls the penguins to leave their home, because if they do not walk to the destination where they will meet their mates and welcome their young into the world, all together and dependent upon each other, their life as penguins will come to an end. And there are no other options, no other ways to fulfill their God-given destiny—the joy of being penguins.

And so they walk, exposing themselves to the harshest, coldest winters on this planet, enduring incredible hardship in which mother and father penguins join together in literally expending themselves in ways that, as the psalmist says, declare the glory of God to those who have eyes to see. *The March of the Penguins* is a story of sacrifice and self-giving; it is a story or parable of love that works through death and resurrection, the wisdom of the cross, the word of life God speaks in creation and in its fullness through Jesus Christ.

Let's listen to Paul again. In his letter to the Philippians, as we have heard this morning, he uses what was a familiar hymn in his day to convey God's master story of love as told in the life, death, and resurrection of Jesus Christ. Now, we should be able to appreciate his pastoral approach; after all, we know how powerful church music, hymns, and songs of praise can be. They affect not only what but how we think. And when we sing, as it has often been said, we pray twice, praising God with both our words and music. Perhaps nothing is better at getting to the heart of who God in Jesus Christ is and what God wants to do with us, which is to convert us from a self-centered life and unite us in a God-centered life. God is at work transforming our longings and reeducating our desires, redirecting our attention to Christ, drawing our lives together in worship of him, which is our witness to what God desires for the whole creation.

And singing God's praises engages our deepest emotions and affections. It not only changes our minds but also moves our hearts and sets our lives in motion, opening us and energizing us to step out in new and often unknown and risky directions in response to the God who is our beginning and our end—as Charles Wesley wrote, "lost in wonder, love, and praise."[45] This is how we should hear Paul's great doxology in Philippians—a glorious hymn of praise to God for the life and death of Jesus Christ, a hymn that "lifts high the cross" to proclaim the power of God in the self-giving love of Christ for the world. This is a message of good news to the church through which we become a living message of good news to the world, our lives taking on the shape of the cross and becoming a living hymn of praise to God through giving ourselves to others as Christ gives himself to us, communicating the fullness of God's love.

When seen from within the master story of love told by Paul, the cross is not only the beginning of our salvation; it is also the means and the goal of salvation, the almighty powerfulness of God revealed in the suffering and death of his Son. Yes, the cross is the goal and climax of Christ's entire life and ministry, his loving obedience to the Father that fulfilled our vocation as God's people, our calling to be a faithful witness to the power of God that the world might know, love, and praise its Creator.

This is why Paul sings with such joyful abandon. Because of his perfect obedience to the Father's will, Jesus neither bowed nor bent the knee to the powers of this world—whether they be religious, political, or popular—and his death was the worst kind of death, a crucifixion, execution among condemned criminals. Yet the goodness, grace, and glory of God is displayed in all of this because Jesus Christ, the Son of God, the Creator of all that is, did not take advantage of his special status, his power, or his privilege; he did not exploit what was rightly his for selfish gain, for his own reputation and success. Neither did he use his power for competence, mastery, or control to give easy answers, bring quick solutions, or produce impressive results. Instead, he renounced all such temptations to self-sufficiency, putting his own concerns and self-interests aside, forgetting himself in constant attentiveness to the Father's love, pursuing the good of a world held in the grip of its own deadly ways, his only desire being

45. "Love Divine, All Loves Excelling," in *The United Methodist Hymnal* (Nashville: United Methodist Publishing House, 1988), no. 384.

that of pleasing the Father, the One whose wisdom he revealed and whose will he accomplished.

I am certain you must be able to hear how radically different, how odd and strange such a life and death must seem when measured by the wisdom and ways of the world. It is certainly not very efficient, effective, impressive, or successful in our I-am-more-famous-than-you-are and got-to-get-ahead world. Can you imagine? Jesus did not succeed by competing, calculating, or pushing his way to the front; neither did he sweet-talk nor charm himself to the top. He was not continually obsessed with having his own way or imposing his agenda on others; he did not first seek what would call attention to himself. He had no public relations or advertising, nor did he work the angles or manipulate people and situations to make himself look good. No, amazingly, not even for good, worthy ends would he stoop to such means.

You see, Jesus was not a pragmatist. For him the ends did not justify the means. His mind, desires, words, and actions were not driven by what might work or what people might like. Instead, he was committed only to a life of prayerful response to the love and wisdom of the Father, who had sent him. And so he was not dependent upon the world's wisdom and ways, not even to reach lost people, not even to save the world. Can you imagine? Even when faced by dreadful pain and the threat of his own death, the end of his ministry and the failure of his mission, the isolation and betrayal of his friends, he steadfastly refused to trust in the world's wisdom and ways to do God's work. Instead, he simply expended himself and gave himself away, pouring out his life in the form of generous, abundant, extravagant, forgiving love, pouring out the life he shares with the Father and the Holy Spirit, the life that is salvation, life that is given and received within our human vulnerability and neediness; this is life in God's kingdom.

I was watching the news on the Sunday after Katrina hit the Gulf Coast. They showed a congregation in the New Orleans area gathered to worship God even though their church building and all their resources and property had been completely destroyed and blown away. They sat out in the hot sun on a concrete slab, which was all that remained, and they offered their prayers and praise to God. According to the world's wisdom, they had lost everything, they possessed nothing, and they were no longer a church; they had nothing left to commend themselves. But according to the wisdom of God—the wisdom of the cross, the almighty powerfulness that works in our neediness, emptiness, loss, and death—they were indeed every bit a church. They were rich, wealthy, blessed, and filled to overflowing by the abundance of God's self-gift in Christ, the Son of God who emptied himself and became a servant all the way to death. And this was their worship, the working out of their salvation, simply resting in their sorrow and loss, their weakness and need, because God in Christ was among them and with them. Jesus Christ crucified and risen is God's strength in our weakness; Christ crucified and risen is God's hope that energizes us to live for God's glory.

So now that we are saved, what is there left for us to do? Worship God. Worship the power of God revealed in Jesus Christ. That's right; turning our attention to God is the true work for which we have been created and redeemed; this is how we are working out our salvation with fear and trembling. We are being saved from the worship of false gods and false powers, saved to offer ourselves to God in the power of Jesus Christ as a daily, continual sacrifice of praise and thanksgiving in giving ourselves to others. And this is God's will at work in us, which he does simply as an expression of the sheer love, joy, delight, and good pleasure he shares with the Son and the Holy Spirit. And there are no other options, no other ways to fulfill our God-given destiny as God's people. As one person has said, "If in this world you love well, you will be killed; but if you do not love, you will die."[46] How odd and strange: life in the form of death, power in the shape of weakness. And so Paul sings:

> Because of that obedience, God lifted him high and honored him far beyond anyone or anything, ever, so that all created beings in heaven and on earth—even those long ago dead and buried—will bow and worship before this Jesus Christ, and call out in praise that he is Lord of all, to the glorious honor of God the Father. (Phil. 2:9–11 *Message* 2138)

46. Herbert McCabe, OP, *God Still Matters*, ed. Brian Davies, OP (New York: Continuum, 2002), 63.

5

Speaking of God:
Preaching as a Scriptural Practice

Now I would remind you, brethren, in what terms I preached to you the gospel, which you received, in which you stand, by which you are saved. . . . For I delivered to you as of first importance what I also received, that Christ died for our sins in accordance with the Scriptures, that he was buried, that he was raised on the third day in accordance with the Scriptures.

—Paul the Apostle, First Epistle to the Corinthians

Throughout their history Christians have generally read Scripture to guide, correct, and edify their worship, faith, and practice, which are essential aspects of the ongoing struggle to live, think, and speak truthfully before the Triune God.[1] Authored by the Spirit, Scripture is the church's book, a living book, and a book about life that in its liturgical interpretation and enactment serves as a kind of sacrament of the Word of God. A living God speaks a living Word, Jesus Christ, and the Holy Scriptures are the written representation of that Word, which

1. Stephen Fowl, "Introduction," in *The Theological Interpretation of Scripture: Classic and Contemporary Readings*, ed. Stephen Fowl (Malden, MA: Blackwell, 1997), xiii.

creates conversation or "sermon" between God and God's people. The church, then, is a people for whom the Bible functions as the canonical source through which the voice of Christ speaks, drawing listeners into communion with its author and primary actor: God the Father, Son, and Holy Spirit.[2]

Aidan Kavanagh comments that "if the Bible needs reclaiming in the church . . . it must follow that the church's worship must be reclaimed as well. . . . It is difficult . . . to see how, when the reciprocal authorities of Bible and worship collapse, the church can maintain its own public identity much less be taken seriously in the public square."[3] If what Kavanagh says is true, that "worship is Scripture's home," then the fundamental form of interpreting Scripture is liturgical, political, and social: "the life, activity and organization of the believing, worshiping community."[4] Scripture is most at home when reverently and receptively read, spoken, and heard within Christian assemblies constituted by prayer, praise, and proclamation. "The knowledge of God is made available to the world in the Church's *kerygma*, and in the Scriptures that confer the saving power and wisdom of its preaching."[5]

Since the knowledge of God disclosed is essentially christological, pneumatological, and thus trinitarian, it is best acknowledged and received within a particular context of Christian belief in which text, interpreter, and the practice of interpretation are continuous with the scriptural witness to the wisdom of God in Jesus Christ. Thus it is the historical witness, the particular memories and practices of the apostolic faith that gave birth to the Christian movement, the redemptive economy of the Holy Spirit, the social reality of the whole church, and the communion of saints that constitute the most fitting framework for scriptural interpretation.[6] Concerning this David Yeago comments:

2. Geoffrey Wainwright, *Doxology: The Praise of God in Worship, Doctrine, and Life* (New York: Oxford University Press, 1980), 149–50; for discussion of the canon, see the collection of essays in Carl E. Braaten and Robert W. Jenson, eds., *Reclaiming the Bible for the Church* (Grand Rapids: Eerdmans, 1995).

3. Aidan Kavanagh, OSB, "Scriptural Word and Liturgical Worship," in Braaten and Jenson, *Reclaiming the Bible*, 136.

4. Nicholas Lash, *Theology on the Way to Emmaus* (London: SCM, 1986), 42.

5. Telford Work, *Living and Active: Scripture in the Economy of Salvation* (Grand Rapids: Eerdmans, 2002), 45.

6. David S. Yeago, "The Bible," in *Knowing the Triune God: The Work of the Spirit in the Practices of the Church*, ed. James J. Buckley and David S. Yeago (Grand Rapids: Eerdmans, 2001), 63. Here I have also benefited from the collection of essays in *The Art of Reading Scripture*, ed. Ellen F. Davis and Richard B. Hays (Grand Rapids: Eerdmans, 2003), esp. "Nine Theses on the Interpretation of Scripture," 9.

Scripture is the standing testimony of the Spirit to the church, for the purpose of forming the church itself as the Spirit's testimony to the nations. The goal of the Spirit's gift can thus be summed up as . . . the building-up of the church; the *telos* of the Scripture's presence in the life of the church is the formation of the church's earthly-historical common life in such a way that the corporate existence of the Christian people in the world bears witness to the Messiah Jesus and to the God of Israel who sent him for the world's salvation.[7]

Gordon Lathrop writes of how the Bible particularly marks corporate worship, giving biblical character to the holy assembly, the meeting between God and his people during which faith is generated, nourished, and guided:

Genuine authority in the Christian community is always grounded in the Bible. . . . The Bible most clearly and properly exhibits its authority in the gathering where it is read, sung, preached, and enacted. The Bible is the assembly's book. . . . That we have a Bible and consider it authoritative may be interpreted as one primary example of the "rule of prayer," the practice and order of the Christian assembly, establishing the "rule of believing." To interpret the meaning of the assembly is to interpret the meaning of biblical faith.[8]

The character of Christian faith and life is mediated by and formed within the liturgical activities of petition, praise, adoration, confession, lament, and celebration. "Everything the church knows, it knows by attending to testimony, listening to words and performing rites that have been given to it."[9] The *lex orandi, lex credendi, lex bene operandi* (law of prayer, law of believing, law of good works) create receptivity and response to the knowledge of God communicated by the apostolic witness in ecclesial memory and practice.[10] Robert Jenson notes that the Reformation added an analogous rule: *lex proclamandi, lex credendi,* "the law of proclaiming is the law of believing." The church's common prayer creates the conditions for orthodoxy (right praise), for thinking and speaking the gospel as doxological speech: "the church, in its prayer

7. Ibid., 63.

8. Gordon W. Lathrop, *Holy Things: A Liturgical Theology* (Minneapolis: Fortress, 1993), 9.

9. Gordon W. Lathrop, *Holy People: A Liturgical Ecclesiology* (Minneapolis: Fortress, 1999), 102.

10. William H. Willimon, *The Service of God: How Worship and Ethics Are Related* (Nashville: Abingdon, 1983), 74–80.

and praise, in their verbal forms and embodied forms called sacrifice, the church's discourse turns and fastens itself to God."[11]

In its ecclesial and liturgical use, the Bible itself is God-centered just as the worship assembly is God-centered in its prayer, praise, and proclamation.[12] Because the end of Scripture's performance is the praise and adoration of God, an essential task of Christian preaching is "to be reminded against our inveterate tendency to forget who God is and who we are, what God's bearing toward us is and what that means for our common life as creatures."[13]

Perhaps nothing is more critical for shaping Christian identity and imagination in our time than the recovery of living remembrance, or commemorative doxology—a traditioned capacity for praise-filled thanksgiving. If this remembrance is lost, the church will be left without a sense of the biblical narrative or the proclamation of the living God, which is knowledge of God's speech and action by which Christian wisdom and character are sustained. Grounded in the narrative of the God of Israel and Jesus Christ, the fundamental pattern of Scripture is embodied within the Christian tradition to mediate the memories and hopes of a people constituted around the baptismal font, Holy Scripture, and communion table.[14] Don Saliers writes:

> Without living remembrance of the whole biblical story there would not be authentic worship, nor could there be such a thing as becoming a living reminder of Jesus Christ for others. Seeking God and embodying holiness in our whole existence is, in great measure, a matter of receiving and exercising the memories of the Scriptures in and through the particular forms of communal traditions. Living our lives open to God requires dwelling in a common history, the teachings, the writings, of the prophets, the witness of the apostles, and the extended memories of the community praying and living in accordance with them through time.[15]

Preaching as a scriptural practice, then, serves the Word in the task of forming and re-forming a people whose sense of past, present, and

---

11. Robert W. Jenson, *Systematic Theology*, vol. 1, *The Triune God* (New York: Oxford University Press, 1997), 13–14.

12. Willimon, *Service of God*, 149.

13. Charles M. Wood, *The Formation of Christian Understanding: An Essay in Theological Hermeneutics* (Philadelphia: Westminster, 1981), 38.

14. Don E. Saliers, *Worship and Spirituality* (Philadelphia: Westminster, 1984), 14–19.

15. Ibid., 17–18.

future is congruent with its story of God and the world. The liturgical use of Scripture cultivates a narrative vision of reality that summons the church toward its true end, a life of praise in response to the Triune God, which is its primary witness to the world. Reflecting on the divine and human natures of Christ, James McClendon writes of two scriptural stories that are indivisibly one: "of divine self-expense and human investment, which constitute the biblical story in its fullness, . . . God reaching to people even before people reach to God, of a God who gives in order to be able to receive, and a humanity that receives so that it shall be able to give."[16]

This story becomes gospel today—good news—when it is remembered and reactualized in the church's proclamation, liturgical celebration, and common life.[17] Like the biblical word, the incarnate Word, and the risen Word, the liturgy of the church is of God, a function of the Word, the communal remembrance of the divine presence and glory received as God's self-revelation. "We stand before it like Moses before the mystery of a burning bush, in awe, reverence, worshipfully. As fallen creatures, there is no other way to stand in the divine presence."[18]

As sacramental discourse, then, the liturgical proclamation of the Word is an instrument of the active and real presence of God, divine address mediated through scriptural speech to accomplish God's purpose, as he wills, by the gift of himself in his Son through the Holy Spirit.[19] Such transformation of life is nothing less than a sacrament of communion with God, the "gospel of Jesus Christ become a people," a sign of humanity on pilgrimage toward the fullness of the kingdom already active in building up the church for the salvation of the world.[20] William Willimon comments on pastoral interpretation and discourse, by which the Word speaks in the Spirit's power to create the church:

> We keep trusting the Bible because we keep meeting God in the Bible. In the words of Scripture we are encountered by the Incarnate Word. We call the Bible "inspired" because the Bible keeps reaching out to us and keeps striking us with its strange truth, keeps truthfully depicting God. God keeps truthfully speaking to us through Scripture as in no other

16. James W. McClendon Jr., *Systematic Theology*, vol. 2, *Doctrine* (Nashville: Abingdon, 1994), 276.

17. John Breck, *Scripture in Tradition: The Bible and Its Interpretation in the Orthodox Church* (Crestwood, NY: St. Vladimir's Press, 2001), 12–13.

18. Kavanagh, "Scriptural Word and Liturgical Worship," 132.

19. Aidan Kavanagh, *On Liturgical Theology* (New York: Pueblo, 1981), 112–20.

20. Ibid., 173–80.

medium. We trust the Bible because on enough Sundays we discover that God's Word has the power to produce the readers that it requires. In the reading of Scripture, the Creator is at work, something is made out of nothing; the church takes form around the words of the Word.[21]

Thus in its community-constituting capacity, Christian Scripture functions not simply as text but as canon, that is, a list of books that are received, read, and prayed in Christian assemblies and that as a single, unified book speaks the Word incarnate in Christ.[22]

As canon, Scripture norms Christian witness as scriptural or evangelical, enabling us to judge whether or not human speech participates in God's self-communicative Word enacted definitely in Jesus Christ. Moreover, as a communal or catholic task rather than an individual endeavor, ecclesial interpretation of Scripture requires judgment congruent with the identity of the Triune God to whom the canon bears witness and the church confesses.[23]

Because the identity of the God whom the church worships is the same as the God revealed in the Bible, the primary form of theological interpretation is the telling of the Bible's story in the liturgy, and the main character of that story is God, the Trinity, who speaks in the Scriptures to create the church and renew its life.[24] "The Christian church is the community that expects to hear God speaking through its Scriptures. It is that community which has been formed and sustained by God who addresses it through those events and words that are preserved for us in the Bible."[25]

As a scriptural practice, then, preaching is a form of primary theology brought to speech in the proclamation of the gospel. Announcing God's saving promises, the communication of the Word incarnate in Christ generates the response of a people who embody the wisdom of Scripture in its liturgical enactment through the whole of life.[26] The language of preaching—speaking of God—is dependent speech, responsive to the

21. William H. Willimon, *Pastor: The Theology and Practice of Ordained Ministry* (Nashville: Abingdon, 2002), 128.

22. Lathrop, *Holy People*, 25.

23. Wood, *The Formation of Christian Understanding*, 100–101; see also the discussion in Kevin J. Vanhoozer, "Scripture and Tradition," in *The Cambridge Companion to Postmodern Theology*, ed. Kevin J. Vanhoozer (Cambridge: Cambridge University Press, 2003), 149–69.

24. Frank C. Senn, *New Creation: A Liturgical Worldview* (Minneapolis: Fortress, 2000), 15–16.

25. Elizabeth Achtemeier, "The Canon as the Voice of the Living God," in Braaten and Jenson, *Reclaiming the Bible*, 119.

26. Senn, *New Creation*, 15–16, 30–35.

movement of Scripture toward its focus in Christ that calls the church to worship the Triune God: remembering the story of the nature and destiny of all things; participating in the surprising drama of creation and redemption; and embodying under the conditions of human finitude and sin the promises of God unfolded by the Spirit to the senses and imagination.[27]

Preaching in a "Tournament of Narratives"

George Lindbeck has argued that at the heart of the current "crisis" of biblical authority are not the questions and debates about inerrancy or inspiration, but rather is the gap between past and present, what God said and what God says now, which is typically described as the need for the church to be "relevant." Modern methods of biblical exegesis, which on the whole remain historically critical, have failed to provide adequate guidance on how the Bible as the Word of God speaks with its own voice in new conditions and situations. Lindbeck thus advocates a critical retrieval of classical, pre-modern scriptural practice that articulates "the liturgically embedded Christological and Trinitarian reading of the Hebrew Scriptures . . . as a Christ-centered narrationally and typologically unified whole in conformity to a Trinitarian rule of faith that was constitutive of the Christian canon . . . an authority inseparable from the rule itself."[28]

In short, for the majority of Christian history the Bible has been read as the "all-embracing story of the present as well as the past dealings of the Triune God with God's people and God's world" that shapes and sustains communal and personal identity in changing circumstances across time and place.[29] Lindbeck argues that a retrieval of classical Bible reading by churches would indeed change the context of many current debates among Christians, shifting the focus to the pastoral office itself as God's instrument for nurturing God's people through Word and sacrament: "What builds up the church is what counts."[30]

27. See the excellent discussion in Rowan Williams, *On Christian Theology* (Malden, MA: Blackwell, 2000), 142–48.

28. George Lindbeck, *The Church in a Postliberal Age*, ed. James J. Buckley (Grand Rapids: Eerdmans, 2002), 204, 208.

29. Ibid., 207.

30. Ibid., 221.

Irenaeus, second-century bishop of Lyons, is a salutary exemplar of classical Bible reading—the interpretation of Scripture as a single, unified, coherent narrative that witnesses to the God of Jesus Christ within the baptismal, eucharistic, and kerygmatic patterns of the church's liturgical life. Arguably the first great postbiblical theologian of the church, Irenaeus, summarized the apostolic witness to the Triune God by means of a Rule of Faith, or Truth, that identifies the one Creator who rules heaven and earth and is worshiped by the church, guides its interpretation of Scripture, informs the content of its preaching, and shapes its imagination and life.[31] Rowan Greer observes that Irenaeus was the first witness to a Christian Bible and provided a framework for its interpretation.

> The church came to insist that the God of Israel was the God of Jesus Christ and also that the significance of the Hebrew Scriptures lay in the testimony they bore to Christ. . . . For Christians, the dialogue between God and his people found its fullest expression in Christ, and so Christ became the key to the whole of Scripture. The theological and even christological convictions that determined how a Christian Bible was to be constituted then became central in shaping the interpretation of that Bible.[32]

For Irenaeus, the church's theology begins with the gracious movement of the Triune God toward creation and humanity. This personal knowledge is received and transmitted in the church's worship and practice, its prayers and catechesis, and the words, images, and stories of the biblical narrative. Thus the fundamental source of the vision or knowledge of God's glory revealed in Christ crucified and raised from the dead was what was accomplished and experienced in the prayer and praise of the church.

Liturgy and theology were intimately related by the new reality entrusted to and experienced by the apostles. The continued presence of

31. For good discussions of Irenaeus, see Eric Osborn, *Irenaeus of Lyons* (Cambridge: Cambridge University Press, 2001); Basil Studer, *Trinity and Incarnation: The Faith of the Early Church*, ed. Andrew Louth (Collegeville, MN: Liturgical Press, 1993); Rowan A. Greer, *Broken Lights and Mended Lives: Theology and Common Life in the Early Church* (University Park: Pennsylvania State University Press, 1986); John Behr, *The Formation of Christian Theology*, vol. 1, *The Way to Nicaea* (Crestwood, NY: St. Vladimir's Press, 2001); John O'Keefe and R. R. Reno, *Sanctified Vision: An Introduction to Early Christian Interpretation of the Bible* (Baltimore: Johns Hopkins University Press, 2005).

32. Rowan Greer, "The Christian Bible and Its Interpretation," in Rowan Greer and James Kugel, *Early Biblical Interpretation*, vol. 3 (Philadelphia: Westminster, 1986), 111.

the crucified and risen Lord was received and extended in assemblies that followed the Lord's command to baptize and to celebrate a supper of bread and wine in remembrance of him:

> Baptism and Eucharist—it is the Lord's command that makes this a *lex orandi* (law of prayer). On the foundation of what God the Trinity accomplishes in these celebrations, and from the communities' experience of them, there developed a history of thought, a history of theology. Some ways of understanding things eventually became normative themselves: a *lex credendi* (law of believing).[33]

The liturgy, therefore, gave rise to both the interpretive framework and the interpretation of the Christian Bible, the apostolic witness to the gospel of Jesus Christ through the medium of Scripture according to the pattern of the *regula fidei*, or Rule of Faith.[34]

For Irenaeus, Christian prayer, the sacraments, Scripture, preaching, virtue, and devotion were all congruent with a trinitarian Rule of Faith.[35] Thomas Torrance comments:

> Knowledge or the truth of God or the truth of the Gospel is not given in an abstract or detached form but in a concrete embodied form in the church, where it is grasped within the normative pattern of the faith imparted to it through the teaching of the apostles, and is therefore to be grasped only in unity and continuity with the faith, worship, and godly life of all who are incorporated into Christ as members of his Body.[36]

The rule or canon for understanding and measuring the scriptural pattern of God's truth is most positively set forth by Irenaeus in a catechetical handbook, *The Proof or Demonstration of the Apostolic Preaching*. This handbook provides a "summary memorandum" of Christian teaching, "the preaching of truth so as to strengthen your faith . . . to understand all the members of the body of truth . . . and receive the exposition of the things of God, so that . . . it will bear your own salvation like fruit."[37]

---

33. Jeremy Driscoll, OSB, "Uncovering the Dynamic *Lex Orandi—Lex Credendi* in the Baptismal Theology of Irenaeus," *Pro Ecclesia* 12, no. 2 (Spring 2003): 214–15.

34. Ibid., 219.

35. See the excellent introduction in Greer, *Broken Lights and Mended Lives*, 1–20.

36. Thomas F. Torrance, *The Trinitarian Faith: The Evangelical Theology of the Ancient Church* (Edinburgh: T&T Clark, 1988), 33.

37. St. Irenaeus of Lyons, *On the Apostolic Preaching*, trans. John Behr (Crestwood, NY: St. Vladimir's Press, 1997), 39. Hereafter references will appear in the text as *Dem*.

The *Demonstration* clearly and comprehensively unfolds the content of the Scriptures, that is, the Old Testament that points to the revelation of Jesus Christ as proclaimed by the apostles. Irenaeus thus sought to assist Christians in recognizing and following the scriptural authority of that preaching by demonstrating that the apostles' proclamation of what has been fulfilled in the death and resurrection of Christ, shaped as it is by Scripture, was indeed prophesied by the same God who created the world, elected Israel, and inspired the Law and the Prophets.[38]

Because the true meaning of Scripture is theological, Irenaeus begins by confessing the Triune God, the source of Christian faith, hope, and love.

> We must keep the rule (canon of faith) unswervingly, and perform the commandments of God, believing in God and fearing him; for he is the Lord, and loving Him. . . . Faith exhorts us to remember that we have received baptism for the remission of sins, in the name of God the Father and in the name of Jesus Christ, the Son of God, who was incarnate, and died, and was raised, and in the Holy Spirit of God, and that this baptism is the seal of eternal life and rebirth to God. (*Dem.* 3)

Irenaeus's confession of the triune name leads to a reading of Ephesians 4:6 that illumines his liturgical and theological vision of Scripture: "One God and Father, who is above all and with all and in us all." This enabled Irenaeus to affirm that everything is created by the Father through his Word, while the Holy Spirit, who is received in baptism, enables us to cry, "Abba, Father," and forms us to the likeness of God (*Dem.* 5). According to Driscoll, Irenaeus's great theological accomplishment was the assertion of concrete, material conclusions—regarding the truth of God and humanity—drawn from the whole economy of God. In its trinitarian dimensions, the economy extends from the creation of all things to the creative work of the Spirit in baptism and anticipates Christ's return in glory to consummate the peace and righteousness of God on earth.[39]

According to Irenaeus these three articles, God the Father, the Son Christ Jesus, and the Holy Spirit, are the order of Christian faith and life and are intimately connected to what happens in the liturgical experience of the church (*Dem.* 7).[40] This is summed up in a story

38. Behr, *Formation of Christian Theology*, 1:112–13.
39. Driscoll, "Uncovering the Dynamic *Lex Orandi—Lex Credendi*," 218.
40. Ibid., 217.

expressing the continuity of Adam and Christ, and of creation and redemption—one all-encompassing divine economy or history, embodied in Scripture, the Rule of Faith, which finds its fullness in the new humanity of the incarnate Word.[41]

> And this is the order of our faith, the foundation of the edifice and the support of our conduct: God, the Father, uncreated, uncontainable, invisible, one God, the Creator of all: this the first article of our faith. And the second article: The Word of God, the Son of God, Christ Jesus our Lord, who was revealed by the prophets according to the character of their prophecy and according to the nature of the economies of the Father, by whom all things were made, and who, in the last time, to recapitulate all things, became a man amongst men, visible and palpable, in order to abolish death, to demonstrate life, and to effect communion between God and man. And the third article: the Holy Spirit, through whom the prophets prophesied and the patriarchs learnt the things of God and the righteous were led in the path of righteousness, and who, in the last times, was poured out in a new fashion upon the human race renewing man, throughout the world, to God. (*Dem.* 6)

Of utmost importance for Irenaeus is that the one God who is Creator and Redeemer of all things is known in the church's liturgy. In the saving activity of the Trinity, those who bear the Spirit are led to the Son, and the Son presents them to the Father: salvation is communion with God (*Dem.* 7). Thus the liturgical knowledge of the Trinity, as given and received in baptism, provides the key or rule for understanding the whole Bible. Robert Wilken concludes, "The rule of faith had a Trinitarian structure whose narrative identified God by the things recorded in the Scriptures, the creation of the world, the inspiration of the prophets, the coming of Christ in the flesh, and the outpouring of the Holy Spirit. . . . The Bible is thus oriented toward a future still unfolding."[42]

The formulation of the Rule of Faith, or Truth, was an urgent pastoral matter for Irenaeus, since the ancient church found itself engaged in a "tournament of narratives."[43] He thus sought to differentiate churchly reading and preaching from that of the Gnostics, whose idiosyncratic interpretations pointed in directions alien to the purpose of a church

41. Greer, *Broken Lights and Mended Lives*, 26–27.
42. Robert Louis Wilken, *The Spirit of Early Christian Thought: Seeking the Face of God* (New Haven: Yale University Press, 2003), 66–67.
43. I have borrowed this term from Rodney Clapp, *A Peculiar People: The Church as Culture in a Post-Christian Society* (Downers Grove, IL: InterVarsity, 1996).

formed by the apostolic witness to the God of Jesus Christ. During the second century, gnostic teachers wreaked havoc in Christian congregations, luring the faithful with their highly popular, creative, novel, and engaging exegetical expertise, claiming they had special channels for getting back to hidden "meaning" in Scripture. For the Gnostics, Scripture was a mine from which to dig spiritual nuggets of wisdom, rearranging its pieces to suit their own individual purposes, while typically creating false gods, without involvement in either the crucified Jesus or the weakness and foolishness of his cross that identifies the church.[44]

Describing the Gnostics, Jenson states, "Their exegesis supposed that scripture is a congeries of sayings and stories and commands and so forth, and that each component bit is a lump of ore from which we may extract precious insight if only we know the technique." Gnostic exegesis regarded Scripture as a discrete set of opportunities to acquire or display private religious knowledge and timeless truths over a temporally embodied ecclesial narrative. Jenson likens this to the homiletic practice of many contemporary preachers who make occasional visits to the Bible in order to abstract individual stories, sayings, wisdom, and rules that are individually exploited by discovering whatever relevant and interesting point, theme, or topic it may inspire.[45]

Irenaeus's great work, *Against Heresies*, exposed and challenged this way of reading Scripture and preaching by demonstrating its failure to discern the larger biblical framework, story, and actors according to the witness of the prophets and apostolic proclamation of the gospel: Christ crucified and raised. Christ himself is the key to discovering and interpreting the Word of God, but it is Christ who also identifies and interprets those who seek him as the truth.[46] According to Irenaeus, because the heretics failed to either grasp or participate in the providential plan of Scripture revealed in Christ, they discovered truth in their own interpretations and ended up preaching themselves.

> Such then is their system, which the prophets did not announce, the Lord did not teach, and the Apostles did not hand down; but which they boastfully declare that they understand better than others. . . .

44. Robert Jenson, "Hermeneutics and the Life of the Church," in Braaten and Jenson, *Reclaiming the Bible*, 95–96; Joseph T. Lienhard, *The Bible, the Church, and Authority: The Canon of the Christian Bible in History and Theology* (Collegeville, MN: Liturgical Press, 1995), 42–52.

45. Ibid., 96.

46. Behr, *Formation of Christian Theology*, 1:33–37.

They attempt to make ropes of sand in applying the parables of the Lord, or prophetic utterances, or Apostolic statements to their plausible scheme, in order that they may have foundation for it. But they alter the scriptural context and connection, and dismember the truth as much as they can. . . . It is just as if there were a beautiful representation of a king made by a skilled artist, and one altered the arrangement of the pieces of stone into the shape of a dog or a fox, and then should assert that this was the original representation of a king. In much the same manner, they stitch together old wives' tales, and wrestling sayings and parables, however they may, from the context, attempt to fit oracles of God into their myths.[47]

On the other hand, Irenaeus's ruled way of reading Scripture was communal and ecclesial, structured according to the trinitarian baptismal formula. The *regula fidei*, or Rule of Faith, served the church's hope of articulating and authenticating a world-encompassing story of the Triune God, whose purpose—the fulfillment of all things in Jesus Christ—is revealed in creation, incarnation, redemption, and consummation: the hypothesis or plan of Scripture. His aim was to assist Christian communities that were striving to remember, retell, and relive the story of faith, hope, and love through their preaching and teaching, participating in the construction of a coherent, overarching narrative of salvation in Jesus Christ, who is God's arrangement or economy "according to the scriptures."[48] Concerning Irenaeus's work, John Behr concludes, "The canon of truth enabled the demonstrations of scripture to describe, accurately, the portrait of a king, Christ: it is a mode of interpretation delivered by the apostles in the proclamation of Christ."[49]

Scripture, then, intends to disclose the truth of God, the world, and human destiny by speaking of the one Jesus Christ, the manifestation of God's purpose for the whole creation as proclaimed by the apostles. Moreover, the Rule of Faith is necessary for discerning the arrangement or economy of Scripture, which renders the apostles' witness to the incarnate Lord, who was announced by the Spirit in the Law and the Prophets. Christ himself is the purpose of the story and its exegesis; thus

---

47. Irenaeus, *Against Heresies* 1.8.1, in The Ante-Nicene Fathers 1, ed. A. Roberts and J. Donaldson, rev. A. C. Coxe (Grand Rapids: Eerdmans, 1953), 326. Hereafter references will be included in the text as *AH*.

48. Paul Blowers, "The *Regula Fidei* and the Narrative Character of Early Christian Faith," *Pro Ecclesia* 6 (1997): 203–4; see the excellent discussion in Francis Young, *Virtuoso Theology: The Bible and Interpretation* (Cleveland: Pilgrim, 1993), 47–65.

49. Behr, *Formation of Christian Theology*, 1:37.

the scriptural texture of the apostolic preaching, the gospel proclaimed in the "wisdom of the Cross," is given voice within the whole canon. The God of Jesus Christ remains the subject and scope of Scripture, which speaks of him in the Word, the incarnate form of salvation.[50]

> The church, dispersed throughout the world to the ends of the earth, received from the apostles and their disciples the faith in one God the Father Almighty, "who made heaven and earth and sea and all that is in them" (Ex. 20:11), and in one Jesus Christ, the Son of God, the incarnate for our salvation, and in the Holy Spirit, who through the prophets predicted the dispensations of God: the coming, the birth from the Virgin, the passion, the resurrection from the dead, and the ascension of the beloved Jesus Christ our Lord in the flesh into the heavens, and is coming from the heavens in the glory of the Father to "recapitulate all things" (Eph. 1:10) and raise up all flesh of the human race, so that to Christ Jesus our Lord and God and Savior and King, according to the good pleasure of the invisible Father, "every knee should bow, of beings in heaven and on earth and under the earth, and that every tongue should confess him (Phil. 2:10–11)." (AH 1.10.1)

The relationship of Scripture, the gospel, doctrine, and the church in history is established in the proclamation of the whole narrative movement to its climax in cross and resurrection. Irenaeus described this as the "recapitulation of all things," or a summary or restatement that provides a way of seeing the person of Christ, the incarnate Word, who defeated the power of sin and overcame death to accomplish the purpose of God revealed through the whole economy.[51] Moreover, the recapitulation of all things in Christ was essential for Irenaeus's theology, since the Gnostics separated Christian content and form: Christ from creation, the Old Testament, and Israel; the divinity of Christ from his humanity; Christians from participation in Christ's suffering and death for the world. By thinking within the faith confessed by the church, revealed in the scriptural narrative, and summarized in the apostles' preaching, Irenaeus affirmed that salvation is not from the world but in and for its perfection, thus overcoming the gnostic division of reality into material and spiritual realms.[52]

50. Behr, *Formation of Christian Theology*, 1:119–24; Greer, *Broken Lights and Mended Lives*, 26–31.

51. Behr, *Formation of Christian Theology*, 1:124–26.

52. Greer, *Broken Lights and Mended Lives*, 25–27; Greer, "The Christian Bible and Its Interpretation," 171–76.

There is, therefore, as I have pointed out, one God the Father, and one Jesus Christ, who came by means of the whole dispensational arrangements (economies) and gathered all things into himself. But in every respect, too, He is man. The formation of God: and thus He took up man into Himself; the invisible becoming visible, the incomprehensible being made comprehensible, the impassible becoming capable of suffering, and the Word being made man, thus summing up all things into Himself so that as in supercelestial, spiritual and invisible things, the Word of God is supreme, so also in things visible and corporeal He might possess the supremacy, and, taking to Himself the pre-eminence, as well as constituting Himself Head of the Church, He might draw all things to Himself at the proper time. (*AH* 3.16.6)

The incarnation represents the culminating economy of God: "The work of the Word in creation and in the Old Testament finds its completion when the Word is made flesh."[53] By attending to the whole narrative of Scripture, Irenaeus contemplated God's work in Christ as articulated in Ephesians 1:9–10: "For he has made known to us in all wisdom and insight the mystery of his will, according to his purpose which he set forth in Christ as a plan for the fullness of time to unite all things in him, things in heaven and things on earth." Paul Blowers observes that "the challenge of Christian identity was to reconstruct the story of Jesus Christ in its dramatic fullness as both the cosmic story—a narrative comprehending the destiny of all creation and all peoples—and as the genuine 'final act' to the peculiar sacred story of Israel."[54]

The subject of Scripture and Christian preaching is Christ seen through the lens of the cross. Christian preaching is, therefore, the concise word of salvation proclaimed by the apostles. It unites the identity of the Word in creation, in Scripture, in the flesh of Christ, and as embodied by the church in history.[55] Interpreting Scripture as the revelation of the Triune God's dealings with the world, the church is invited to discover its life within that providential story, thus becoming itself a witness to God's purpose to unite and perfect the creation through the Son and by the Spirit, for the Father's glory.[56]

53. Greer, *Broken Lights and Mended Lives*, 37.

54. Blowers, "*Regula Fidei*," 203–4.

55. Behr, *Formation of Christian Theology*, 1:127–33.

56. Colin E. Gunton, *The One, the Three and the Many: God, Creation and the Culture of Modernity* (Cambridge: Cambridge University Press, 1993), 225–31; Wilken, *Spirit of Early Christian Thought*, 25–49.

Irenaeus's theological wisdom guided preachers to read each text of Scripture with the whole Bible in mind and to locate each individual sermon text within the whole canon. Christian Scripture is a whole because it is the whole narrative of the one Triune God, and to follow the whole story preachers must know the whole story's plot and its characters. The church, moreover, does know the plot and characters of the scriptural narrative; and because the church is a continuous community with the story's actors and narrators, it has no need to make the Bible relevant for listeners, but must learn to see or imagine itself as one with God's people across time, as a single community created by the Spirit through the Word of God.[57] As Rowan Greer notes:

> From one point of view, the Rule of Faith was limited as a unifying framework for interpreting scripture. It did not settle the question of method, nor did it solve problems of detail in theological, moral, and spiritual exposition of the Bible. But from another point of view, what seem to be limitations are precisely what enable the task of interpretation. Built into the patristic vision of exegesis is the conviction that the Christian's theological vision continues to grow and change, just as the Christian life is a pilgrimage and progress toward a destiny only dimly perceived. The framework of interpretation, then, does not so much solve the problem of what scripture means as supply the context in which the quest for that meaning may take place.[58]

Irenaeus's theological and pastoral wisdom helps to illumine important contemporary challenges related to the interpretation of Scripture and proclamation of the gospel. For example, many preachers continue to visit the Bible in search of useful ideas, topics, and illustrations to explain how Christianity might be functionally useful and personally meaningful for their listeners. However, few inhabit the narrative world of Scripture so as to speak its language with the Christian wisdom displayed by exemplars such as Irenaeus, who preached to form a holy people identified by the story of Christ that embodies the mission of God to the world. Much contemporary preaching tends to follow the "great reversal" that dominated modernity.[59] This has become a matter of translating and fitting the biblical story into another world constituted by that range of experience or understanding open to anyone

57. Jenson, "Hermeneutics and the Life of the Church," 98.
58. Greer and Kugel, *Early Biblical Interpretation*, 198–99.
59. See the excellent discussion in Charles L. Campbell, *Preaching Jesus: New Directions for Homiletics in Hans Frei's Postliberal Theology* (Grand Rapids: Eerdmans, 1997), 117–88.

possessing "common sense," rather than incorporating that world into the scriptural narrative of the Triune God's dealings with Israel and the church. Hauerwas comments on this popular view of preaching as a form of "communication," stating,

> The notion of communication too often assumes that what one person has to say to another must "in principle" be capable of being understood. Certain words may need explaining, and so on, but finally the speaker will be able to make himself or herself understood. In that sense preaching is not about communicating, but is rather to challenge our presumption or our "understanding." . . . Preaching is meant to challenge the presumption that our "understanding" is sufficient to hear the gospel. Preaching rightly requires us to be transformed if we are to hear what is being proclaimed.[60]

Ironically, this apologetic strategy of "relevance" is situated within a tradition of interpretation that reflects the widespread notion that it is possible to understand the Bible without the spiritual or moral transformation that occurs through participation in a particular tradition. It is therefore dependent upon a view shared by both literalistic fundamentalists and biblical critics, namely, that Scripture should make rational sense to anyone abstracted from its performance in the story and practices of the Christian community.[61] Commenting on this approach to Christianity and the Bible, Rodney Clapp states:

> Now I would suggest that Christian discipleship is better served by the model of apprenticeship than the model of how-to manual. . . . Books on application, how to apply the Bible, flourish only because we have lost a sense of discipleship as apprenticeship. If we do not have a viable community to help us participate in the story where we are, we can only grasp at the inferior substitutes of application manual—written as if from beyond space and time, for no particular time and place.[62]

Following the work of John Milbank, Hauerwas notes that when explanation of a spiritual domain of meaning in terms of efficient causation is our primary mode of understanding, the result is nihilism in which all

---

60. Stanley Hauerwas, "Introduction" in William H. Willimon and Stanley Hauerwas, *Preaching to Strangers: Evangelism in Today's World* (Louisville: Westminster John Knox, 1992), 10.

61. Stanley Hauerwas, *Unleashing the Scripture: Freeing the Bible from Captivity to America* (Nashville: Abingdon, 1993), 15–38.

62. Clapp, *A Peculiar People*, 137.

that remains is the will to power.[63] This itself is a matter of discernment within a particular community, since when the Bible is read according to the church's faith in the Triune God (i.e., as a liturgical book), the church is summoned to its first political task and primary loyalty: worshiping and proclaiming the "true God truly" while resisting the fallen powers and idolatries of the world.[64]

Irenaeus read the story of the Bible as both true and saving, as a liturgical book proclaiming that the Father's purpose for the cosmos *is* the Word made flesh, the person of the Son, Jesus Christ, crucified and raised from the dead, in whose image we are being conformed by the justifying, sanctifying, perfecting work of God the Holy Spirit. Salvation *is* communion with the Triune God.

Preaching the Narrative of Salvation

Preaching as a scriptural practice springs from the Word, Jesus Christ, who is narrated in Scripture and performed in the Spirit as "public, fleshly fact" for particular purposes in particular places and times. Nicholas Lash notes that because God's Word *is* God himself, the appropriate human response of the church in its praise, confession, and petition "is to find and fashion our human finitude in the world in the form of discipleship, a following according to the truth enfleshed, enacted, made finite and particular, arrested, tried and crucified."[65]

When the church attunes its life to the voice of God in the canonical story, it discovers that what Christ said and did he still wishes to say and do, just as Christ will continue to speak and do these things until God's reign comes in its fullness.[66] Such speaking and hearing occur most readily when we allow ourselves to be taken up into the drama of Scripture, to become actors in its pastoral and ecclesial roles. Richard Hays affirms that "where Scripture speaks as a living word, it creates communities whose lives are hermeneutical testimonies, embodying the word, making its speech palpable. . . . Scripture, then, continues to

63. Stanley Hauerwas, *Performing the Faith: Bonhoeffer and the Practice of Nonviolence* (Grand Rapids: Brazos, 2004), 144–45.
64. For putting the matter this way, I am indebted to Stanley Hauerwas, *Disrupting Time: Sermons, Prayers, and Sundries* (Eugene, OR: Cascade, 2004), 181–82.
65. Lash, *Way to Emmaus*, 42.
66. Don E. Saliers, *Worship as Theology: Foretaste of Glory Divine* (Nashville: Abingdon, 1994), 182.

speak in order to call into existence the community in which it can be heard rightly."[67]

Thus Scripture's canonical plot is constituted by divine initiative and derivatively by human response. It is a living conversation initiated by and through God with God's people for its liturgical enactment in the world. James McClendon observes:

> God *summons* Abraham and *fulfills* Sarah; God *frees* Israel; God *anoints* David; God *punishes* but *restores* a rebellious nation; God *sends* Jesus, *accepts* his death, and *raises* him from the dead; God *pours forth* the Spirit; in the end the risen Christ *returns*. Each of these divine-action initiatives both requires and enables a human response which is taken up into the divine action; the people, *chastised*, *renew* their covenant faithfulness; Jesus at the Jordan and again in Gethsemane *accepts* his ministry; Spirit-filled believers *speak* in new tongues; the faithful church *expects* the coming of Christ in his kingdom at the end. In sum, God acts and enabled people to answer; in the broadest sense this elicited answer is their reasonable worship (Rom. 12:1).[68]

In the preaching of the Word a whole new world is given; the Spirit activates and moves the narrative of Scripture from a collection of texts to an interpretation of a past event realized in the present that summons the church to go on as participants in God's story. "In the act of proclamation, of standing before the community and speaking the Word aloud, we become the word we utter. At this moment the narrative is no longer a literary story, but the very life of the community."[69]

1 Corinthians 10:1–13

Visit a church on Sunday morning—most any will do—and you will likely find a congregation comfortably relating to a deity who fits nicely within precise doctrinal positions; or a deity who lends almighty support to social crusades and political causes; or a deity who conforms to individual expectations and spiritual experiences.[70] But

---

67. Richard B. Hays, *Echoes of Scripture in the Letters of Paul* (New Haven: Yale University Press, 1989), 168.

68. McClendon, *Systematic Theology*, 2:376; emphases are in the original.

69. Susan Wood, "The Liturgy," in Buckley and Yeago, *Knowing the Triune God*, 106.

70. The first three paragraphs of this sermon are indebted to Donald W. McCullough, *The Trivialization of God: The Dangerous Illusion of a Manageable Deity* (Colorado Springs: Nav-Press, 1995), 13–14.

you will not likely find much awe or mystery. The only sweaty palms will be those of the preacher unsure whether the sermon will go over, whether it will work, as we like to say; the only shaking knees will be those of the musicians about to perform.

The New Testament warns us: "Offer to God an acceptable worship, with reverence and awe; for our God is a consuming fire" (Heb. 12:28–29). However, in many churches reverence and awe have been replaced by a yawn of familiarity, a desire for comfort, and a promise of convenience. The consuming fire has been domesticated by a religion designed for consumption, domesticated into a candle flame, perhaps adding a bit of religious atmosphere or ambiance but without searing heat, blinding light, or power to purify God's people. Even preaching, which once proclaimed a living Word to call and create a people to be participants in the grand drama of creation and redemption authored by God, has been reduced to a self-help method of explaining spiritual things, a handy technique by which we gain better control of our lives: Witness the huge popularity of sermons or talks, as some now like to call them, that offer tips to make it through the week, principles for spiritual success, and rules for realizing your potential, increasing self-esteem, and acquiring happiness.

"Why do people in churches seem like cheerful, brainless tourists on a packaged tour of the Absolute?" asks Annie Dillard. She continues:

> On the whole, I do not find Christians, outside the catacombs, sufficiently sensible of the conditions. Does anyone have the foggiest idea what sort of power we so blithely invoke? Or, as I suspect, does no one believe a word of it? The churches are children playing on the floor with their chemistry sets, mixing up a batch of TNT to kill a Sunday morning. It is madness to wear ladies' straw hats and velvet hats to church; we should all be wearing crash helmets. Ushers should use life preservers and signal flares; they should lash us to our pews. For the sleeping god may wake some day and take offense; or the waking god may draw us out to where we can never return.[71]

Just about everything in the gospel of Jesus Christ runs counterintuitive to the religious habits and spiritual inclinations of North Americans. We live in a culture that tells us, again and again, from one end of the theological spectrum to the other, that Christianity must either change or die. In fact, I have heard this warning so many times in the

71. Annie Dillard, *Teaching a Stone to Talk* (New York: Harper & Row, 1982), 40–41.

last twenty-five years that it seems easier to begin believing that the refusal to change, especially a refusal to change how we do church, as the popular saying goes, has become the most recent addition to the seven deadly sins.

If there is a defining characteristic of the twenty years I spent in pastoral ministry, it was that of constant conflict and controversy over how we do church. And while the season of Lent is about change, it is about the kind of change only God can work in us—which is called repentance—a change of mind and life, and most important, a change of who or what we worship. This is change that comes only as we heed the warning spoken in the Word of God: "Flee from the worship of idols" (1 Cor. 10:14 NRSV).

Now, perhaps you may be thinking, "He's not talking about us, since those words were addressed to the Corinthians, and everyone knows how messed up they were. They lived in a culture that was very different from ours, and besides, we have so many more tools, techniques, and wonderful technology for ministry than they did, so surely we cannot be idol worshipers. We are just sincere, nice people who want to be effective, who are just looking for a little religious help that will make the lives of people a little better."

So were the Corinthian Christians, my friends. And they too were sincere and desired only to be effective and to find a little help from God. But Paul tells them after a brief review of the tragic story of Israel in the wilderness: "The same thing could happen to us. . . . We must be on guard so that we never get caught up in wanting our own way as they did. . . . We must never try to get Christ to serve us instead of us serving Christ." And the story of Israel is the story we share with the Corinthians, a story of God's mighty power to deliver, faithful provision, providential guidance, and gracious promises. But this is also a story of human arrogance and presumption, the source of pride and its diverse and destructive expressions: rebellion, indifference, ingratitude, and infidelity. Yes, we are quite capable of taking God's love and gracious gifts for granted, of viewing God as an indulgent parent who simply never says no to us, of reducing God to something we can use or control.

Paul adds that this story, as it has been told in Exodus, Numbers, and Deuteronomy, has "danger" written all over it; it has been written down so that we will not foolishly repeat the mistakes and moral failures of our spiritual ancestors. And we are part of the same story, since in Jesus Christ we have been called and are being saved by the same God, we are just as capable of messing up as they were.

I suspect that we are not so readily inclined to hear these words as good news, as gospel, are we? But Paul is writing and bearing witness from a position that begins with God; yes, believe it or not, he begins with God, a move we are not so accustomed to hearing these days when many preachers are quite happy to announce "It's about you!"

But because Paul knew Scripture, he also knew he was not simply free to make up his own mind; nor was he free to choose his message based on whatever topic he might think meaningful, interesting, or relevant. And because he knew Scripture, he saw that in Jesus God had brought the life of Israel to its fulfillment, so that the Christian life is one in which we now share their vocation and their calling to be dependent on God and to be made different by God. And Paul also knew that our call to faithful obedience possesses the power to make us into a holy people whose love and loyalty to a holy God will most often appear to the world as rather odd and strange.

But what is most striking about the apostle's words of wisdom is that the cultural irrelevance of the church in Corinth—and we need to remember that they were just a small, peculiar minority in that big, diverse city—was not, surprisingly, their primary problem. Contrary to many of our contemporary prophets, the apostle Paul—with his memory shaped by Torah, the Law, and Prophets, Israel's story and its way of life and worship with God, and with his understanding of Torah shaped by Jesus the crucified Messiah and Son of God—announces that idolatry, not irrelevance, is the greatest threat to God's people. Our greatest need is for freedom from idolatry to worship the one, true, living God, as was made clear at Mt. Sinai: "I am the LORD your God, who brought you out of the land of Egypt . . . you shall have no other gods before me" (Exod. 20:2–3).

Now perhaps you are thinking that the Corinthians' situation was very different from ours; they were involved in the idolatrous practice of eating meat sacrificed to idols and attending meals in temples that were built to serve pagan gods. But let's be serious; none of us are participants in pagan rituals, are we? Well, exercise your imaginations for a moment to consider what idolatrous practices pull at us today. More than likely they draw us into activities and customs that cultivate in us opinions, attitudes, habits, and actions that the culture tells us are normal, acceptable, sensible, helpful, and most certainly harmless. Or more deceptively, they tell us that these things are neither religious nor spiritual; that they don't aim to control our lives with godlike claims and power, and if they do require some degree of allegiance, they do so to an extent that is basically mild and poses no threat to the church or its faith. Now, if you believe this line of thinking, just try to remove the American flag from a church sanctuary and see what kind of response you provoke.

And it's not only the temptation to make God the god of my and our nation. There are other temptations that pull at us just as powerfully: the god of my comfort who solves my problems and makes me happy; or the god of my success who helps me achieve my life goals; and then, there is the god of my family or the god of my favorite group; why, we can even reduce God to the god of our church, but not of those other congregations or denominations. It is remarkable how useful a god can be once we no longer make worshiping him—as God—the primary purpose or end of our life.

I suspect that in the increasingly post-Christian time in which we find ourselves, we will see a sharp increase of subtle temptations to adapt or accommodate the wisdom of the one, true God to the many wisdoms of this world; and we will continue to feel a strong pull to prop up the power of God revealed in the weakness of Jesus Christ with a little help from the powers of this world in exchange for a little more churchly survival or success. For many in our culture, and even many within the church, have persuaded us to believe that the only story we have is the story that tells us we have no story other than the story we have chosen for ourselves.

Thank God for the witness of the apostle Paul, who in his wisdom invites us to find safety—salvation—in believing that we have been made participants in Israel's story, the story of Israel's God revealed in light of Jesus Christ. May we never forget that this story is about a gracious and merciful God who has first spoken to make us his own. Our vocation is not to change Christianity in order to save it; rather, our vocation is to be changed, to be made holy by the power of Jesus Christ, the Son of God and Savior of the world. This truth moved Martin Luther to write that the whole gospel, the marvelous, wonderful good news, is contained in these words: "You shall have no other gods before me." Do you hear God calling us today?

6

Speaking of God: Preaching as a Beautiful Practice

Late have I loved you, beauty so old and so new; late have I loved you.

—Augustine, *Confessions*

As the practice of homiletic artistry, preaching is the oral expression of divine truth and goodness incarnate in the Word communicated by the Spirit to fashion the church into a living sign of the doxological beauty of the Triune God. To be a preacher is to be taken up into the activity of God's self-communication, which itself is an activity of receiving and being conformed to the knowledge and love of God within the liturgical life of the church. Thus the preacher is the handiwork of God, a "sacramental" expression of divine beauty displayed in Christ and in God's glory manifested in the harmony of Christian speech and life. Through the wisdom and eloquence of the Word, God, the master rhetorician, evokes and gives form to the church's witness of praise.[1] In his treatise on the Trinity, Augustine unfolds a God-given human

---

1. See the discussion of preaching in Richard Viladesau, *Theology and the Arts: Encountering God through Music, Art, and Rhetoric* (Mahwah, NJ: Paulist Press, 2000), chap. 4; I have also

desire for that which is true, delightful, and good in the sacramental beauty of God's temporal revelation:

> That after this meaning, then, the Lord said, "Why askest thou me about the good? There is none that is good but One, that is, God," is probable upon these proofs which I have alleged, because that sight of God, whereby we shall contemplate the substance of God unchangeable and invisible to human eyes (which is promised to the saints alone; which the Apostle Paul speaks of as "face to face"; and of which the Apostle John says, "We shall be like Him, for we shall see Him as He is"; and of which it is said, "One thing have I desired of the Lord, that I may behold the beauty of the Lord," of which the Lord Himself says, "I will both love him, and will manifest myself to him," and on account of which alone we cleanse our hearts by faith, that we may be those "pure in heart who are blessed for they shall see God": and whatever else is spoken of that sight (which whosoever turns the eye of love to seek it, may find it most copiously scattered through all the Scriptures), that sight alone, I say, is our chief good, for the attaining of which we are directed to do whatever we do aright.[2]

A vision of the Triune God's perfect love, beauty, and blessed delight informs Augustine's theology of language, since all signs of human speech are situated within the Triune God's love and joy: the Father's speaking of the Son and the Son's response to the Father.[3] Christian speech cannot be learned as a technique or skill. Rather, it is a gift that is received in attending to the Word, who indwells Scripture, the liturgy, and the sacraments; it is God's self-giving that draws human creatures into the knowledge and love of their Creator. Thus Christ himself is the language and life of the church, the first Word of a conversation prompted by the Spirit within the loving discourse of the Father and Son.[4]

In *De doctrina christiana*, Augustine sketched an analogy of the Word, connecting the incarnation and human speech within the economy of redemption, emphasizing the efficacy of Christ and the example of

---

benefited from the discussion in James K. A. Smith, *Introducing Radical Orthodoxy: Mapping a Post-Secular Theology* (Grand Rapids: Baker, 2004), chap. 6.

2. Augustine, *The Trinity* 1.13.31, cited in Michael Hanby, *Augustine and Modernity* (New York: Routledge, 2003), 30.

3. Ibid., 31–40.

4. Ibid., 37; see also the illuminating discussion in Oliver Davies, *A Theology of Compassion: Metaphysics of Difference and the Renewal of Tradition* (Grand Rapids: Eerdmans, 2001), 251–87.

his humility—the foolishness of preaching in which the Word speaks wisely, sweetly, and persuasively to save.[5] The saving efficacy and self-humiliation of Christ is embodied in the diverse literary form and style of Scripture, which transforms its readers into expressions of the self-giving, dispossessed character of the Word, and into echoes of the love, joy, goodness, and beauty of the God who speaks.[6] Through the mediating activity of the Spirit in Scripture, the analogous relationship between the Word and human words becomes a means of graced, dramatic participation in Christ, the speech of God incarnate. Augustine writes:

> How did he come except that "the Word was made flesh, and dwelt among us"? It is as when we speak. In order that what we are thinking may reach the mind of the listener through the fleshly ears, that which we have in mind is expressed in words and is called speech. But our thought is not transformed into sounds; it remains entire in itself and assumes the form of words by means of which it may reach the ears without suffering any deterioration itself. In the same way the Word of God was made flesh without change that he might dwell among us. (*DDC* 1.13.12)

The whole of *De doctrina christiana* can be read as an extended performance of Christian speech, since Augustine's aim in writing was the conversion of his readers—the cultivation of the wisdom, virtues, dispositions, and affections necessary for hearing and speaking of God. Thus the robust theology of divine activity or grace that underlies books 1–3 informs Augustine's description of Christian preaching as the effect of the Holy Spirit, that is, a miracle of speaking and hearing that cannot be produced by human ingenuity or skill, but rather is a gift received in the church's self-offering and sacrifice of praise evoked by the presence of God in Christ.[7]

5. Telford Work, *Living and Active: Scripture in the Economy of Salvation* (Grand Rapids: Eerdmans, 2002), 56–59.

6. David Dawson, "Sign Theory, Allegorical Reading, and the Motions of the Soul in *De doctrina christiana*," in *De doctrina christiana: A Classic of Western Culture*, ed. Duane W. H. Arnold and Pamela Bright (Notre Dame, IN: University of Notre Dame Press, 1995), 131–44.

7. For interpretations of *De doctrina christiana*, see Arnold and Bright, *De doctrina christiana*; and Carol Harrison, *Augustine: Christian Truth and Fractured Humanity* (Oxford: Oxford University Press, 2000), chaps. 2–3; see also the comments on the church in Davies, *Theology of Compassion*, 274–76; see the integrative, theological interpretation of *DDC* in David Tracy, "Charity, Obscurity, and Clarity: Augustine's Search for Rhetoric and Hermeneutics," in *Rhetoric and Hermeneutics in Our Time*, ed. Walter Jost and Michael J. Hyde (New Haven: Yale University

Augustine's reflections in book 4 are less a theory of rhetoric or homi-letics than an extended reflection on preaching as theological rhetoric: participation in the trinitarian discourse of love that generates Christian speech. The Word of the Father is communicated by the Spirit, who draws, delights, and fills to overflowing both speakers and listeners with an ardent love and desire for the God whose wisdom and beauty orders all things to their true end. God's truth and goodness form the heart of Christian witness and preaching; even the outward word of proclamation imitates the trinitarian movement of divine knowledge that is accompanied by self-giving and desiring love.[8]

Augustine's description of preaching centers in divine love and en-joyment, a human participation in the truth, beauty, and goodness of God that is discovered in creation and Scripture; and the expression of divine wisdom and eloquence that moves human hearts from idolatry to the praise of God. Already in book 1, Augustine had established the true end of Christian worship and life—knowing and loving God by attaching oneself to God simply for God's sake. In other words, this end is the delight and enjoyment of God and others in the love of God that engenders happiness and holiness. It is the praise of God that sustains the church in this pilgrimage as it is drawn by the sacramental beauty of divine love revealed in Christ.

> The things therefore that are to be enjoyed are the Father and the Son and the Holy Spirit, in fact the Trinity, one supreme thing, and one which is shared in common by all who enjoy it. . . . In fact it is better just to say that this Trinity is the one God from whom all things, through whom all things, in whom all things (Rom. 11:36). . . . So what all that has been said amounts to . . . is that the fulfillment and the end of the law and the end of all the divine scriptures is love (Rom. 13:8; 1 Tim. 1:5). . . . So in order that we might know how to do this and be able to, the whole ordering of time was arranged by divine providence for our salvation. (*DDC* 1.5.5, 1.35.39)

Book 4 is the goal or end to which the whole of *De doctrina christiana* moves: the proclamation of the Triune God, whose knowledge, wis-dom, and love re-forms the church into the beauty of Christ through

---

Press, 1997), 254–74; a more comprehensive study to which I am indebted is William Harmless, *Augustine and the Catechumenate* (Collegeville, MN: Liturgical Press, 1995).

8. John C. Cavadini, "The Sweetness of the Word: Salvation and Rhetoric in Augustine's *De doctrina christiana*," in *De doctrina christiana*, ed. Arnold and Bright, 164–72.

the Christian practices of doxology, discipleship, and devotion. God is the Divine Orator, and Scripture's substance and style mediate God's rhetoric. God's rhetorical motive is the saving intention of Scripture—the Father's divine generosity or self-giving spoken in the Son, or Word, and breathed forth in the Spirit, or Love.[9]

The divine artistry inscribed in the scriptural narrative has the character of wisdom and eloquence, which delights, captivates, and persuades us, rather than teaching us something (since knowledge puffs up), of the divine generosity and goodness that is creation's source and end. The content of Scripture, then, engenders the form of its speech: God's truth and goodness, expressed in an abundance and excess of self-giving love that creates and redeems all things.[10] Moreover, the form of this love is the beauty of Jesus Christ, the art of God incarnate, who is the object of Christian adoration and imitation.[11] Just so, the gift of the Word, in an analogous manner, becomes incarnate in preachers, suffusing them with the wisdom and righteousness of Christ, the effect of the Spirit, who kindles faith, hope, and love. Carol Harrison comments:

> There is sort of a hermeneutical circle here: love is the hermeneutical principle of Scripture; delight is that which inspires love; beauty is that which inspires delight; truth is that which inspires beauty; what man loves is the truth. It is therefore essential for Augustine that Scripture be shown to be beautiful, be made delightful, if its true end is to be attained. . . . God has chosen to motivate man's fallen will to the true and good through the delight occasioned by His beautiful revelation of Himself—and this includes, centrally, Scripture and preaching.[12]

At the heart of Christian faith and life is truthful acknowledgment of the love of God. "All creation is a work of God's love; Jesus Christ is God's giving of himself in love to restore and fulfill all creation. The Holy Spirit is the pouring out of this love in endless transformation and fresh creativity. In praising God the church confesses and celebrates in contemplative wonder, awe and astonishment the revelation and

---

9. Work, *Living and Active*, 59–60.

10. James Patout Burns, "Delighting the Spirit: Augustine's Practice of Figurative Interpretation," in *De doctrina christiana*, ed. Arnold and Bright, 189–92.

11. See the discussion in Aidan Nichols, OP, *The Art of God Incarnate: Theology and Image in Christian Tradition* (London: Darton, Longman & Todd, 1980).

12. Harrison, *Augustine*, 76.

self-giving of such love."[13] Moreover, the sweetness or persuasiveness of God's voice, or speech, is embodied in the person of Christ, the Mediator, who in his self-humiliation has made himself the road traversed by fallen humanity from the exile of sin and death into communion with the Triune God.[14] Ralph Wood comments:

> True worship of the true God—worship which alone can enable evangelical intimacy with the One who is high and lifted up—lies in nothing other than such ugly but holy beauty. To proclaim Christ's beauty is . . . not to give way to any sort of comforting pleasantness but to be schooled in the angular realism of the cross. Any sermon that can be preached without the illumination of its shadow-creating Light is sure to be ugly in the ultimate sense, however lovely its immediate appeal.[15]

The glory of God's beauty is expressed in the person of Christ, the Way, Truth, and Life, whose truth and goodness is manifested through the pilgrimage of the church.

> Furthermore, we are still on the way, a way however, not from place to place, but one traveled by the affections. And it was being blocked, as by a barricade of thorn bushes, by the malice of our past sins. So what greater generosity and compassion could he show, after deliberately making himself the pavement under our feet along which we could return home, than to forgive us all our sins once we had turned back to him, and by being crucified to root out the ban blocking our return that had been so firmly fixed in place? (*DDC* 1.17.16)

This is a journey "traveled by the affections" through which the heart's desires are drawn from and through created things to perceive the beauty of their true end within the fullness of trinitarian love. As an expert in the art of rhetoric, a master "peddler of words" and "professional liar," Augustine knew well the enchanting power of human speech and its capacity for harm when separated from God's truth and goodness. In the *Confessions* he tells the story of his professional success, of his vanity and pride, of the self-serving ways of his old life prior to conversion. Augustine viewed his former vocation in clas-

13. Daniel W. Hardy and David F. Ford, *Praising and Knowing God* (Philadelphia: Westminster, 1985), 71–74.

14. Cavadini, "The Sweetness of the Word," 164.

15. Ralph C. Wood, *Contending for the Faith: The Church's Engagement with Culture* (Waco: Baylor University Press, 2003), 147–48.

sical rhetoric, the art of persuasion, as being not only vain but also dishonest: "In all innocence I taught my pupils crafty tricks, not to enable them to secure the death of an innocent man, but on occasion to acquit a guilty one."[16]

Integral to Augustine's conversion was entering into a whole new way of thinking, desiring, and speaking. Augustine viewed his previous success, by which he valued language for its utility and capacity to control, as morally insufficient for Christian preachers since the educational system of classical rhetoric and its use were bound up with decadence and deceit. As he discovered, the greater the deceit, the more the praise. According to Augustine, rhetoric was "mendacious folly," and oratory was "wordy and polished falsehood," its use aimed at worldly riches and success: "I studied the authorities on rhetoric and desired to excel therein, an aim leading to damnation and puffed up with the joys of human vanity" (*Confessions* 9.2.2; 3.4.7; cf. 8.6.13).[17]

Whose Rhetoric?

Augustine's struggle with the moral demands presented by the power of words sheds light on the challenges presented by contemporary homiletic practice that is characterized by "the turn to the listener."[18] In this popular vision of preaching, almost everything is predicated upon the exercise of rhetorical skill and technique for bridging what are perceived as significant gaps: a communicative gap between speaker and listeners, an epistemological gap between Bible and culture, a metaphysical gap between God and the world. Left unexamined, however, is the extent to which such assumptions have been shaped by a sacred/secular vision of reality, a diminishing of ecclesial identity, the privatization of religion, and a gnostic understanding of Christianity.[19]

16. Augustine, *Confessions*, trans. Henry Chadwick (New York: Oxford University Press, 1991), 4.2.2. Hereafter references will be included in the body of the text.

17. See the discussion in M. L. Clarke, *Rhetoric at Rome: A Historical Survey* (New York: Routledge, 1996), 148–54; Harrison, *Augustine*, 46–53.

18. Thomas G. Long, "And How Shall They Hear? The Listener in Contemporary Preaching," in *Listening to the Word: Studies in Honor of Fred B. Craddock*, ed. Gail R. O'Day and Thomas G. Long (Nashville: Abingdon, 1993), 167–88.

19. See the excellent discussion in Smith, *Introducing Radical Orthodoxy*, chaps. 4–5; for a communication perspective on the "gaps," see John Durham Peters, *Speaking into the Air: A History of the Idea of Communication* (Chicago: University of Chicago Press, 2000), 263–72.

Moreover, Augustine's theological rhetoric challenges what is perhaps the most unquestioned homiletic assumption of our time: that the primary task of preaching is a matter of finding the right rhetorical technique, homiletic style, and evangelistic strategy to translate and render Christianity useful, appealing, relevant, and entertaining on terms dictated by a consumerist culture.[20] This understanding of preaching—often described as "effective communication" and typically operating within an unacknowledged gap between divine and human speech, or the Word and human words—in practice, shifts the weight of dependence from the efficacy of the Spirit to an almost exclusive dependence on human personality, ingenuity, method, and skill.[21] The Christian practice of preaching, or as Augustine conceived of it, sacred rhetoric—the liturgical expression of God's truth and love revealed in the gospel—has been reduced to a tool for transmitting an abstract, minimally Christian message to religious consumers.[22]

Thus in its neglect of theological wisdom—owing primarily to a preoccupation with the means of communication rather than the truth of the One of whom we speak—such preaching arguably conveys, through both substance and style, a sense of God's absence. Ironically, such forms of communication, which are promoted as "cutting-edge" or "state of the art" and admired for their novelty and innovation, are actually quite old. William Willimon argues in *Peculiar Speech: Preaching to the Baptized* that the prevailing tendency to split apart the message and method of preaching—a preoccupation with "how to" preach rather than the "who, to whom, what, and to what end" of preaching—is a contemporary manifestation of nineteenth-century liberalism, which proposed that the focus of sermons shift from the pulpit to the people, from the theological convictions of the church to the immediate personal concerns of the congregation. Nor is it a coincidence that during this period rhetorical form and style played a much more prominent role in preaching than did theology, a homiletic characteristic that has continued into the present.[23]

20. Here I am following James F. Kay, "Reorientation: Homiletics as Theologically Authorized Rhetoric," *The Princeton Seminary Bulletin* 24, no. 1 (2003): 16–35; William H. Willimon, *Peculiar Speech: Preaching to the Baptized* (Grand Rapids: Eerdmans, 1992); Willimon, *The Intrusive Word: Preaching to the Unbaptized* (Grand Rapids: Eerdmans, 1994).

21. See here Willimon, *Peculiar Speech*, 47–57; Willimon, *Intrusive Word*, 15–25.

22. On Augustine's "sacred rhetoric," I am following Deborah K. Shuger, *Sacred Rhetoric: The Christian Grand Style in the English Renaissance* (Princeton, NJ: Princeton University Press, 1988), 14–54.

23. See Kay, "Reorientation: Homiletics," 17–20, 26–30.

This predominately rhetorical approach has proved to be highly successful in North American contexts, especially where homiletic effectiveness is measured by the achievement of quantifiable results and the satisfaction of popular demand for exciting, entertaining communication. This method, however, exacts a particularly heavy theological price since, if preaching is not adjusted to meet the "deeply felt needs" of listeners, a preacher risks the loss of hearers, who in the contemporary marketplace of religious desire are free to shop for a more personally accommodating speaker and message.[24] Thus when homiletic style is determined by listener demand rather than the content and purpose of Scripture, the rhetoric of preaching is made extrinsic to the subject matter of preaching: God and his Word have been separated.

A commitment to consumerist religion has produced forms of preaching based on scarcity and privation and informed by a technology of desire that defines listeners according to one's own self-perceived needs. This commitment, however, requires communicative strategies more congruent with the market economy that rules democratic nation-states than with the church's triune economy of grace. God is thus rendered as functionally useful—not as the One whose extravagant, superabundant self-gift of divine goodness is lavishly poured out on creation in generous love, but as the commodity that fulfills human needs and satisfies human lack. This practice is shaped by a "grammar" of thinking and speaking that is derived from modernity's logic of rationalism, liberalism, and capitalism.[25]

Ironically, assumptions that drive this kind of communicative "effectiveness" have produced forms of popular religion that in their zeal to compete for a share of the religious market on the terms dictated by a consumerist culture have set themselves against the claims of the gospel they presume to proclaim. By subordinating the scriptural and theological substance of preaching to popular style, such pragmatic strategies point listeners toward alternative claims and allegiances— most prominently the market and state—that in their particular wisdom are ordered toward the self and its freedom to choose, rather than toward Word and Spirit, which reorder human desire to participate in the triune communion of self-giving love.[26]

24. I am indebted here to Philip Kenneson, "Selling (Out) the Church in the Marketplace of Desire," *Modern Theology* 9, no. 4 (October, 1993): 319–48.
25. Smith, *Introducing Radical Orthodoxy*, 244.
26. Ibid., 247–59.

The implications of such human-centered communicative strategies are the displacement of God, the debasement of Christian speech, and the deformation of human desires, which have been divorced from the mystery of holiness, "the supremely transforming art."[27] Lost in an enthusiasm for reaching people is the vision of the Triune God revealed in the particularity of Christ's own speech and life; the glory of his humble obedience, suffering, death, and resurrection by which he assumed the ugliness and deformity caused by sin and restored humanity to the radiance and beauty of divine truth and love.[28]

If preaching is abstracted from this trinitarian wisdom, then the grace, beauty, and "style" of Jesus—the love, joy, delight, and pleasure of the Father that rested upon him in the Spirit—is also subject to separation from his mission as the incarnate Word—who he is, what he did and suffered, and what he spoke as the Son of God who embodied the gospel of the kingdom. Thus a readily accessible, decontextualized "human" Jesus serves to underwrite pragmatic models of communication that emphasize the actions, choices, and preferences of individual speakers and listeners. Once the task of preaching is reduced to finding the "right" style of communication by imitating the example of Jesus, Augustine's analogy of the Word has been overturned, and the preaching of Jesus becomes a projection of the preacher's own desires: as a model of sincerity and authenticity, as a popular and effective communicator who meets listeners' needs. This reduction of preaching to style is the homiletic expression of "anti-intellectualist romanticism" that represents the dissolution of a christological vision of human being and action, a vision that is necessary if preaching is to remain a theologically informed practice. Such theologically informed practice is characterized by the audible Word of God becoming incarnate in Scripture and being given voice through human speech in a manner consonant with the material substance of the Word enacted in baptism and the Eucharist, which are the "visible words of God."[29]

27. Don E. Saliers, *Worship as Theology: Foretaste of Glory Divine* (Nashville: Abingdon, 1994), 210.

28. Carol Harrison, *Beauty and Revelation in the Thought of Saint Augustine* (Oxford: Clarendon, 1992), 230–38; here it is interesting to note the affinity of Rick Warren's work with Bultmann's program of demythologization. See Brevard S. Childs, "On Reclaiming the Bible for Christian Theology," in *Reclaiming the Bible for the Church*, ed. Carl E. Braaten and Robert W. Jenson (Grand Rapids: Eerdmans, 1995), 1–18.

29. In trying to understand these issues, I have been indebted to the argument in Steve Long, *John Wesley's Moral Theology: The Quest for God and Goodness* (Nashville: Abingdon, 2005), 67–70. See also the discussion in Robert W. Jenson, *The Visible Words of God: The Interpretation*

The theological rhetoric of Augustine demonstrates that without the doctrine of the incarnation, the "Word being made flesh" that creates the conditions of Christian speech, the transcendent cannot inhabit the immanent, the intelligible and sensible ways of knowing remain divided, and the words of Scripture and of sermons cannot serve as a sacramental medium for the power and wisdom of God who saves.[30]

As David Hart comments, "The incarnation is the Father's supreme rhetorical gesture, in which all he says in creation is given perfect emphasis. . . . If Christ, the eternal Word, is the Father's 'supreme rhetoric,' then the truth of the evangel is a very particular kind." He continues:

> As Word he [Christ] comes as a word among words, a discourse among discourses, a particular rhetoric that stands at odds with many of the rhetorics of the world; as the living infinite that passes by every boundary as form, Christ's dramatic and formal concreteness comprehends all the signs of creation by reordering them according to his own form; his own series, his own practice and history. Which is to say his kingdom is not of this world, that the thrones and principalities and dominions that preside over the world often speak a language inimical to the language of creation—the discourse of the gift—and must be overcome by the language that Christ instaurates in himself. No division can finally be drawn between the style of God's address in Christ and the content of what it reveals; and it is a style of being that stands contrary to many of the fashions of this world, its romances of power, its hierarchies of truths, its prudential violences and narratives of rights, rules, and possessions. He is the *ratio* of all things, but is also a word of contradiction, a sword of division.[31]

A primary focus on questions of "how to" communicate fails to address the central vocation of preachers, which is to be listeners, to respond in prayerful attentiveness and loving devotion to the rhetoric of God's Word, to cultivate a way of thinking and speaking congruent with the wisdom and eloquence of God communicated through the

---

and Practice of Christian Sacraments (Philadelphia: Fortress, 1978); Oliver Davies, *The Creativity of God: World, Eucharist, Reason* (Cambridge: Cambridge University Press, 2004).

30. Smith, *Introducing Radical Orthodoxy*, 185–230; James K. A. Smith, *Speech and Theology: Language and the Logic of Incarnation* (New York: Routledge, 2002), 114–50; see the chapter on the sense of delight in Don E. Saliers, *Worship Come to Its Senses* (Nashville: Abingdon, 1996), 33–47.

31. David Bentley Hart, *The Beauty of the Infinite: The Aesthetics of Christian Truth* (Grand Rapids: Eerdmans, 2003), 327, 330.

language of Scripture. Nor do such strategies give sufficient consideration to the persuasiveness of the Holy Spirit, the love that attracts, delights, and draws both speakers and listeners to the beauty of God's holiness revealed by the Word. In the end, what makes the message and method of preaching unique is not something in its doing; rather, it is the wisdom and power of God given voice in Christ's dying and rising. As Richard Lischer observes, "The New Testament . . . offers no explanation or rules for preaching, but only the affirmation of a mystery in which we are privileged to participate."[32]

As a community of praise, the church is taken up by the Spirit in expressions of extravagant, overflowing communication through which it "participates in the movement of God and celebrates his abundance while being shaped by his word and opened to a new future."[33] Rowan Williams comments:

> There is a kind of convergence between the idea of a practice of generosity as sharing in and making visible the character of a generous or welcoming God, and the experience of "anti-rhetoric" of human inarticulacy and unskilledness in verbalizing the nature and purposes of God. The practice of the ethical life by believers is a communicative strategy, a discourse of some sort; and equally the speech of believers is an ethical matter, morally and spiritually suspect when it is too fluent, too evidently grounded in the supposedly superior quality of the speaker. A form of religious persuasion that insists upon its right to possess or control its own outcome, whether by appeal to status or privilege, or by insistence upon its own excellent performance fails to communicate its intended matter, which is the action and nature of God.[34]

Viewed from this theological perspective, pragmatic and functional uses of language are incongruent with the truth, beauty, and goodness of the gospel that gives preaching its content and expression: the overflow of delight and free praise of God, a generosity and foolish abundance far beyond all needs and practicality. Christ the living Word unites message and method, just as Christ the Head of the body creates the context of salvation—an ethos of excess and generosity, the love of God and neighbor, which invites and draws creation toward communion with God. The presence of the Word and Spirit creates the conditions for

32. Richard Lischer, "Resurrection and Rhetoric," in *Marks of the Body of Christ*, ed. Carl E. Braaten and Robert W. Jenson (Grand Rapids: Eerdmans, 1999), 14.

33. Hardy and Ford, *Praising and Knowing God*, 120.

34. Rowan Williams, *On Christian Theology* (Malden, MA: Blackwell, 2000), 256–57.

affirming divine love as the power of our very being, the source and end of all our yearning, needs, and desires, and the true ethic (ethos) from which all worship, preaching, evangelism, and mission spring. Hardy and Ford comment:

> The crucified and resurrected Jesus Christ is therefore at the heart of the method as well as the content of Christian mission. He is also at the heart of the Christian community and of Christian praise and knowledge of God. Jesus is our praise, and through him the God of living perfection invites others deeper into his life, dealing with everything that spoils it . . . setting the problems of life, such as poverty, broken hearts, imprisonment, bereavement, lack of confidence, and the destruction of cities and social fabric over generations, in the context of good news and praise, the glory of God.[35]

Sacred Rhetoric

Forms of preaching that presume only to be "practical" help to illumine obstacles to reuniting homiletic content and form within the being and activity of the Triune God, who speaks in generating the Son, or Word, and pouring forth the Spirit, or Love. This divine speaking is sacred rhetoric.

When situated within this trinitarian vision, preaching is a form of graced participation in God's expression of himself in the Word, an inspired witness of praise through which God the Father lovingly communicates himself in the abundant generosity and joy of self-giving—the eternal, endless, overflowing source of all being, happiness, pleasure, and delight in the Spirit, who evokes and indwells the praise of the church. In stark contrast to the rhetoric of scarcity and privation that is defined by listeners' felt needs, aims toward production, serves consumption, and is driven by a technology of desire, Augustine began with the rhetoric of God's truth and beauty displayed in the heightened, poetic speech of Scripture, a rhetoric that is a purposeless art of abundance grounded in the character of God's goodness.[36]

As a practice of divine beauty, preaching participates in the knowledge and love of God, who crafts beautiful preachers and inspires

---

35. Hardy and Ford, *Praising and Knowing God*, 149–52.

36. See the excellent discussion of need and privation in Smith, *Introducing Radical Orthodoxy*, 247–54.

beautiful preaching, which is the harmonious embodiment and articulation of Scripture's content and form. As a work of divine grace (or divine artistry expressed in incarnate beauty), the art of preaching draws both speakers and listeners to "see" the presence of Christ in their midst, in the form of the intelligent order of love that constitutes the union of Christ and the church in the world.[37]

Augustine's theological art challenges us to see the excellence of divine wisdom and eloquence expressed in Christ, through whom the Spirit regenerates and reorders human desire toward its end in God. Although Augustine acknowledged that rhetoric may play a limited role in preaching, he emphasized more the gift of divine rhetoric embodied in the Word, who with great compassion humbled himself to become our neighbor and whose loving obedience enables renunciation of desire to control others through the power and eloquence of words. "It is our love of God which is a reflection of God's love for us and is a transforming power which makes us conform to the beauty of the divine nature."[38]

According to Augustine, the style of Scripture cannot be used to achieve predetermined effects, but is the spontaneous accompaniment of words that are true, "like wisdom coming from her house (that is, from the breast of the wise) followed by eloquence as if she were an inseparable servant who was not called" (*DDC* 4.6.10). Wisdom and eloquence cannot be separated; the art of speaking wisely cannot be learned by applying rules for speaking well, but by immersing oneself in the truth communicated by the sacred authors. In Christ the message and method of preaching are reconciled: "Scripture teaches nothing but charity." Augustine describes this homiletic art:

> Just as he (the listener) is delighted if you speak agreeably, so in the same way he is moved if he loves what you promise him, fears what you threaten him with, hates what you find fault with, embraces what you commend to him, deplores what you strongly insist is deplorable; if he rejoices over what you declare to be a matter of gladness, feels intense pity for those whom your words present to his very eyes as objects of pity, shuns those who in terrifying tones you proclaim are to be avoided; and anything else that can be done by eloquence in the grand manner to move the spirits of the listeners, not to know what is to be done, but to do what they already know is to be done. (*DDC* 4.12.27)

37. David L. Schindler, "Religion and Secularity in a Culture of Abstraction: On the Integrity of Space, Time, Matter and Motion," *Pro Ecclesia* 11, no. 1 (Winter 2002): 80–94.
38. Davies, *Theology of Compassion*, 81.

Speech that is suffused with divine beauty is best learned in a manner that is similar to the way a child learns a language, not by following rules, but in the practice of learning to listen and to speak (*DDC* 4.3.5). Sacred eloquence is more like a gift than a tool, effected more "through the purity of prayers than through the skill of oratory" (*DDC* 4.15.32).

Thus, in book 4 of *De doctrina christiana*, Augustine highlights the difference between classical and Christian rhetoric by offering sketches of preachers who embodied the wisdom and eloquence of the Word. For example, the preaching of Amos, Paul, Cyprian, and Ambrose communicates the message of charity—love of God and neighbor—which is the sum of what Scripture teaches. At the same time, their manner or style of speaking communicates the grace of charity that was demonstrated by Christ, who in his ministry renounced possessiveness and control (*DDC* 4.5.8–4.28.61).

Not coincidentally, during the time leading to his conversion, Augustine developed a strong interest in the preaching of Ambrose, but quickly discovered he was enchanted more by the latter's homiletic style, "the charm of his language," than by Christ who was the subject matter of the sermons but who left him contemptuous and bored. Over a period of time, however, Ambrose, in both his character and words, communicated the truth of Christ, which entered Augustine's heart and led him to a gradual change of mind (*Confessions* 5.13.23–5.14.24).

Augustine concluded that rhetoric must simply be seen for what it is: a technology of words, an art or technique that can be used for either good or ill. A combination of effective technique, persuasive power, and theological indifference can indeed make rhetoric a dangerous tool. Preaching that is shaped only by rhetorical rules and judged only by rhetorical effectiveness can easily be co-opted by the drift of popular art forms, reduced to mere entertainment, and used as a means of manipulating and doing violence to others.[39]

It is important to understand Augustine's criticism of rhetoric in light of a desire to depict preaching as theological rhetoric, or as a revelatory art that communicates the truth of God in its temporal beauty. For these theological reasons, preaching will proceed with a certain amount of "studied neglect" in its deployment of the art of persuasion. Human eloquence must be subordinated to and transfigured by the truth of divine wisdom. On the other hand, Augustine continued to believe

39. See the excellent discussion in Harmless, *Augustine and the Catechumenate*, 346–58.

that rhetoric might play a subordinate role in preaching—to serve the discovery of wisdom in Scripture's vivid, sensuous, and dramatic events—and to assist in the communication of divine beauty through the breadth of Scripture's figures, narratives, parables, metaphors, and images.[40] In the *Confessions*, Augustine celebrated both the revelatory and rhetorical art of Scripture in which God, the Master Rhetorician, continues to address human listeners through its exquisite tapestry of saving events and verbal signs:

> What wonderful profundity there is in your utterances! The surface meaning lies open before us and charms beginners. Yet the depth is amazing, my God, the depth is amazing. To concentrate on it is to experience awe—the awe of adoration before its transcendence and the trembling of love. . . . But, those immature in the faith, who are of good hope, are not alarmed by the language of your book, humbly profound and rich in meaning contained in few words. (*Confessions* 12.14.17; 12.30.41)

Most important is the truth that is spoken, since speaking God's truth in love is a sacrifice of praise that pleases even more than the style in which it is spoken. Commenting on Augustine's understanding of Christian speech, Carol Harrison states, "There is no divorce between style and substance, words and meaning, signs and signification, in a Christian context, because the former are sacraments of the latter. In this sense, too, then, the former cannot be taken as ends in themselves . . . but are to be so 'used' so that their truth can ultimately be enjoyed."[41] For Augustine, Scripture must be treated as sacramental, as an incarnate form of Christian revelation that inspires desire and love, delights and purifies, and demands an imaginative, image-making apprehension of the Word more characteristic of a poet or artist than a philosopher.[42]

The beauty of preaching is in the joy of proclaiming the truth of God. It is the pleasure of inviting others to see the beauty of Christ, who appears through the medium of the church's language and life. Augustine asserts:

40. Harrison, *Augustine*, 211–12; see also the excellent discussion in Robert W. Bernard, "The Rhetoric of God in the Figurative Exegesis of Augustine," in *Biblical Hermeneutics in Historical Perspective*, ed. Mark S. Burrows and Paul Rorem (Grand Rapids: Eerdmans, 1991), 88–99.

41. Harrison, *Augustine*, 65.

42. Ibid., 66–67; see the excellent description of Augustine's practice in Harmless, *Augustine and the Catechumenate*, chap. 9.

> Therefore Christ is our knowledge, and the same Christ is our wisdom. He himself implants in us faith concerning temporal things. He himself shows forth the truth concerning eternal things. Through Him we reach on to Him: we stretch through knowledge to wisdom; yet we do not withdraw from one and the same Christ "in whom are hidden all the treasures of wisdom and knowledge."[43]

The aim of preaching is to direct listeners toward the truth that is self-communicating, to the good willed by God and made attractive through the sweetness of his love. The Word itself is invested with the character of rhetoric or persuasion. It appears to the eye as beauty, as possessing a certain splendor, as an intrinsic, luminous, graceful style that attracts and kindles love of love itself.[44] It is the efficacy of grace that draws listeners to embrace their own being through faith. So inspired by the Spirit and the grace that springs from desire and delight, the self is transfigured within the fellowship of love shared by the Father and the Son.[45]

> That he might give it (the soul) what He commands, and may, by inspiring into it the sweetness of His grace through His Holy Spirit, cause the soul to delight more in what He teaches it, than it delights in what opposes his instruction. In this manner it is that the great abundance of His sweetness—that is the law of faith—His love which is in our hearts, and diffused, is perfected in them that hope in Him, that good may be wrought by the soul, healed not by the fear of punishment, but by the love of justice.[46]

As the Mediator between God and humanity, Christ has reincorporated an estranged creation into the life of God. This mission, however, is inseparable from the meaning of Christ's incarnation and passion, a meaning that is manifested in the beauty of creation and the restoration of its goodness as the expression of divine love.[47] Augustine affirms:

> "Let us love, because he first loved us." We did not yet love him: by loving we are made beautiful. . . . Our soul, my brethren, is ugly because

43. Saint Augustine, *The Trinity*, trans. Edmund Hill, OP (Brooklyn, NY: New City, 1991), 13.19.24.

44. Hanby, *Augustine and Modernity*, 61–62.

45. Harrison, *Augustine*, 75–77, 186–89; see the fascinating discussion in David Bentley Hart, *The Beauty of the Infinite: The Aesthetics of Christian Truth* (Grand Rapids: Eerdmans, 2003), 289–317.

46. Cited in Hanby, *Augustine and Modernity*, 81.

47. Ibid., 28.

of sin: by loving God it becomes more beautiful. . . . He first loved us, Who is always beautiful; and what were we when He loved us, but foul and ugly? But not to leave us foul but to change us, and from deformity to make us beautiful. How shall we become beautiful? By loving Him who is always beautiful. In as much as love grows in you, in so much beauty grows; for love is itself the beauty of the soul.[48]

It is not surprising, then, in the light of such divine beauty and love expressed in Christ, that Augustine was reluctant to establish rules for preaching. Instead, he advised preachers to be conformed to the rule of charity, that is, to the beauty of Christ displayed in the substance and style of Scripture: love of God and neighbor. Nor is it surprising that Augustine counseled pastors to be prayers before speakers, since prayer schools us to know and enjoy God rather than autonomy, to delight in God's truth and goodness rather than self-sufficiency, and to rest in God rather than seeking control of our lives or the lives of others.

> But whether you are at this very moment about to preach to a congregation, or give a talk to any kind of group, or whether you are on the point of dictating something that is to be preached to a congregation, or to be read by anyone who wishes and is able to, you should pray that God may put good words into your mouth. (*DDC* 4.30.63)

Augustine's robust confidence in the efficacy of preaching is grounded in an economy of divine grace and human desire. Christian rhetoric effects the breaking of pride, inspiring progress toward loving God as God, toward delighting in and enjoying (but not using) God as God, toward delighting and enjoying all creation in the love of God, and toward becoming a human expression of doxological beauty. Thus divine grace restores integrity between the message and medium of preaching within a holy conversation that binds Christ and the church in communion. As Augustine comments in a homily on 1 John,

> You see here, my brethren, a great mystery. The sound of our words strikes the ear, but the Master is within. . . . For my part, I have spoken to all; but those who hear not the inward speech of that same anointing, those whom the Holy Spirit teaches not inwardly, go home untaught. . . . He that teaches is the inward Master, Christ and his inspiration. Where that inspiration and anointing are lacking, the noise of words is in vain. . . . This then is our word to you: whether we plant or water through

48. Cited in Harrison, *Beauty and Revelation*, 232.

our speaking, we are nothing. All is of him who gives the increase, even God: that is, his anointing that teacheth you concerning all things.[49]

This is the wisdom of faith that is communicated through Scripture, through its verbal images and graceful style by which the Spirit awakens recognition, responsiveness, repentance, sorrow, confession, and lament. Because our human loves and yearnings define us—we are what we love—our loves and desires must be redirected toward their true end in God. Thus the voice of the Spirit speaks through the impassioned Word, drawing the intellect and will toward the truth and goodness of God.[50]

Because God speaks through the language of Scripture, its words and the things to which they point are one. But the language of Scripture is also sacramental; it is the inspired Word of God that veils, honors, and guards the truth. Scripture, therefore, meets its listeners at many levels, in an abundance of analogical expressions, through which God inhabits human speech. For this reason, Scripture's style possesses more than ornamental or illustrative value; the style of Scripture is intrinsic to Scripture's wisdom, just as the beauty of Christ is intrinsic to his truth and love.[51] In preaching, human speech is surrendered to this mystery.

> Who knows what we should say or what should not be heard through us at any given moment except the One who sees the hearts of all? Who then, can insure that we say the right thing and in the right way, save that One in whose hand both we and our speaking are held? (*DDC* 4.15.32)

Augustine situated his description of preaching within the vision of theological wisdom that enlivens the whole of *De doctrina christiana*: the goodness of creation, the incarnation of the Word, the resurrection of the body, the outpouring of the Holy Spirit, the reality of Christ and the church, and the friendship of Christian people. This style of grace-filled, Spirit-inspired speaking reflects the beauty of intelligent love in its scriptural, liturgical, and sacramental expressions: Christ, the Wisdom of God.[52]

---

49. *Homilies on the First Epistle of St. John*, in *Augustine: Later Works*, ed. and trans. John Burnaby, Library of Christian Classics (Philadelphia: Westminster, 1965), 285.

50. Shuger, *Sacred Rhetoric*, 223–40.

51. Harrison, *Augustine*, 77–78; see the excellent discussion in Thomas G. Long, *Preaching and the Literary Forms of the Bible* (Philadelphia: Fortress, 1989).

52. See the discussion in Catherine Pickstock, *After Writing: On the Liturgical Consummation of Philosophy* (Malden, MA: Blackwell, 1998), 44–48; see also Robert W. Jenson, "Beauty," in *Essays in Theology of Culture* (Grand Rapids: Eerdmans, 1995), 147–55.

Within this economy of grace, words must be seen as more than deaf, mute objects that exist to serve a functional purpose within a cause-and-effect world, just as words must be seen as more than tools that can be deployed according to the rules or logic of prediction, mastery, and control. As gifts that participate in God's good creation, words have been redeemed by the beauty of God's language and life disclosed in Christ and Scripture. So illumined by grace, preaching is charged with new significance, to render expressions of divine wisdom through the beauty of human speech.[53]

It is in worship, through the Spirit's indwelling love, that we are illumined to "see" the glory of the Father and the Son, offering praise to the "attractiveness of God" for which we are being redeemed to share.[54] Stanley Hauerwas comments:

> Perhaps no place are beauty and goodness more united than in the truthful speech liturgy requires. The language of prayer is exacting, an exactness that fosters over time—elegance. The prayers of the church, unlike our prayers, have been honed to say no more and no less than what must be said to confess sin, praise God, to respond with thanksgiving to the gift of the Eucharist. Liturgy is the source of the word-care necessary to be beautiful and good—beautiful and good because by constant repetition we have learned the habits necessary to speak truthfully.[55]

Revelation 21:1–6

I am accustomed to reading and preaching this passage from the book of Revelation at funerals and have had many occasions to use it over the years. But I think that limiting our use of Revelation for dealing only with disaster or at the time of death—at the end of life—limits our vision of the goodness and glory of God that is being revealed in our midst today. The vision disclosed in Revelation is the true end or

---

53. See the discussion of language, poetics, and speech in Davies, *Theology of Compassion*, 165–95; Alistair I. McFadyen, *The Call to Personhood: A Christian Theory of the Individual in Social Relationships* (Cambridge: Cambridge University Press, 1990), 44–61; Edward Farley, *Practicing Gospel: Unconventional Thoughts on the Church's Ministry* (Louisville: Westminster John Knox, 2003), 93–106.

54. Here I am indebted to R. P. C. Hanson, *The Attractiveness of God: Essays in Christian Doctrine* (Richmond: John Knox, 1973).

55. Stanley Hauerwas, *Performing the Faith: Bonhoeffer and the Practice of Nonviolence* (Grand Rapids: Brazos, 2004), 163.

goal of life, the destiny of creation that has been taken up into the life of Jesus Christ, our Risen Lord. John provides us with a stunning picture of the presence of the living God dwelling among us here and now in the Spirit's power.

And do you not find it significant that while the story of the Bible begins with a garden, it nevertheless ends in a city, a holy city, the new Jerusalem; a city inhabited and illumined by the splendor of God's glorious presence, the Lord enthroned, surrounded, praised, loved, and adored by redeemed humanity? This is all of God; it is certainly not our doing; rather, it is the handiwork of God, who from the very beginning has and continues to speak the story of creation and salvation to a glorious conclusion, a life of praise and delight that he has lavished upon us in his Son through the gift of the Spirit.

What if we were to read John's vision with imaginations shaped by the Word and sanctified by the Spirit? What if we were not only to look *at* John's vision, but to look *with* and *through* John's vision to behold, to discover the end, the goal, the glorious destiny, which through the mystery of grace presses in on us today, surrounding us who live somewhere in the middle between the beginning and the end of the story.

To live by faith and not by sight, as we Christians certainly do, is to have a very real sense of living in the middle of the story, does it not? We certainly believe that God is at the beginning of all things, and we believe that God is at the conclusion of all life. In John's striking words, God is Alpha and Omega, the beginning and the end. Now, it is common for us to assume that the beginning was good: "And God saw everything that he had made, and behold, it was very good" (Gen. 1:31). And we agree that the conclusion will be good: "Then I saw a new heaven and a new earth" (Rev. 21:1). This would seem to say that everything in between the beginning and the end of God's grand story is also good. But it doesn't turn out that way, as we experienced in the days since September 11 and again as we watched helplessly while the fury of Katrina was unleashed on the Gulf Coast of the United States.

On these terrible days our expectations for uninterrupted goodness were harshly interrupted. But the truth of the matter is that the World Trade Center bombing and the widespread disaster wrought by Katrina are only two very large-scale and unforgettable examples of the countless smaller and, sad to say, unnoticed and forgotten losses—the experience of death and the diminishment of our humanity. Relationships grown cold, turned sour, and ended; hurt, rejection, and disappointment from those we love; life that is often unjust and senseless; decisions and answers that are not as evident, easy, or apparent as we expect; and even failure and discouragement that accompany our noblest, Christian intentions. As John says, we know all too well the reality of tears, pain, sadness, darkness, suffering, and death.

And all of this happens in a life that at its beginning was very good, that at its conclusion will be completed according to God's glorious and loving design and purpose.

Friends, the story of Jesus Christ is what makes it possible for us who live somewhere in the middle to face the ugly details, the deep disappointments, the unexpected disasters, the meaningless routines, the absurdity of evil, the destruction of life, and the darkness of death. As it has been said many times, if our gospel, our story, will not preach in a cancer ward, then it is not worth preaching, hearing, or believing.

After the terrible bombing on September 11, I tuned in each night to get an update, listening to Dan Rather and the CBS news. Rather was busy at work, interpreting and preaching for us; he was announcing news, a certain kind of cultural "gospel," making large claims that sounded rather like the end-time vision of John. Do you remember it? Dan Rather, our visionary prophet in New York, repeating over and over with such finality, "The terrorist bombings of September 11 have changed our lives forever. Our life will never be the same." I ask you, just where did he get this news? Who revealed these things to him? Whose story was he reading? What revelatory vision had been given for him to behold?

And this happened again as I tuned in each evening for an update on what was happening in New Orleans, Mississippi, Alabama, and other states near and far, where displaced Americans—"refugees" as some took to calling them—were hanging on to life by a thread, desperately grasping for any sign of hope and order in the midst of horrific, destructive, violent chaos: a bottle of water, a cot, a box of military food, a hug, a reunion with lost loved ones, medical attention that may have meant the difference between life and death, and perhaps most important, news of what has happened to their homes. Each night as I watched and listened, I heard news being announced, a cultural gospel with all of its interpretations, explanations, and speculations; a story being told that, whether we are aware of it or not, teaches us how to make sense of God, our common humanity, and the world. Have you heard this? Whose story are we to believe? Whose story do you believe? Of what story are you a part?

In the story of Scripture, we Christians see New York City and New Orleans through the eyes of John's vision, the vision of a holy city, the new Jerusalem; a city that the living God is lovingly calling into being through his Word and Spirit; a city whose citizens surround the throne of the innocent, suffering Lamb who was slain, the Lamb of God who takes away the sins of the world.

We see the World Trade Center bombing and the devastation of Katrina from within the story we not only read but also inhabit. A story illumined by the grace of the Holy Spirit and authored by the Triune God himself, the One who is Alpha and Omega, the beginning and end of all that is. And at the center of this story is Jesus Christ, his way of life, his suffering, his death, and his resurrection. And the coming of God's Son is the decisive turning point; he is the person and decisive event on which the final destiny of the whole universe turns. But apart from God's gracious Word, God's self-communication in the self-giving love of his Son, we would never know these things on our own, especially with our minds so colored by catastrophic events such as 9/11 and Katrina.

And because of him, because the Son of God has come and assumed our humanity, because he lived, died, and was raised up and exalted to reign at the Father's right hand, our lives have been changed forever. Thank God that we, along with the whole creation, will never be the same! And why is this so? Because if our gospel, our story, will not preach at Ground Zero in Manhattan, if our story will not play in the flooded streets of New Orleans or in the rubble and ruins of the Gulf Coast shore, then it will not preach at all.

Friends, our risen Lord is here among us today. Can you hear him announcing: "Behold, I am making all things new!" May God grant us the imagination, nourished by the Word and sanctified by the Spirit, to see and to make the connections between what is visible and invisible, between heaven and earth, to see our past, present, and future in light of the story of Jesus Christ, the revelation of the Father's self-giving, suffering love with and in the world.

For the living God is busily at work making all things new, a new creation. He is even making this of us; we who are citizens of this world, we who once were in bondage to the powers of sin, evil, and death, and we who lived in fear due to the restlessness of our scattered loves and desires. He has made us citizens of a heavenly city, the new Jerusalem, which has come down to earth in Jesus Christ our Lord, whose kingdom knows no end. Amen.

7

Speaking of God: Preaching as a Pilgrim Practice

There we shall rest and we shall see; we shall see and we shall love; we shall love and we shall praise. Behold what shall be in the end and shall not end.

—Augustine, *City of God*

Preaching as a pilgrim practice calls the church to remember and to hope, thus forming its identity as an end-time people whose witness is in "looking for the city that is to come." In the Lord's Day worship, the eschatological vision of the church is shaped in hopeful anticipation of seeing the final advent of the crucified and risen Christ, who will come to "judge the living and the dead."[1] The heart of the New Testament proclamation is that through the Son, the Father is leading the whole created universe—cosmos and history—to the ultimate fulfillment of the kingdom (Eph. 1:9–10).[2] In its celebration of Word and sacrament,

---

1. Daniel L. Migliore, "From There He Will Come to Judge the Living and the Dead," in *Exploring and Proclaiming the Apostles' Creed*, ed. Roger E. Van Harn (Grand Rapids: Eerdmans, 2005), 178–90.
2. Aidan Nichols, OP, *Christendom Awake: On Re-energizing the Church in Culture* (Edinburgh: T&T Clark; Grand Rapids: Eerdmans, 1999), 222.

the church is transformed to see that the whole creation is a gift whose purpose is to praise its Creator. This purpose, however, is understood doxologically and eschatologically only through the constant telling and retelling of the story of creation and redemption: "remembering the future."[3]

The virtue of Christian hope, then, is based on God's promise that humankind is made for God and cannot find beatitude except in union with him. Thus the character of the hope that constitutes the church's witness is shaped by the mission of God, *missio dei*: the reality given the mission of Christ to which the Spirit draws the church in drawing the world to God.[4] As Robert Jenson comments, "The church has a mission: to see to the speaking of the gospel, whether to the world as a message of salvation or to God as appeal and praise."[5]

Francis Mannion has written of the renewal of the church's commemorative doxology, which in its remembrance looks forward to the fullness of the reign of God.

> Liturgy must again become solemn and glorious, profound and ecstatic, serene and exuberant, weighty and festive. The play of heaven needs its earthly counterpart, and the earthly must take on the superabundance of the festival of the heavenly city. Such a vision will serve to restore praise-filled energy, delight, awe, and fascination regarding the divine mystery that is at the heart of the liturgy. Visually powerful liturgical art and architecture have a crucial agency in sustaining and generating the doxological expressivity of the liturgy. These rebound profoundly upon all that occurs within a place of worship so conceived and arranged. . . . The language is not that of the everyday, but of the New Jerusalem.[6]

As a community of praise, the church lives by pointing to the resurrection as the restoration of God's good order in a creation held captive by the power of death. This hope of glory, which belongs to God, is

3. This phrase is taken from Don E. Saliers, *Worship as Theology: A Foretaste of Glory Divine* (Nashville: Abingdon, 1994), 217.

4. Daniel W. Hardy and David F. Ford, *Praising and Knowing God* (Philadelphia: Westminster, 1985), 137–67; Barry A. Harvey, *Another City: An Ecclesiological Primer for a Post-Christian World* (Harrisburg, PA: Trinity Press International, 1999), 1–63; Saliers, *Worship as Theology,* 224–30.

5. Robert Jenson, *Systematic Theology*, vol. 1, *The Triune God* (New York: Oxford University Press, 1997), 13.

6. M. Francis Mannion, "Rejoice, Heavenly Powers! The Renewal of Liturgical Doxology," *Pro Ecclesia* 12, no. 1 (Winter 2003): 58–59.

the source of our gladness as creatures: "that now we do not have to do the work of God."[7] Robert Jenson offers a poetic vision of this end-time hope:

> Let us say: there will be a universally encompassing liturgy, with the Father as the bishop enthroned in the apse and the apostles as the presbyters around him and the redeemed of all times as the congregation and the angel-driven creation as the organ and orchestra, and the tomb of all martyrs as the altar, and the Lamb visibly on the altar, and the Spirit as the Lamb's power and perception, and the music and drama and sights and aromas and touches of the liturgy themselves the Life who is worshipped.[8]

The proclamation of the gospel is a sign of Christ's victory; it is an instrument of the Spirit who reconciles all things through the wisdom and power of the cross. Through its weekly performance of the gospel story, the church gives voice to the apostolic witness that points to the age to come.

> In the death and resurrection of Jesus Christ, the giving of the Holy Spirit, and the creation of the new community of God's people among the nations, God acted decisively to deliver humanity and the cosmos from the powers of "the present evil age" and inaugurated "the age to come" in which God's triumph over the powers is revealed or "apocalypsed" to Paul among the nations.[9]

Telford Work observes that the use of the Bible in the life of a pilgrim people makes sense only when seen in light of this telos of God's self-involvement in the world, a telos that involves the salvation of persons "for the eternal glory and worshipful enjoyment of God."[10] The church does not undertake this journey for its own benefit but rather for the sake of the world. And although the wisdom of salvation is mediated through the church to the world, the church's life is given in glad receptivity to the Spirit's bestowal of the Father's self-gift of salvation in

7. Stanley M. Hauerwas, *Wilderness Wanderings: Probing Twentieth-Century Theology and Philosophy* (Boulder, CO: Westview, 1997), 201.

8. Robert W. Jenson, *Systematic Theology*, vol. 2, *The Works of God* (New York: Oxford University Press, 1999), 430.

9. Douglas Harink, *Paul among the Postliberals: Pauline Theology beyond Christendom and Modernity* (Grand Rapids: Brazos, 2003), 17.

10. Telford Work, *Living and Active: Scripture in the Economy of Salvation* (Grand Rapids: Eerdmans, 2002), 313.

Christ: "called according to the Father's will, hearing in faith, repenting, being justified, then sanctified, and finally glorified."[11]

Augustine's grand narration of the Christian story, *The City of God*, depicts the church's identity as a pilgrim people ruled by Christ, "resident aliens" being led by the Word and sustained by the Spirit as they journey toward the attainment of eternal happiness with the saints in the heavenly city.[12] Reading the world through the lens of Scripture, Augustine came to see history as an open-ended narrative involving two cities with opposing ways of life, devoted to either love for God or love for self. However, the church in history remains a thoroughly mixed body that continues to struggle with the power of sin and its effects at work in the powers of the earthly city until attaining the eschatological peace of the city of God. Concerning this, Robert Wilken comments:

> Christians . . . belonged to a community whose end lay outside of history, and whose company was even larger than the church. Its history extended back into the history of Israel, and it included men and women who had lived in former times, the saints who had gone before; and it awaited others who were not yet born (or already born) who would one day become its citizens. . . . The church is that part of the city of God which is on pilgrimage. . . . The church lives in the company of a much larger community.[13]

As the city on pilgrimage through time, the church is characterized by a particular way of life, the gift of divine wisdom by which it worships the Father, Son, and Holy Spirit. Thus in worship the means and destination of the journey are one and the same. Without true worship and love for God, moreover, there can be no human fulfillment, happiness, or genuine life in community since the just live by faith in God and justice is found only where God is worshiped, where the justice due to God is rendered. All human life is directed toward the good that is God, and all actions come to fulfillment and perfection in the

11. Ibid., 305.

12. Augustine, *The City of God*, ed. David Knowles, trans. Henry Bettenson (New York: Pelican, 1972); cited hereafter as *CoG*.

13. Robert L. Wilken, "Augustine's *City of God* Today," in *The Two Cities of God: The Church's Responsibility for the Earthly City*, ed. Carl E. Braaten and Robert W. Jenson (Grand Rapids: Eerdmans, 1997), 35; see also the discussion in Nicolas M. Healy, *Church, World and the Christian Life: Practical-Prophetic Life* (Cambridge: Cambridge University Press, 2000), 54–56.

God who is both Lord and the desire of all human hearts. In the new Jerusalem, therefore, the peace for which the city of God now yearns is inherently social; that is, it is a mutual fellowship that human beings share together in communion with God and in enjoyment of God. "Thus the greatest gift the church can give the world is to be itself, offering itself to God and bearing witness to the justice due God."[14]

> Justice is found where God . . . rules an obedient city to his grace . . . so that just as the individual righteous man lives on the basis of faith which is active in love, so the association, or people, of righteous men lives on the same basis of faith, active in love, the love with which a man loves God as God ought to be loved, and loves his neighbor as himself. But where this justice does not exist, there is certainly no "association of men united by a common sense of right and by a community of interest." (CoG 19.23)

For Augustine, the earthly pilgrimage of the city of God is directed by Holy Scripture, since God, the highest good, is its source and end. Because the church derives its faith and wisdom from Scripture rather than itself, it should not despair of the goodness of God, even during this time of pilgrimage and exile from the Lord (CoG 19.19). On the other hand, faith and wisdom are gifts bestowed upon a pilgrim people who in acknowledging their human constraints, sins, limits, and death confess dependence on God.[15] This is the virtue of humility, which is prized in the city where the love of God and neighbor rules (CoG 14.13). Such humility reflects the glory of Christ, which is acquired through participation in a shared life of prayer and devotion within a community of common memory, bound together in common service, and which shares a common hope. "Only people schooled in the religious life can tell the difference between serving the one God faithfully and bowing down to idols."[16] As Rowan Greer comments:

> I think what Augustine means is something like this. Human life for the elect is a long pilgrimage or convalescence. And just as a sentence does not make sense until the period is placed at the end of it, so our

14. I am following the excellent discussion in Robert L. Wilken, *The Spirit of Early Christian Thought: Seeking the Face of God* (New Haven: Yale University Press, 2003), 186–211.

15. On the epistemic humility and the "pilgrimage of testimony," see Rodney Clapp, *Border Crossings: Christian Trespasses on Popular Culture and Public Affairs* (Grand Rapids: Brazos, 2000), 19–32.

16. Wilken, *Early Christian Thought*, 209–10.

pilgrimage does not achieve its meaning until we arrive at our destination. There in the City of God we shall be able to have for the first time a retrospect over our entire life. And for the first time we shall see that all our loving and knowing was informed by the presence of God. The perfection of our loving and knowing will be accompanied by the perfection of our remembering. And God's presence is the proper object of all three activities. Moreover, we shall not only see our own lives this way, we shall see one another in the same light. The pilgrimage of the Christian life is, then, a constant struggle to remember, to know, and to love. But these activities will find their completion only in the Christian destiny. Then the image of God will be achieved. Then no clouds will obscure our vision of God's presence. The broken lights that characterize our perceptions of God's redeeming work in this present order will be united in the face-to-face work for which we now yearn.[17]

According to Augustine, in this earthly pilgrimage a willingness to listen and be led is of particular importance in discerning the wisdom of Christ, since the human mind, darkened by sin, has to be trained and purified. This transformation, the renewing of the mind and reordering of desire, illumines the way and goal of faith, which is the Son of God himself. Because the Son did not abandon his divinity when he assumed our humanity, he was able to establish the path to God through One who was God (*CoG* 11.2).

> As man he is our Mediator; as man he is our way. For there is hope to attain a journey's end when there is a path which stretches between the traveler and his goal. . . . As it is, there is one road, and one only, well secured against all possibility of going astray; and this road is provided by one who is himself both God and man. As God, he is the goal; as man, he is the way. (*CoG* 11.3)

Moreover, Christ the Mediator has indeed spoken, in former times through prophets and later through his own words, and after that through the apostles, communicating the wisdom of God that leads to salvation. And Christ continues to speak through Scripture, revealing himself as God's wisdom and way: "He also instituted the Scriptures, those which we call canonical. These are the writings of outstanding authority in which we put our trust concerning those things we need to know for our good, and yet are incapable of discovering by our-

---

17. Rowan A. Greer, *Broken Lights and Mended Lives: Theology and Common Life in the Early Church* (University Park: Pennsylvania State University Press, 1986), 90.

selves" (*CoG* 11.3). Scripture's voice, then, is living and active: "For Scripture is concerned for man, and it uses such language to terrify the proud, to arouse the careless, to exercise the inquirer, and to nourish the intelligent; and it would not have this effect if it did not first bend down and, as we may say, descend to the level of those on the ground" (*CoG* 11.4).

Telford Work has written of the eschatological character of Scripture, which is known in the end-time gathering of God's people through the "presence in absence" of Jesus. "The Bible's performance makes the absent Lord present in the coalescing assembly of his disciples." It is the concrete life of the church that reveals the public side of Scripture's performance by its people. Work observes that it is the marks of the church that tie Scripture's qualities to the qualities of the church that bears it, shapes it, preserves it, and performs it. This relationship, between Scripture and tradition, locates the Bible's work within the diversity of communities that comprise the church of Jesus Christ as it journeys toward its final destiny. He comments:

> The Bible is an agent in the divine economy of salvation, whose terrestrial focus is the Church. It is not the Word *in extra*, but the Word *ad extra*—in creation, redemption and *eschaton*. This means that in the age of the Church, it is the Word of the Church. Its speech is God's words to himself, to the Church, and to the world; and the Church's words to God, to itself, and to the world. Because Israel and the Church occupy the middle position in this divine-human verbal exchange, Scripture plays an instrumental role in all the Church's activities, from its worship and glorification to its evangelization of the world.[18]

Thus the pilgrimage of the church, the heavenly city in the world, is evangelical in nature; it is of God, it is universal in scope, it is catholic. Augustine asserts, "She calls out citizens from all nations and so collects a society of aliens, speaking all languages" (*CoG* 19.17). Robert Jenson comments:

> Just so the church now is truly the people of God and the body of Christ and the Temple of the Spirit. For, it is what creatures may anticipate from God that is their being. Just so also, the church is grounded in God himself, the *Eschatos*. All creatures are moved by God to their fulfillment in him; the church is doubly so moved, as

---

18. Work, *Living and Active*, 313–14.

one among God's creatures and as the creature that embodies that movement for others.[19]

As the voice of Christ, Scripture possesses both divine character and agency in the economy of salvation, thus building up the church as a visible witness to the gathering of the nations for the praise and knowledge of God. Augustine writes in the *Confessions*:

> I now began to believe that you would never have conferred such pre-eminent authority on the scripture, now diffused through all lands, unless you had willed that it would be a means of coming to faith in you, and a means of seeking to know you. . . . The Bible offered itself to all in very accessible words and the most humble style of diction. . . . It welcomes all people to its generous embrace, and also brings a few to you through narrow openings. Though the latter are few, they are much more numerous than would be the case if the Bible did not stand out by its high authority and if it had not drawn crowds to the bosom of his holy humility. (*Confessions* 6.6.8)

Jenson has suggested that in a world that has lost its story, its beginning and end in God, and which no longer believes itself to inhabit a narratable world, the church herself must be that world. The church must become that place where we behold our destiny, where we see what is to become of us; a story of humankind called from nowhere, ex nihilo, toward its proper place, a promised polis, the new Jerusalem, a city "not built by human hands."[20] That city will be a place and time of true glory, of endless love and praise, the doxological fulfillment of humanity before the throne of God.

> The reward of virtue will be God himself, who gave the virtue, to-gether with the promise of himself, the best and greatest of all possible promises. For what did he mean when he said, in the words of the prophet, "I shall be their God, and they will be my people"? . . . He will be the goal of all our longings; and we shall see him forever; we shall love him without satiety; we shall praise him without wearying. This will be the duty, the delight, the activity of all, shared by all who share the life of eternity. . . . Nothing will give more joy to that City

---

19. Jenson, *Systematic Theology*, 2:172.

20. Robert W. Jenson, "How the World Lost Its Story," reprinted in *The New Religious Humanists*, ed. Gregory Wolfe (New York: Free Press, 1997), 142–43; Nicholas Lash, *The Beginning and the End of "Religion"* (Cambridge: Cambridge University Press, 1996), 233–34.

than this song to the glory of Christ by whose blood we have been set free. There the precept will find fulfillment: "Be still, and know that I am God." (*CoG* 22.30)

The work of Samuel Wells helps to illumine the kind of storytelling that characterizes the church on this journey—a story that is more fitting for saints than heroes.[21] On the one hand, the heroic storyteller is in charge and must intervene to make things turn out right; thus the hero remains at the center of the story, since a heroic story is always about the hero and what the hero accomplishes. On the other hand, the saint is at the periphery of a story that is really about God; the story told by the saint celebrates who God is and what God has done, and while the saint may not be strong, brave, clever, or opportunistic, the saint is faithful, since the story of the saint is told to celebrate faith in God's faithfulness to his promises (*Improvisation*, 43).

Saints, then, tell a story that is different from the story told by heroes. Hoping in God, saints have no need to tell a story that will compete with the world and its stories, since Christ has already fought for and secured in abundance love, joy, peace, faithfulness, gentleness, and all the gifts of God communicated in the story of the gospel. Thus when the story goes wrong for the hero, all rests on the hero's action. On the other hand, when the story goes wrong for the saint, failure opens out to repentance, forgiveness, reconciliation, and restoration, since the saint lives as a member of God's new creation. Thus the stories we tell are congruent with how we see the world and with the way we live. Wells concludes that while the hero acts in isolation, saints tell a story about God, drawing from the wisdom of the whole church and communion of saints to reveal their dependence on God and each other (*Improvisation*, 43–44).

The church's story is a five-act play. Act 1 is creation, act 2 is Israel, act 3 is Jesus, act 4 is the church, and act 5 is the eschaton. Wells writes:

The principles and the narrative of the first act continue through the three that follow; the covenant of the second act is alive and significant in the third and fourth; the theme of the third is the key to understanding all the others; and the character of the fourth, the "holy city" is at least partly preserved, though transformed, in the fifth. (*Improvisation*, 53)

21. Samuel Wells, *Improvisation: The Drama of Christian Ethics* (Grand Rapids: Brazos, 2004); cited hereafter as *Improvisation* in the text.

In the course of this drama there are countless opportunities and temptations to lose patience, hope, perspective, direction, and timing. For example, we may perceive ourselves in the wrong place, believing we are in act 1 as the authors of our own story, or that we are in act 5 and responsible for its outcome. We may also mistakenly identify ourselves with Jesus in act 3, rather than seeing ourselves as his church in act 4. At the same time, we may choose to enjoy the play as spectators, from a distance, presuming the whole story is for us and about us rather than God, who authors our life and whose promises secure our future (*Improvisation*, 55).[22]

Moreover, because Christians live in that forgiveness won by Christ's death and resurrection, they are free, in faith, to make honest mistakes in their ongoing improvisations of the story. Wells argues persuasively that since Christians live in the fourth act of this five-act play, they have permission to improvise as saints, which means they do not have to make everything come out right as heroes, nor do they have to correct the failures of the previous three acts—as God. God's people have only to use the resources of the first three acts in light of the anticipated outcome, faithfully playing with and within the circumstances in which they find themselves. And because the church knows that God, rather than itself, is the goal or end of the play, it is under no compulsion to be original or creative. The church is thus free to employ the resources of the first three acts rather than creating its own, while at the same time continuing to hope for the final act, the glory of the creation's destiny in God. The whole drama is therefore characterized by the joy of communion with God, past, present, and future, through God's self-gift of Christ and the Spirit (*Improvisation*, 55–56).

> Baptism takes the Christian from a one-act play to a five-act play. In baptism, Christians are taken into a drama, where God has created them and others for a purpose, where Israel has answered a call and pursued a vocation, where Jesus has become one like them and has conquered sin and death, where the Spirit has empowered the church to follow Christ, and where God will end the drama when he sees fit. Christians find their character by becoming a character in God's story. They move from trying to realize all their meaning in their own lives to receiving the heritage of faith and the hope of glory. They move from fearing their

22. I have also benefited from the work of Craig G. Bartholomew and Michael W. Goheen, *The Drama of Scripture: Finding Our Place in the Biblical Story* (Grand Rapids: Baker, 2004).

fate to singing of their destiny. For this is the effect of God's story: it transforms fate into destiny. (*Improvisation*, 57)

Discovering God's Purpose: Figured Out or Figured In?

Ephraim Radner has argued that as a pilgrim people, the church apprehends the form of Christ, the form of its own life, and the form of the world within the words of Scripture. "In addition to referring to God's own being, the form of Christ connotes the very things that speak of him—the Scriptures, the Church and even the world in its own way."[23] Radner offers an extensive description of the spiritual and figural meaning of Scripture, which is grounded in the fundamental scriptural form of Christ himself, the Word, or original form, before all things and through whom all things are made. In Christ, the form of God's being and will is revealed, and in Christ the being and will of all things are perceived since they exist for God and by God, so that reality is given in direct reference to God (*Hope*, 12).

Radner argues that to behold or to see the form of Christ is to move toward understanding the world in and through him; to apprehend Christ in his form as given by Scripture is to perceive in him something of the time, shape, purpose, and meaning of creatures. Thus Christ as a form stated by Scripture is the likeness and form of God (2 Cor. 4:4; Phil. 2:6; Col. 1:15) and the literal likeness and form of a human slave obedient to death on a cross (Rom. 8:3; Phil. 2:6–11). Because this form is taken by him in all its complexity and temporal details, "the form of Christ is what all truthful speech about God entails and to what the Scriptures first refer" (*Hope*, 13). It is the form of Christ that gives rise to those signs and figures by which we attempt to speak and manifest the truth of God.

Thus within the practice of spiritual and figural meaning, a figure "is nothing else than something that God makes for the sake of speaking about himself" (*Hope*, 13). All things have been created to speak of Christ, who in his form—through whom and for whom all things are made—allows as a gift of grace particular objects, moments, and persons to become indicators of the Spirit. The language of Scripture, then, does not refer to meaning in life or purpose or to something that

23. Ephraim Radner, *Hope among the Fragments: Broken Church and Its Engagement of Scripture* (Grand Rapids: Brazos, 2004), 11; cited hereafter as *Hope*.

can be abstracted or "figured out" from the Bible. Rather, Scripture, as the object of God's creating hope, is itself a referent—"something whose meaning is made up primarily in Christ's giving of himself and showing himself through its forms" (*Hope*, 13–14). We cannot "figure out" God's purpose as if it were a problem to be solved or question to be answered; we must allow ourselves to be "figured in" for participation in the providential force of Christ's speech, through which Scripture and the church are given voice in history.

Radner observes that, for Augustine, the events of salvation are in themselves God's speech in history, which indicates not only the events and actors but also the Scriptures themselves as objects of God's providential economy in which the whole world is found. Augustine saw this truth given in the incarnation of the Word. As "speaker of words and creator of new words and speakers," . . . "the Word of God tabernacling in human life, Christ makes the Father known within the world of human created beings, yet, as their creator, he makes possible the forms of praise by which the knowledge of God finds its true end." Christ in the form of God points directly to God, but as the form of a slave he points indirectly to God through the servant's joy of adoration—the Scriptures and the church, which is his body (*Hope*, 14).

Following Augustine, Radner concludes that within a trinitarian assertion of the coming of Israel's Messiah in the incarnation of God's Son, the words of Scripture are the words of God spoken by the Spirit that give the form of God's work in history. By perceiving itself to be located within the providential activity of God, the church discovers afresh the form of its life, destiny, and meaning, "the stance of hope that constitutes the fruit of apprehending scriptural providence in the first place—a stance whose power to transform lives into the figure of God's redemptive will would place us in the form of Christ's mind" (*Hope*, 17).

Thus in the form of Christ, who draws all forms of ecclesial existence into himself, the church cannot be an instrumental tool but only a revelatory form of its own. "The Church's witness is of hope, and indeed the hopefulness of its promised future, is given in disclosure of Christ in time: and Christian faithfulness is revealed in subjection of life to this inescapable sway of the Church's disclosure herself" (*Hope*, 18). It is futile, even arrogant, to imagine that we are capable of devising programs for "figuring out" God's purpose, reinventing the church, or choosing our life. Only in the form of Christ, as given in Scripture, is the church enabled to discover its location within God's providence;

only by divine mercy and forgiveness is the church "figured in" the form of Christ's death and resurrection and thereby conformed to the gospel for God's mission within the particularities of place and time (*Hope*, 18–19). Radner comments:

> Searching for Christ amid all the Scriptures is but another way, in rela-tionship with the Bible, of describing how the human creature stands in the world with respect to God and is called to stand ever more firmly. To live in the world as it truly is—that is, as God's world, the God revealed in Christ—is to read Scripture in a figural way. Similarly, to read Scripture in a way that can uncover this God in all corners of its textual universe is to learn to live truly in this world, God's world, as it is. (*Hope*, 100)

Radner's insightful work directs our attention to the need for learning to interpret in a manner that bears hopeful witness to the lordship of Christ, who holds together Scripture, history, the church, and Christian faith in conformity with the object of Christian worship: the Triune God (*Hope*, 174–75).

John David Dawson also has commented extensively on the practice of figural reading, which involves the church in a drama of discerning the point of existence and identifying its place in it. This practice is figured as a journey through various states of transformation from a former mode of life to an ultimate end. He writes:

> The overwhelming presumption of classical Christian figural reading . . . is that the Christian Bible is read Christianly when it is seen to depict the ongoing historical outworking of a divine intention to transform humanity over time. Moreover, Christian figural readers insist that the history of Israel, Jesus of Nazareth, his immediate followers, and the Church are all somehow ingredients in this overarching divine intention. That intention and its outworking in history are regarded as alternately clear and obscure, reliable and unpredictable. Figural readers turn to the text of the Bible for clues and models useful for unraveling as much as they can of what they think they discern as the mysterious working of God in the lives of people over time.[24]

Thus in a world of competing and violent interests, the most faithful service the church can render is to embody the weakness and humility

24. John David Dawson, *Christian Figural Reading and the Fashioning of Identity* (Berkeley: University of California Press, 2002), 216.

of the wisdom of Israel and of the form of life displayed by its crucified Lord, thereby disclosing a fundamental truth about human beings and society: without true worship and love for God there can be no human fulfillment, happiness, or genuine communal life. We are made in the image of God, and are restless until we find our rest in God.[25]

In a post-Christendom world the formation of ecclesial identity as God's people requires that our liturgical gatherings be characterized by attentive, reverent reception and performance of the biblical script—a communal sacrifice of praise to the Triune God, whose love creates, redeems, and perfects all that is. As Jenson notes:

> The church must herself be a communal world in which promises are made and kept. . . . It is the whole vision of an eschaton that is now missing outside the church. The assembly of believers must therefore itself be the event in which we may behold what is to come. . . . If, in the post-modern world, a congregation or whatever wants to be "relevant" its assemblies must be unabashedly events of shared apocalyptic vision. "Going to church" must be a journey to the place where we will behold our destiny, where we will see what is to become of us.[26]

We are the stories we inhabit, tell, perform, and celebrate. The purpose of reading and preaching is the formation of a people who indwell a real, substantial, living world in accordance with the sense of Scripture's commands and promises, its will and wisdom: God is making a world of peace, for love of God and love of others. Wilken comments:

> The church is a social fact as well as an eschatological sign. It draws its citizens into a shared public life with its distinctive language, rituals, calendar, practices, institutions, architecture, art, music, in short, with its culture. Though it joins with others to promote the good of society in which it lives, its end is with the heavenly company of angels. "With us," says Augustine, "they make one city of God." That part of this city, "which consists of us, is on pilgrimage," and "the part which consists of the angels, helps us on our way." The church is not an instrument to achieve other ends than fellowship with God. It serves society by being unapologetically itself and bearing witness to the justice that alone makes human community possible, the justice due God. The greatest gift the church can give society is a glimpse, however fleeting, of another city,

---

25. Robert Wilken, *Remembering the Christian Past* (Grand Rapids: Eerdmans, 1995), 60–61; Wilken, "Augustine's *City of God* Today," 28–31.

26. Jenson, "How the World Lost Its Story," 147.

where the angels keep "eternal festival" before the face of God. . . . By offering itself to God as a living sacrifice, the church's life foreshadows the peace for which all men and women yearn, the peace God alone can give.[27]

In a particularly intense way, sermons exemplify the struggle to hear the Word that forms the church, which as a community is "figured in" the narrative of Scripture that illumines fullness of peace with God and neighbor. Preaching to a pilgrim people is a summons to live in God's world, according to God's wisdom, and with hope in God's providence, which makes possible the knowledge and praise of God's goodness for creation's true end, which is God's glory. Sermons are improvisations of the gospel, which is freshly illumined in liturgical gatherings through a canonical conversation that guides the church as a community of friends on the journey toward God's kingdom. These improvisations involve the calling of a people for the praise and service of God; glad remembrance of the coming of Christ, the promised Messiah of Israel and Savior of the nations; and the anticipation of his return in glory to consummate the kingdom in which God will be all in all.[28] As Stanley Grenz and John Franke comment,

> Viewed in light of the Christian life as performance, the Christian tradition becomes the historically extended, socially embodied context in accordance with which the contemporary community is being called to interpret, apply and live out—that is, to perform in the here and now—the communally formative narrative given in the canonical texts.[29]

A sermon, then, is not a solo performance but belongs to the whole company of the gospel. "To be made a part of God's speech lies at the heart of the Christian understanding of God. In short, our God is a performing God who has invited us to join in the performance that is God's life."[30] That performance is the liturgy: it is the work of a pilgrim

27. Wilken, *Early Christian Thought*, 210–11.

28. On "pilgrimage catechesis," see Brent P. Webb-Mitchell, *Christly Gestures: Learning to Be Members of the Body of Christ* (Grand Rapids: Eerdmans, 2003), 166; see also the discussion of "peregrinational catechesis" in Reinhard Hütter, *Suffering Divine Things: Theology as a Church Practice* (Grand Rapids: Eerdmans, 2000), 190–93.

29. Stanley J. Grenz and John R. Franke, "Theological Heritage as Hermeneutical Trajectory: Toward a Postfoundationalist Understanding of the Role of Tradition," in *Ancient and Postmodern Christianity: Paleo-Orthodoxy in the 21st Century, Essays in Honor of Thomas C. Oden*, ed. Kenneth Tanner and Christopher A. Hall (Downers Grove, IL: InterVarsity, 2002), 239.

30. Ibid., 77.

people, the vocation of praise in which the church is conformed to the wisdom of Christ.[31] As Kevin Vanhoozer notes, the church's liturgical performance will never be more than amateur theater since it performs for the love of it, for the love of God's Word, for the love of the world as God's good creation. And what the church loves doing best is commemorating, celebrating, and communicating Christ. "It is God's love that impels the drama along, and our love for God that compels our participation in it. Doctrine directs us to what alone is worthy of our loving attention—God's worded and embodied love—just as it directs our fitting participation in it."[32]

1 Samuel 2:18–20, 26; Luke 2:41–52; Colossians 3:12–17

The Gospel lesson for this Sunday, on the Feast of the Holy Family, is about Jesus, Mary, and Joseph. And if you were listening to the story when it was read a few minutes ago, you probably realized that on this day the holy family was not a very happy family. There was a certain amount of confusion and tension in the air, created by the surprising absence and presence of Jesus, which they simply did not understand. Already, early on in the story, there is something mysterious about Jesus; there is something about him that evokes awe, even astonishment, an element of surprise that will only increase throughout the course of his public ministry and its fulfillment through death on a cross and resurrection from the grave. This child of Israel and son of Mary will not be domesticated by the claims of this world. As God's Son, his loyalty to God's kingdom will remain constant, despite increasing pressure to conform to the expectations of others in the form of temptation, rejection, suffering, and in the end, even death.

In his story of Jesus, Luke quickly moves us from birth through boyhood to the beginnings of adulthood and accountability. And it is no accident that this scene takes place in the temple, where Israel gathered in the presence of God and for the praise of God; where Israel gathered to express love and loyalty to the One who delivered it from slavery in Egypt; where Israel remembered the goodness of the One who graced its life with divine wisdom revealed in Torah, the Law, the gift of covenant love. In fact, Israel's Torah and temple, its way of wisdom

31. Ibid., 98–99.
32. Kevin J. Vanhoozer, *The Drama of Doctrine: A Canonical-Linguistic Approach to Christian Theology* (Louisville: Westminster John Knox, 2005), 442.

and worship, provide the setting for the opening scenes of Luke's story of Jesus. Nor is it a coincidence that Luke's story of Jesus ends in the temple. At the end of the story, after his death and resurrection, after his greater Exodus and Passover had fulfilled Israel's way of wisdom and worship, the disciples return to the temple, where they praised God for the great things he had done. Luke's story of the gospel begins and ends in praise of the God of Israel, the God and Father of our Lord Jesus Christ, Creator and Redeemer of heaven and earth.

I was walking my dog one night a few weeks ago, around the time when Christmas lights were starting to go up. Most were rather typical: configurations that look like Santa Claus, candy canes, reindeer, Christmas trees, snowflakes, and other assorted designs. But one house really caught my eye. On the front lawn were three brightly lit crosses, with the one in the center raised up above the others. Can you imagine? Crosses for Christmas! Why, this is what we are accustomed to seeing during Lent and Easter. But I think those folks got it just right. It is Christmas, *Christ's mass*, which means the remembrance of Christ's death and the celebration of his continued presence with us in Holy Communion. We remember and celebrate his birth as Son of God in light of his cross and resurrection, just as we remember and celebrate our new birth as children of God in light of our baptism into Christ's death and resurrection. It is only in light of the beginning and end of the story of Jesus Christ that we are able to make sense of the beginning and end of our lives as his people.

But at the point in the story where we find ourselves this morning—in the temple with Jesus, Mary, and Joseph—all signs of Jesus's special nature and mission have been given either to or through other actors in the story of God and Israel: the words of the prophets; angelic messengers; Mary his mother; Mary's sister Elizabeth, mother of John the Baptist; Zechariah the elderly priest; the poor shepherds; and faithful, pious Simeon and Anna. On this day, however, after his parents frantically search to find their lost son who was busily occupied in the temple, Jesus affirms his identity within the story and vocation of Israel, in whose common life God's purpose for God's human creation is made known.

This is a revealing moment, the first time Jesus speaks in Luke's Gospel: "I must be about my Father's business." Now, this is not a story about Jesus the whiz kid who has been identified as one of the brightest and the best among the gifted and talented; you know, a candidate for the National Spelling Bee, or the Governor's School, or the National Honor Society; perhaps someday even a Rhodes Scholar. Jesus is neither a creative genius nor a rebellious hero. The story is actually more mundane and therefore significant for us. The Son of God lived humbly and obediently before God and among family and friends, growing and maturing in both body and spirit, in wisdom and character; blessed by God and all who knew him, a source of delight and gladness to all around him. Now, what are we to make of this?

The Nicene Creed confesses that "for us and for our salvation, he came down from heaven and became human." And here, in the faith of the church, we are at the heart of the matter. In fact, the birth and boyhood of Jesus, as well as the whole life and ministry of Jesus, is the work of God in which the Son of God takes to himself our fallen world, our sinful, human flesh, and lives in it a life of faithful, loving praise on our behalf, doing the will of his Father, walking according to God's wisdom, and following God's way. And an essential part of the vocation of Jesus, which he learned through the Scriptures, traditions, and practices of Israel, is that he must learn for us the wisdom we have lost through sin and foolishness, that he must overcome our idolatrous and destructive ways, and that he must restore and complete our lives and destiny as creatures made to share God's image. He must restore us to communion with God.

St. Irenaeus, a bishop during the early centuries of the church, proclaimed, "The Word of God, our Lord Jesus Christ, through his transcendent love, became what we are, that he might bring us to be even what he is himself."[33] At Christmas we celebrate a great exchange. We have received a wonderful and surprising gift: fully God, the Son descended into ignorance and humiliation; fully human, he advanced in wisdom and stature, demonstrating his full participation in our life for the salvation of humanity and the whole creation.

And this learning and maturity took place in two particular ways that follow the pattern of the surprising story of young Samuel in our Old Testament reading. First, by sitting at the feet of Israel's teachers, and second, by participating in the faithful obedience and worship offered to God by the human family in which he was born and raised: Torah and temple, wisdom and worship. Jesus acquired godly wisdom, a kind of "knowing how" shaped within God's covenant love and by loving obedience to God's law. As a member of God's people, his

---

33. Irenaeus, *Against Heresies* 5.preface, in The Ante-Nicene Fathers 1, ed. A. Roberts and J. Donaldson, rev. A. C. Coxe (Grand Rapids: Eerdmans, 1953), 526.

memory and hope were nourished through regular celebration of the story of God's deliverance and promises, enabling his growth in grace and deepening gratitude for God's continued presence, blessings, and gifts to his people.

Contrary to many popular, contemporary approaches to church, this is not a matter of simply acquiring a little bit of information and the right technique for application in everyday life to get results; neither is this something that can be learned in just a short amount of time and with a minimal amount of effort or personal investment. In fact, much of our foolishness stems from the presumption that we can figure out how to get a handle on the mystery of God; that we can produce and package Christianity as a religious commodity, marketing a tamed Jesus to meet the needs and expectations of spiritual seekers and consumers; you know, three tips to help you make it through the week, twelve steps to an effective church, five keys for self-esteem and happiness, ten principles for living with passion and realizing your potential.

I wonder, though, is it really that simple and easy? Is such self-help religion sufficient for the flourishing of our human vocation and destiny as children of God, a vocation that calls us to grow in wisdom and character, conformed to the image of Jesus Christ crucified? In his book *Not the Way It's Supposed to Be*, Cornelius Plantinga writes of what godly wisdom both requires and makes of us:

> In the literature of Scripture, wisdom is, broadly speaking, the knowledge of God's world and the knack of fitting ourselves into it. The wise person knows creation. She knows its boundaries and limits, understands its laws and rhythms, discerns its times and seasons, respects its dynamics. She understands that creation possesses its own integrity and significance apart from her claim on it and quite apart from any possibility that creation will make her happy. The wise person gives in to creation and to God—she does the first because she does the second. She knows that the earth itself is the Lord's and so is its fullness. She knows that wisdom is itself the Lord's and so is its fullness. She knows some of the deep grains and features of the world because she knows its maker. In the biblical view, the wise are righteous and good and the righteous and good are wise: these are people who love and fear God, affirm God's world, live gladly within its borders, and make music and praise according to divine time and key signatures.[34]

34. Cornelius Plantinga Jr., *Not the Way It's Supposed to Be: A Breviary of Sin* (Grand Rapids: Eerdmans, 1995), 115.

Through the coming of Jesus Christ to assume our human life, the church has been raised up as a school of wisdom for the worship of God in a world awash with information and technique, yet still a world that, in all of its foolishness, continues desperately seeking for goodness, truth, and love. And we have found this wisdom, not by looking within ourselves, but by sitting at the feet of him who came into a world lost in darkness and the foolishness of sin and idolatry and in bondage to a host of false gods and destructive powers. In our seeking we have been found by the One whose glad loving obedience to the Father in loving service to others, especially among the least, the last, the lowliest, and the littlest, learned wisdom for us all.

I will never forget an incident that opened my eyes to see how this wisdom takes form in the world. It was the Christmas season, and my son, who was a member of his elementary school chorus, had gone to sing at a local nursing home. The home was right down the road from the church, so I decided to drop in on that late December afternoon to listen. They set up for the concert in the dining room, and they began to gather the residents there. Many had to be transported in wheelchairs or on hospital beds. Others managed to straggle in with the help of canes and walkers. During the concert, most of the residents gave little evidence they could hear or recognize the Christmas carols and songs that were being sung by the children.

But at the very last selection everything suddenly changed; and I tell you, it was one of the most amazing things I have ever witnessed. The children began to sing "Amazing grace! how sweet the sound, that saved a wretch like me! I once was lost, but now am found, was blind, but now I see." As soon as this old hymn began in that nursing home room, filled with seemingly passive, unresponsive residents, everything suddenly came to life. Many of them strained to stretch their hands upward toward heaven, struggling with frail, feeble voices to mouth the words. Some could only groan in ways that were not even intelligible; but I tell you, it was heavenly music to my ears. I could hear through those desperate groans and feeble voices the sounds of a heavenly hymn of praise: "Glory to God in the highest, peace on earth and God's favor to all the people." It was praise born of humility, a graced wisdom that enables us to acknowledge, in life and death, our utter dependence on the goodness of God.

This is the "politics of praise" to which the Holy Spirit is conforming us as God's beloved children; it is a way of wisdom that is our worship, a living witness to God's glory, salvation taking form among us in Jesus Christ, our crucified Savior. Our salvation in Christ is our schooling in the politics of praise, in which we are granted the gift of wisdom to know, love, and delight in the Triune God. Drawn into the love and joy of the Father and the Son, we are discovering in our kinship with each other the fulfillment of our human love and desire, our destiny of praising and knowing God.

My brothers and sisters, through Christ's cross and resurrection we have been set free from the powers of darkness and death and transferred into the light and life of God's kingdom. In the sacrament of baptism, we have been joined as the temple of the Holy Spirit in which Christ, the Word by whom all things have been made, dwells in the midst of his body, the church. For we are God's new creation, conformed by the Spirit to the Son for the communion of love and joy he shares with the Father. And because he nourishes us with his life in the Holy Meal we share together, we are strengthened to grow into his character and wisdom, to offer ourselves as a sacrifice of thanksgiving to the One who alone is worthy of such praise. Hear again the apostle Paul's witness to God's self-gift of Christ, who with the Spirit has bound us to himself with the Father's love.

> Put on then, as God's chosen ones, holy and beloved, compassion, kindness, lowliness, meekness, and patience, forbearing one another and, if one has a complaint against another, forgiving each other; as the Lord has forgiven you, so you also must forgive. And above all these put on love, which binds everything together in perfect harmony. And let the peace of Christ rule in your hearts, to which indeed you were called in the one body. And be thankful. Let the word of Christ dwell in you richly, as you teach and admonish one another in all wisdom, and as you sing psalms and hymns and spiritual songs with thankfulness in your hearts to God. And whatever you do, in word or deed, do everything in the name of the Lord Jesus, giving thanks to God the Father through him. (Col. 3:12–17)

Amen.

Preaching as Hope

Preaching as a pilgrim practice embodies the hope of God in a world awash in cynicism and credulity. Perhaps nothing is more debilitating for the contemporary church than hopelessness or acedia, a form of depression that lives on the border of despair. Without the virtue of hope, which is nourished within us by God's peace in Christ and the love that the Spirit pours into our hearts, we are vulnerable to fads, easy answers, and quick fixes—the many reduced or reinvented expressions of Christianity that promise much but are insufficient to build up a people created, redeemed, and destined to share the image of the Father given in the Son, which is the glory revealed in the weakness and foolishness of the cross that shines brightly among us through the Spirit's beauty.

If our speech is to be worthy of the God whom we worship, then our preaching will be doxological—orthodox—resonating with right praise and glory. Speaking of God will be discoursing in the Spirit that witnesses to the gospel of Jesus Christ, crucified and raised from the dead, the Lord of heaven and earth who will return in glory to consummate God's kingly reign of love, joy, peace, and righteousness.

Preaching as a pilgrim practice thus forms a people who embody a genuine story of hope—the mission of God—and embrace a way of life that is true, good, and beautiful—the wisdom of God—and who are generous and self-giving in their enjoyment of others and the goodness of creation—the love of God. Paul Wadell writes:

> We need a people who steadfastly witness that God's promises are real. If the Christian story is anything, it is a story of unabashed and jubilant hope because it tells us that a God who fashioned us from love and who lives with us in love will never abandon us. It tells us of a God who was generous enough to share life with us and who wants to give us everything God has: God's perfect peace, God's everlasting joy. We who are already sharers in divinity are summoned to partake in God's life completely, and there is no more hopeful story than that.[35]

35. Paul J. Wadell, *Becoming Friends: Worship, Justice, and the Practice of Christian Friendship* (Grand Rapids: Brazos, 2002), 135.

Epilogue

The center of the Gospel is that in Jesus Yahweh communicates himself wholly to us. There are two fundamental things to be said about Jesus: one is that he is the word of Yahweh, the self-communication of God, the other is that he is the meaning of history. . . . Jesus is the word, the language of God which comes to be a language for man. . . . The church makes the presence of Christ articulate as a language, as an interpretation of the world, as a means of communication.

> —Herbert McCabe, *Law, Love and Language*

Speaking of God: On Changing the Subject

Christian Preaching: A Trinitarian Theology of Proclamation has aimed to "change the subject" of Christian preaching—from human speakers to the Triune God. It has been written as an extended essay in practical theology: theological reflection on the practice of preaching within the church's trinitarian wisdom or "grammar" of faith. Unlike authors who limit the discussion of preaching to how-to matters of homiletic method and technique, I have not written about sermon design, style, delivery, illustrations, PowerPoint, video clips, popular culture, sociological trends, or any other number of secondary matters that continue to dominate our attention more than the Word of God.

My aim in writing has been with a larger and longer view in mind. Speaking of God requires theological rather than pragmatic justification—a "knowing how" that is learned by attending to the "who, whose, to whom, what, how, and to what ends" of preaching. Thus

205

the subject matter of preaching and the condition of our knowing—orthodoxy or right praise—requires that our thinking, feeling, and speaking be purified by the illumination of the gospel through the Spirit's witness in Scripture and its exemplification in the story of the church. This vision of proclaiming the gospel has thus been situated within the church's worship and confession of the Triune God, the centrality of the incarnation, and the testimony of the Spirit, so that our speaking might be more truthful and fitting in ministry to the One with whom and of whom we speak—*theological*—and more truthful and fitting in ministry with those whom God calls through the foolishness of preaching to be conformed to a crucified Lord—*pastoral*.[1]

The proclamation of the gospel evokes a vision of preaching that is constituted by a life-engendering, divine-human conversation. This is the "homily" of God's self-communication in the mystery of creation, covenant, commandment, and the incarnate Christ—the divine "sermon" made efficacious by the Spirit who enlivens the church as the embodiment of God's human speech and its response in the world. We therefore speak because we have been called and authorized to answer the saving eloquence of God, who indwells the creation and redemption of all things. Through the ministry of the Word, Christ is made audible and visible in the speech and life of the church to transform it into a visible sign by which the Spirit draws the world toward its true destiny, dignity, and delight: loving communion with the Triune God.

The purpose of this book has been to encourage members of the homiletic community to embrace a renewed—but not original—way of seeing and articulating a vision of preaching as an integrative movement of theological and pastoral wisdom in service to the gospel of Jesus Christ in light of (1) Christian proclamation as a response to and participation in the gospel as it is spoken and revealed by God in Christ through the whole narrative of Scripture, and (2) proclamation as both a gift of the Holy Spirit and a human vocation that creates and builds up the church as a people transformed by the Word to indwell the world of the gospel of Christ narrated by Scripture. In the end, speaking of God is the gift of redeemed listening and speaking, the work of the Spirit by which the church is reconciled for faithful obedience in loving union with the Son for the Father's praise and glory. It is only in speaking *under* the claims of the gospel that our words are

---

1. See the discussion of theological justification for Christian language in Bruce D. Marshall, *Trinity and Truth* (Cambridge: Cambridge University Press, 2000).

taken up by the Spirit's power to awaken the church in astonishingly life-giving speech. Philip Turner aptly summarizes the largeness, challenge, and glory of this homiletic task:

> The gospel is a complex message in the form of a narrative account of who God is and what God is up to that includes but far exceeds either the liberal or evangelical gospel. I take it that the good news is summed up in the great creeds of the church which confess that the biblical narrative renders for us one God whom we know as Father, Son, and Holy Spirit, who alone created the worlds, who elected Israel as his special people so that all peoples would come to know and love the one true God, who in the fullness of time sent his Son to reconcile through his sacrificial death the peoples of the earth and to restore the order of creation. This son ascended to the right hand of God, the Father, who sent the Spirit to those who receive the Son and bound them together in his body the church, who will come again to judge the peoples of the earth and who, through the Spirit, will bring all things to their intended end and perfection.[2]

At home within the trinitarian economy of creation and salvation, preaching may best be understood as pastoral discourse within a larger tradition of doctrine, devotion, and discipleship. Speaking of God is a form of primary theology, or personal knowledge and love that is nourished in savoring Scripture's wisdom within the church's worship of God. The beauty or excellence of preaching is evinced in the overflowing abundance of doxological speech, a gift engendered by God—focused wisdom in the self-forgetful yet fully engaged habits fitting for the elevation and enjoyment of God. Preaching is thus an inherently liturgical activity, the celebration of the gospel in sermon and sacrament, which are the ordinary means by which the church is taken into an economy of language and life through which God is active within the world.

The first call of the church, then, is to be a listening community, to recognize, rejoice in, and respond to the mission of the Triune God—the presence of the Word and Spirit that manifests the wisdom and generosity of divine love for creation. As a pastoral practice, preaching provides liturgical direction for a pilgrim people to participate in the drama of the universe, a communal performance of God's promises and saving

---

2. Philip Turner, "The Powerlessness of Talking Heads," in *The Strange New World of the Gospel: Re-evangelizing in the Postmodern World*, ed. Carl E. Braaten and Robert W. Jenson (Grand Rapids: Eerdmans, 2002), 79.

purposes displayed in the narrative of Scripture and centered in the mission of Christ. In the mystery of Christ, who indwells the language and life of the church, the astonishing gift of the Word is spoken through the self-giving and vulnerable love epitomized in the cross: this is the eloquence of the gospel by which the Spirit creates living faith.

Thus the wisdom of preaching is acquired through learning to read Scripture as a theologically diverse but unified world that coheres in Christ, a world that is the drama of salvation from creation to consummation: who God is in what God does for humanity from the beginning to the end of the world. At the center of the narrative of creation and sanctification is the incarnation, the Son of God made flesh. All that precedes Christ's coming, all that accompanies it, and all that follows must be understood in relation to him. Thus the logic of this reading is that the mystery of Christ and the church is a body created by the Spirit, the *totus Christus*, or the whole Christ, which is being made visible as the sacrament of God's communion with the world. Oliver Davies comments:

> Scripture stands at the heart of the self-communication of God in history since biblical texts make present kinds of human speaking which are interpenetrated by and formed within the creative rhythms of revelatory divine speech. Old and New Testament are compilations of hymns, historical narratives, dramatic interludes, stories, dialogues, songs, texts of thanksgiving and celebration, prophecies and parables, aetiologies and genealogies, proclamations and affirmations, ethical and legal codes, which are inwardly shaped by divine speaking. This is the distinctive characteristic of Scripture, that it is constituted as a form of testimony, as a witness to God's unfolding presence in history, in and through the creative power of the divine Word. But Scripture is also something other than the testimony of others, for it opens up to us new ways of speaking. Through our reading of Scripture, we come to inhabit utterances that are already shaped by the divine communicative presence. Our own voices enter the voices of others who have been reformed by the power of divine speech, and we learn new modes of speaking and listening. Scriptural reading is the slow learning of these new practices of speaking.[3]

To become a preacher, then, is to be formed into a certain kind of character within a distinctive community and particular way of life.

3. Oliver Davies, *The Creativity of God: World, Eucharist, and Reason* (Cambridge: Cambridge University Press, 2004), 75.

As members of the history of a practice and bearers of a tradition, we are made stewards of a gospel that has been handed down through the centuries by the work of the Spirit in the church.[4] Davies observes:

> It is the Spirit that allows us, if we allow the Spirit, to enter the biblical world. It allows us to "hear" the divine voice that speaks within the biblical world and to become integrated into the perichoretic speaking, and kenotic way of life, which circulates within the Gospels and their Hebrew foundation. As Trinitarian, the Spirit is a participation in the economic life of God. Its movement within us, in the domain of biblical reading and interpretation, is at the same time the discovery that the power of God has preceded us: the Word of which we read is already present to us, as Word and Spirit of the world, in the act of reading. . . . We put on the "mind of Christ" when we read Scripture in and through the Spirit; we become one with his body the Church in a conforming of the self with the divine logic of Scripture which shapes us in a new celebratory and compassionate form of life.[5]

There may be no more urgent need in our time than for preachers to be schooled by salutary exemplars in the logic of Scripture, which shapes the language and grammar of preaching. Rather than new methods and techniques, we would do better to learn from the practice of others whose demonstrated wisdom has called the church to bear witness to the gospel in the world: God's "rhetoric of peace." Richard Lischer observes:

> Reconciling speech is not our native language, it comes from outside us in the testimony of Scripture and the lyricism of worship, languages that even the believer may find awkward to use in the marketplace. But because of our baptism and the work of the Holy Spirit, this new way of talking now wells up within us and our communities. We preach toward reconciliation and also from a reservoir of forgiveness that, had we not received it and shared it among ourselves, we could not speak it. We

---

4. On the theological nature of the pastoral office, see William H. Willimon, *Pastor: The Theology and Practice of Ordained Ministry* (Nashville: Abingdon, 2002), 11–53, 331–36; see the discussion of social "characters" within a community and tradition in Alasdair MacIntyre, *After Virtue: A Study in Moral Theory* (Notre Dame, IN: University of Notre Dame Press, 1984), 27–31; I am indebted to the excellent discussion of tradition by Stanley Grenz and John Franke, "Theological Heritage as Hermeneutic Trajectory: Toward a Nonfoundationalist Understanding of the Role of Tradition," in *Ancient and Postmodern Christianity: Paleo-Orthodoxy in the 21st Century, Essays in Honor of Thomas C. Oden*, ed. Kenneth Tanner and Christopher A. Hall (Downers Grove, IL: InterVarsity, 2002), 215–39.

5. Davies, *Creativity of God*, 121.

participate in something larger and better than our inherently violent disposition toward enemies. This something Paul terms the ministry of reconciliation. We have found our role in God's script at last.[6]

Contrary to much contemporary conventional wisdom, a sermon is not a time for talking *about* an ancient text, for sharing biblical "nuggets," or for discussing relevant topics; nor is it a time for anecdotes from the preacher's recent experience or musings on the state of contemporary culture. The Word we proclaim is neither about a text nor about ourselves. Within the testimony of Scripture, both message and messenger are conformed to Christ, who with the Spirit emboldens us to say, "Our Father who art in heaven, hallowed be thy name. Thy kingdom come, Thy will be done, on earth as it is in heaven." Christ himself is both speaker and speech, calling those "longing for a better homeland" to be citizens of a new Jerusalem, that is, the new heavens and new earth the Spirit is creating as the dwelling place of the Triune God.

Seen from this longer and more hopeful perspective, popular forms of moralistic preaching—principles for application, rules to live by, "life situations," and "life lessons"—are simply shortsighted, communicating forms of "practical atheism" that turn attention to the self and its efforts rather than to the amazing goodness and astonishing glory of God. In this way, people are made "the thing[s] to be enjoyed, and God the sacramental thing to be used in the service of their own enjoyment."[7] Moreover, when used as a tool for motivating listeners to do what they ought, should, and need to do, preaching sounds less like the gospel of Christ as believed by the Christian community and more like a gospel of privatized self-help and self-improvement defined by the culture of marketing and management.[8] In the end, however, such problem-centered, issue-oriented, "practical" forms of speaking communicate a vision of God, the church, and the world that empties the gospel of God's self-gift in Christ. As Hardy and Ford note:

> Praise is the primary form of the communication of the gospel, the sheer enjoyment and appreciation of it before God, "even when there is no point at all." . . . The essence of mission and evangelism is in the intrinsic

6. Richard Lischer, *The End of Words: The Language of Reconciliation in a Culture of Violence* (Grand Rapids: Eerdmans, 2005), 163–64.

7. Telford Work, *Living and Active: Scripture in the Economy of Salvation* (Grand Rapids: Eerdmans, 2002), 317.

8. Here I have found helpful the argument in Jeremy Carrette and Richard King, *Selling Spirituality: The Silent Takeover of Religion* (New York: Routledge, 2005).

worth, beauty and love of God, and the joy of knowing and trusting him. The gospel is that all sin, evil and suffering, all need and want, can now be seen in the perspective of the resurrection of Jesus Christ in which God acts in such a way that the realistic response is joy. Even beyond this, it is the joy of love between us and God, the ultimate mutuality and intimacy. Recognizing and responding to this God inevitably leads to evangelism and mission as acts of love and celebration, longing for others to share in something whose delight increases by being shared.[9]

For theological reasons, pragmatically driven evangelistic strategies misunderstand the gospel at the deepest level by *offering abstract messages, a discarnate gospel, and forms of human salvation that in practice communicate a "real absence" of God's presence and power in the church, with humanity, and for the world.* Only the glory of the gospel embodied in the humility of Christ can draw us back to the "rough ground" of Christian speech: the Word taking flesh among a people in need of reform. This is a sign of the "real presence" of its Lord. Bruce Marshall comments:

> The church's ongoing communal life is always subject to correction, at every point, by the gospel. But the church, precisely as the historically particular community on the way from Pentecost to the return of Christ, is itself a part of the gospel in light of which its present speech and action are subject to reform. So the reform of the church's present belief and practice will very likely take a different concrete form than it would if the church did not belong to the gospel, if, in other words, the gospel could be spoken in abstraction from the church.[10]

The gospel, therefore, cannot be separated from the speech of its human agents, since its authority encompasses both divine and human activity within the economy of grace. Moreover, this larger theological vision informs our understanding of divine efficacy and is the source of confidence that in the ministry of the Word, preacher and listeners are made graced participants in the movement of God to humanity through the work of the Spirit. Most significant, however, is that the saving knowledge and love of God originates entirely with the Triune God, and that this wisdom is disclosed in the history of God's dealings

9. Daniel W. Hardy and David F. Ford, *Praising and Knowing God* (Philadelphia: Westminster, 1985), 149–50.

10. Bruce D. Marshall, "The Church in the Gospel," *Pro Ecclesia* 1, no. 1 (Fall 1992): 39–40.

with the world as focused in Jesus Christ, the "communicability" of the Father and the Son who speak creation, redemption, and consummation in the mystery of grace. As Samuel Wells observes:

> The sermon proclaims that the God who acted in the story of Israel, came in Jesus and was alive in the early church is living and active today. . . . It is a moment when heaven comes down to earth, when the truth of the way God acts in history and God's longing for the restoration of friendship with his people comes face to face with the reality of human intransigence and fragile striving. It is a moment when Christians rediscover who they are by seeing, face to face, who God is. It is a moment when earth comes to heaven, when the truth of what humanity is in sin is re-described by the glory of what humanity is in Christ. It is an incarnational moment, one in which God's divinity meets our humanity in the spoken word, and the congregation discovers that God became what we are so that we might become what God is. It is a resurrection moment, when the apparent givens of sin, death and evil are stripped away and possibilities of humanity in the new creation are transformed.[11]

Changing the subject from ourselves to the Triune God will require learning to ask questions of Scripture, ourselves, and the world in ways that are congruent with the One of whom we speak.[12] For example: *How does Scripture witness to the character, action, and speech of God? What sin or sins does this scriptural text uncover or address? What virtues or examples of faithful obedience does this scriptural text describe or display? How does this scriptural text proclaim the gospel of God's self-communication in Jesus Christ? What is God speaking or doing? What is God teaching, commanding, seeing, inviting, persuading, encouraging, promising, forgiving, blessing, cursing, and so on? Is there anything being spoken in this scriptural text that is surprising? What is odd or strange? How is this scriptural text a Word to and with the church? What is this Word doing to form, sustain, correct, encourage, build up, and empower disciples? How is it doing this? Where and how have I seen this Word being spoken and enacted in the life of the church, among Christian people, or in the world?*

Rather than assessing sermons in light of audience response—compliments, criticisms, what listeners may like or may not like, what is

---

11. Samuel Wells, "Hearing God Out," *Christian Century* 122, no. 9 (May 3, 2005): 223–32.

12. A number of the following questions have their origin in Dr. Richard Lischer's class syllabus for the basic preaching class taught at Duke Divinity School from 1996–2001.

popular, relevant, cutting edge, etc.—our thinking and speaking will become more truthful if judged by criteria congruent with the gospel, the "whole Christ" of whom we speak: *Who is the God speaking in this sermon? What is God speaking and doing? Who are the people being addressed by God? Who are they being called to become and what are they being called to do in response to the Word? Is the context and scope of the sermon love of God and neighbor? Does the sermon position preacher and people within the trinitarian self-communication of creation, redemption, and consummation? Does the language of the sermon form Christ? Does the preacher demonstrate passion for the Word? Does the preacher show an adequate knowledge of his or her listeners in light of the wisdom communicated in Scripture? Does the sermon demonstrate relevance to the gospel in this particular place and time? Does the sermon invite listeners to hear and respond to God in ways that are fitting for who they are and the conditions of their life? Does the sermon "preach" itself through its style and expression? Do the preacher's language and life embody the gracefulness of gospel speech? Does the language make Christian sense? Does the sermon call attention to the delighting, compelling, and attractive nature of God?*

Speaking of God: Preaching as Doxological Speech

Augustine argued passionately and persuasively that our humanity is unfolded within the transcendent love of the Trinity through the Father's sending of the Word and Spirit. This generous and abundantly flowing love, which creates and embraces all of reality, is mediated through the Son by the gift of the Spirit, who elicits our attention and stirs us to delight in, enjoy, and desire Christ the Word, who himself reveals the knowledge and love of the Father. Our life is constituted and upheld in doxological confession, through participation in the downward conde-scension and self-giving of trinitarian love, which evokes our personal response and gathers up our self-offering of thanksgiving and praise in response to the prior activity and gift of grace. And though this is fully God's communicative activity, it is also fully our own; God lets us be so that we might hear and respond, drawing us into communion and friendship with himself and each other to flourish within the truth, goodness, beauty, and delight of his love.[13]

13. Hanby, *Augustine and Modernity*, 27–71.

Rowan Williams argues that the glory of God is not seen in results but rather in the delight and joy of seeing God's nature, in inviting others to give glory, to know and enjoy God, in being glad that God is God and that we are God's creatures. Instrumental and functional understandings of God and correlative standards of glory simply fail to sense the joy of knowing and loving God for God's sake. We do not preach in order that needs might be met or for what God might do for us by being useful. Rather, we preach because we have been transformed by the truth and goodness of God, who communicates himself in teaching, delighting, drawing, loving, claiming, and blessing others.[14]

Only the discipline of God-focused liturgical celebration is capable of opening us to receive the grace of God's self-gift in Christ, who restores our life to communion in the triune love.[15] Moreover, delighting in the humble love of Christ extends even into the manner of our speaking, "to the dispossession of language and power, rhetorical skill and expertise, to giving way in the fractured and failed character of Christian speech, to the vulnerability and awkwardness of human voices in proclaiming it."[16] In short, preaching "works" when we renounce our means and methods of making it work.

Speaking of God, then, is part of the movement of the story of God's people and their language toward the focus of cross and resurrection that is the movement of Scripture.[17] As Williams notes,

> Language about God is kept honest in the degree to which it turns on itself in the name of God, and so surrenders itself to God: it is in this way that it becomes possible to see how it is still God that is being spoken of, that which makes the world a moral unity. Speaking of God is speaking to God and opening our speech to God's; and it is speaking of those who have spoken to God and who have thus begun to form the human community, the unrestricted fellowship of holiness, that is the only kind of universal meaning without the tyranny of a total perspective.[18]

14. Here I have benefited from the discussion in Mark A. McIntosh, *Mystical Theology: The Integrity of Spirituality in Theology* (Malden, MA: Blackwell, 1998).

15. On African-American preaching, see Henry H. Mitchell, *Celebration and Experience in Preaching* (Nashville: Abingdon, 1990); see also Albert Borgmann, *Power Failure: Christianity in the Culture of Technology* (Grand Rapids: Brazos, 2003).

16. Rowan Williams, *On Christian Theology* (Malden, MA: Blackwell, 2000), 256.

17. Ibid., 57; see also Kevin J. Vanhoozer, *The Drama of Doctrine: A Canonical Linguistic Approach to Christian Theology* (Louisville: Westminster John Knox, 2005), 442.

18. Williams, *On Christian Theology*, 8.

In the end, Christian speech is judged according to the truthfulness of its subject and doxological intent: faithfulness in directing attention to the truth, beauty, and goodness of the Triune God of whom we speak. *Speaking of God is ecstatic speech, the self-emptying or giving away that opens us to yield ourselves and our words to the Word of the Father, which is the revelation of the Son in whom we delight and to whom we are drawn by the Spirit's movement of self-giving love.*[19] Freed from anxious striving for the purposeless activity of experiencing the gospel, our hearts return to rest in God, which is the activity of praise that is our eternal duty, dignity, and delight.

St. Augustine describes the glory that is both the means and the end of our journey:

> The reward of virtue will be God himself, who gave the virtue, together with the promise of himself, the best and greatest of all possible promises. . . . He will be the goal of all our longings; and we shall see him forever; we shall love him without satiety; we shall praise him without wearying. This will be the duty, delight, the activity of all, shared by all who share the life of eternity. (*CoG* 22.30)

19. See the excellent discussion in McIntosh, *Mystical Theology*, 47–53.

Index